DOCTOR WHO
THE TWELFTH DOCTOR

VOL 1: TERRORFORMER

"Has every trademark of a classic, Moffat-written episode."
MIND OF THE GEEK

"The art and coloring is terrific!"
DOCTOR WHO NEWS

"Nails the tone of the show."
COMIC BOOK

"The art is fantastic!"
WIRED

"I loved it!"
AIN'T IT COOL NEWS

"Highly recommended!"
COMIC OF THE DAY

"Exciting, fast-moving, funny and mysterious."
GEEK MOM

"Sublime. Makes you tick days off on your calendar until the next issue is out!"
WARPED FACTOR

"One HELL of a
Doctor Who story."
MY GEEKY GEEKY WAYS

"Colorful and fun!"
NEWSARAMA

"Feels like an episode of the series!"
HOW TO LOVE COMICS

"Very interesting and beautiful."
FANGIRL NATION

"The artwork is beautiful."
NERDLY

"Captures the humor of Capaldi's Doctor."
KABOOOOOM

"Full of harrowing action and intrigue!"
GIANT FREAKING ROBOT

"A must-read book."
IMAGES UNPLUGGED

"If you are a Whovian, this is definitely for you!"
RETRENDERS

"An excellent tale!"
TM STASH

"I thoroughly enjoyed this!"
PROJECT FANDOM

TITAN COMICS

SENIOR EDITOR
Steve White

TITAN COMICS EDITORIAL
Lizzie Kaye, Tom Williams

PRODUCTION SUPERVISORS
Maria Pearson,
Jackie Flook

PRODUCTION CONTROLLER
Obi Onuora

STUDIO MANAGER
Emma Smith

CIRCULATION MANAGER
Steve Tothill

SENIOR MARKETING & PRESS OFFICER
Owen Johnson

MARKETING MANAGER
Ricky Claydon

ADVERTISING MANAGER
Michelle Fairlamb

PUBLISHING MANAGER
Darryl Tothill

PUBLISHING DIRECTOR
Chris Teather

OPERATIONS DIRECTOR
Leigh Baulch

EXECUTIVE DIRECTOR
Vivian Cheung

PUBLISHER
Nick Landau

Special thanks to

Steven Moffat, Brian Minchin, Matt Nicholls, James Dudley, Georgie Britton, Edward Russell, Derek Ritchie, Scott Handcock, Kirsty Mullan, Kate Bush, Julia Nocciolino, Ed Casey, Marcus Wilson and Richard Cookson for their invaluable assistance.

DOCTOR WHO: THE TWELFTH DOCTOR VOL 1: TERRORFORMER
HB ISBN: 9781782761778 SB ISBN: 9781782765011

Published by Titan Comics, a division of Titan Publishing Group, Ltd. 144 Southwark Street, London, SE1 0UP.

A CIP catalogue record for this title is available from the British Library. First edition: June 2015.

10 9 8 7 6 5 4 3 2 1

Printed in China. TC0293.

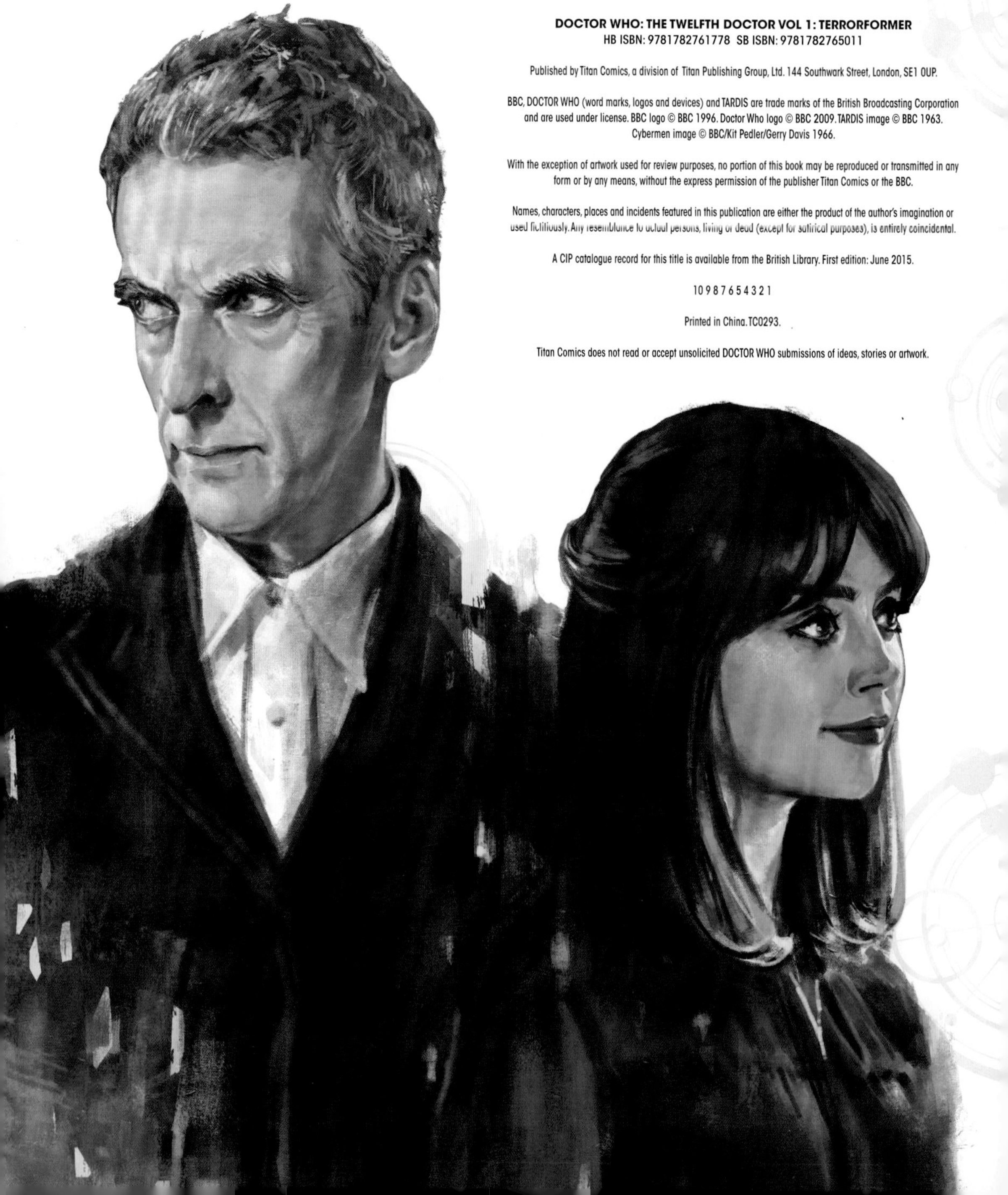

DOCTOR WHO
THE TWELFTH DOCTOR

VOL 1 : TERRORFORMER

WRITER:
ROBBIE MORRISON

ARTIST:
DAVE TAYLOR
WITH MARIANO LACLAUSTRA

COLORISTS:
HI-FI
LUIS GUERRERO

LETTERS: RICHARD STARKINGS
AND COMICRAFT'S
JIMMY BETANCOURT

EDITOR:
ANDREW JAMES

ASSISTANT EDITOR:
KIRSTEN MURRAY

DESIGNER:
ROB FARMER

TITAN
COMICS

www.titan-comics.com

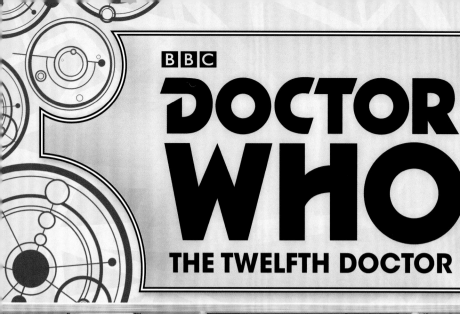

BBC

DOCTOR WHO

THE TWELFTH DOCTOR

POLICE PUBLIC CALL BOX

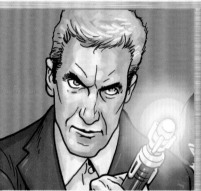

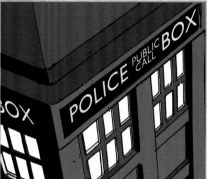

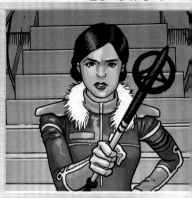

THE DOCTOR

An alien who walks like a man. Last of the Time Lords of Gallifrey. Never cruel or cowardly, he champions the oppressed across time and space. Forever traveling, the Doctor lives to see the universe anew through the eyes of his human companions!

THE TARDIS

'Time and Relative Dimension in Space'. Bigger on the inside, this unassuming blue box is your ticket to unforgettable adventure!
The Doctor likes to think he's in control, but more often than not, the TARDIS takes him where and when he needs to be...

CLARA OSWALD

Clara Oswald, the Doctor's 'Impossible Girl', has stuck with the Doctor through thick and thin, witnessing all manner of strange, wonderful and terrifying things in his company!
Now a teacher at Coal Hill School, she juggles her 'real life' on Earth with her secret adventures aboard the TARDIS!

PREVIOUSLY...

After a thousand years of war on the planet Trenzalore, the Doctor regenerated into a brand-new incarnation! Clara struggled at first to reconcile the Doctor's new face with that of her closest friend, but the pair are now back in the saddle of cosmic adventure, even if this new Doctor is a brusquer and more unpredictable – the kind of Doctor who wishes people would just *get out of his way* and let him get on with the business of saving them!

When you've finished reading the collection, please email your thoughts to doctorwhocomic@titanemail.com

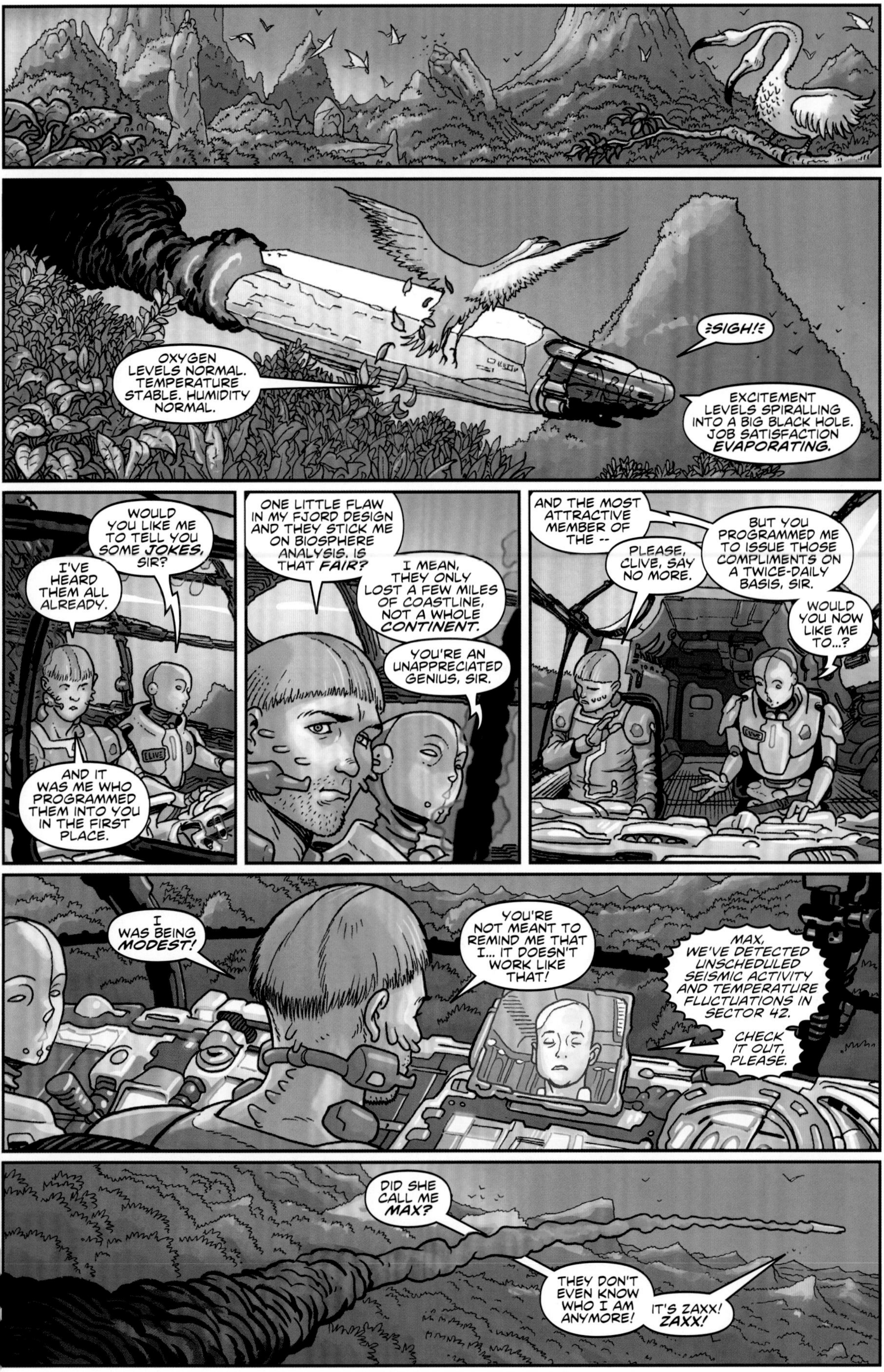

OXYGEN LEVELS NORMAL. TEMPERATURE STABLE. HUMIDITY NORMAL.
SIGH!
EXCITEMENT LEVELS SPIRALLING INTO A BIG BLACK HOLE. JOB SATISFACTION EVAPORATING.
WOULD YOU LIKE ME TO TELL YOU SOME JOKES, SIR?
I'VE HEARD THEM ALL ALREADY.
CLIVE
AND IT WAS ME WHO PROGRAMMED THEM INTO YOU IN THE FIRST PLACE.
ONE LITTLE FLAW IN MY FJORD DESIGN AND THEY STICK ME ON BIOSPHERE ANALYSIS. IS THAT FAIR?
I MEAN, THEY ONLY LOST A FEW MILES OF COASTLINE, NOT A WHOLE CONTINENT.
YOU'RE AN UNAPPRECIATED GENIUS, SIR.
AND THE MOST ATTRACTIVE MEMBER OF THE --
BUT YOU PROGRAMMED ME TO ISSUE THOSE COMPLIMENTS ON A TWICE-DAILY BASIS, SIR.
PLEASE, CLIVE, SAY NO MORE.
WOULD YOU NOW LIKE ME TO...?
I WAS BEING MODEST!
YOU'RE NOT MEANT TO REMIND ME THAT I... IT DOESN'T WORK LIKE THAT!
MAX, WE'VE DETECTED UNSCHEDULED SEISMIC ACTIVITY AND TEMPERATURE FLUCTUATIONS IN SECTOR 42.
CHECK IT OUT, PLEASE.
DID SHE CALL ME MAX?
THEY DON'T EVEN KNOW WHO I AM ANYMORE!
IT'S ZAXX! ZAXX!

LAVA? WHAT THE HELL'S THAT DOING HERE?
ZAXX TO TERRA-SPHERE CONTROL. THERE'S MORE THAN JUST TEMPERATURE FLUCTUATIONS GOING ON HERE.
I'M STARING AT A LAVA-POOL WHERE -- ACCORDING TO DESIGN SPECIFICATIONS -- THERE'S MEANT TO BE A 'CRYSTAL-CLEAR FRESH-WATER LAGOON, IDEAL FOR SKINNY-DIPPING'.
CONTROL? CONTROL, ARE YOU READING ME?
WHOA!
START HER UP, CLIVE, WE'RE OUTTA HERE. PLAYING HOP-SCOTCH WITH MOLTEN LAVA ISN'T IN MY CONTRACT.
CLIVE, OPEN THE DOOR.
I'M SORRY, SIR.
YOU HAVE BEEN JUDGED INSIGNIFICANT.
YOUR CONTINUED EXISTENCE WOULD BE AN EMBARRASSMENT TO THE UNIVERSE.
WHAT DID YOU SAY?
HAS SOMEONE ELSE BEEN FOOLING WITH YOUR PROGRAMMING? WHO WAS IT?
C'MON, LET ME IN!

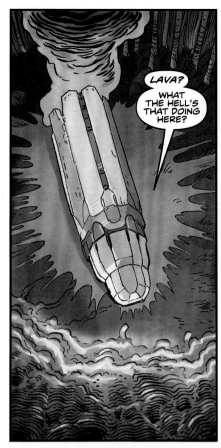

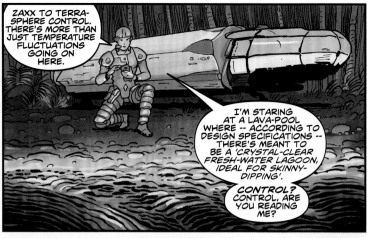

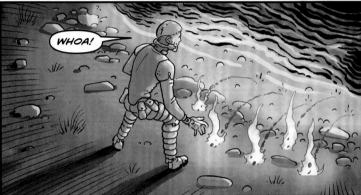

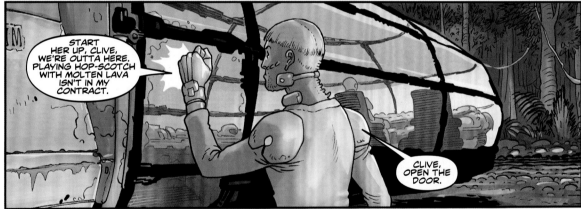

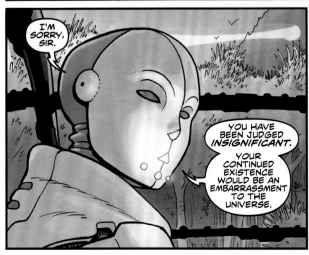

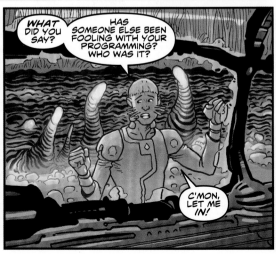

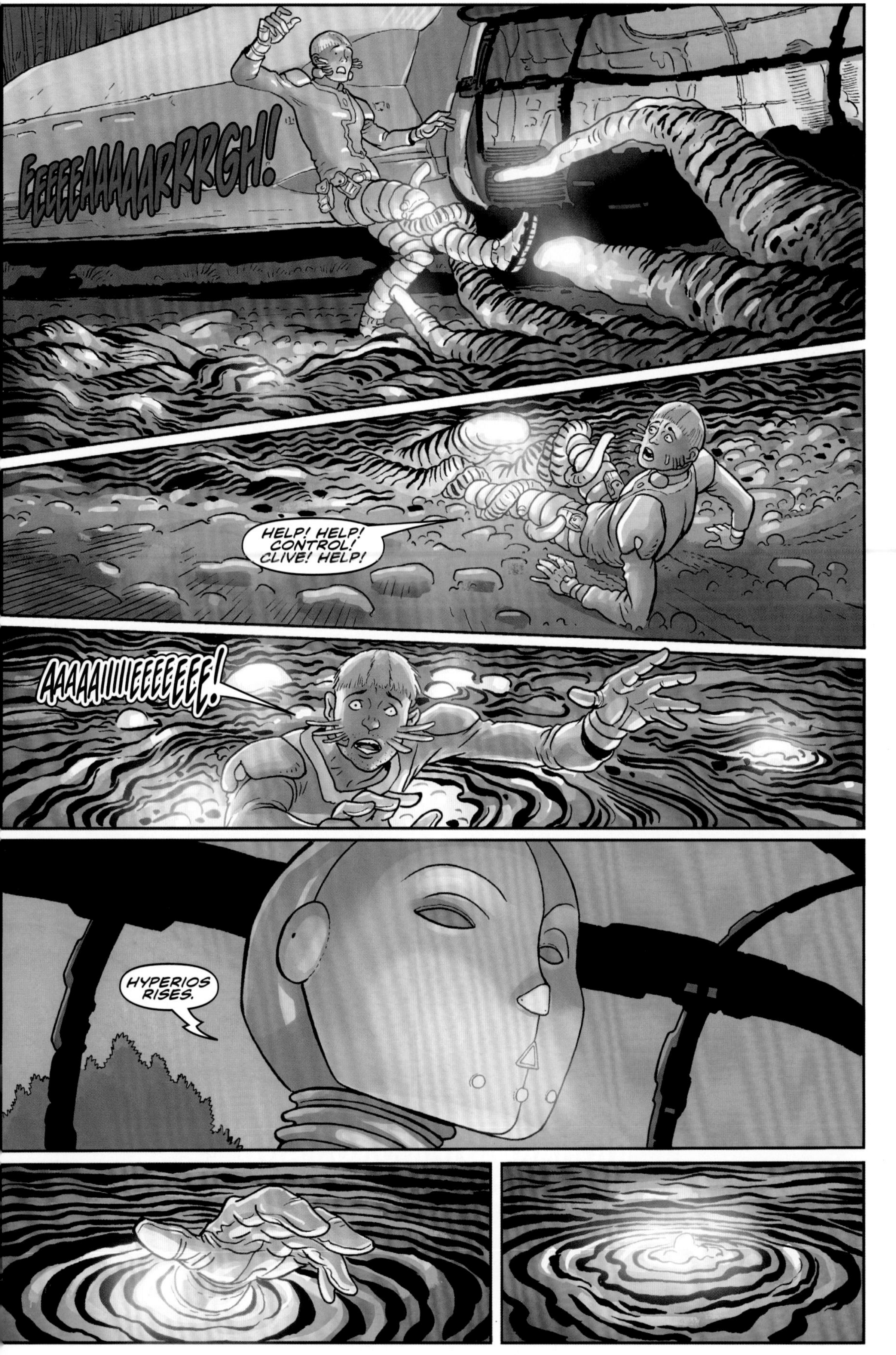
EEEEEAAAAARRRGH!
HELP! HELP! CONTROL! CLIVE! HELP!
AAAAAIIIIIEEEEEEE!
HYPERIOS RISES.

BBC

DOCTOR WHO

THE TWELFT
TERROR

WRITER
ROBBIE MORRISON

LETTERER
RICHARD STARKINGS AND
COMICRAFT'S JIMMY BETANCOURT

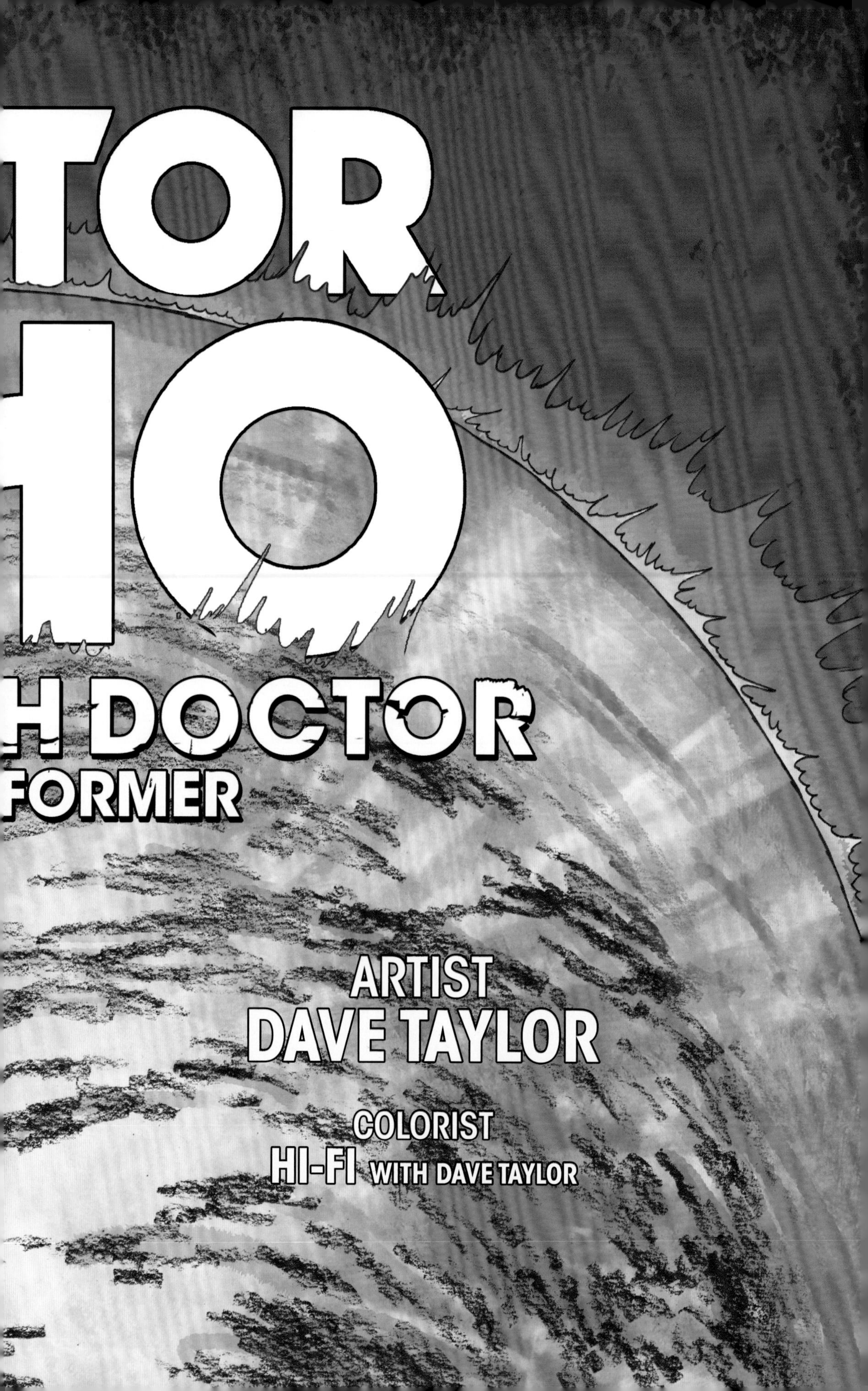
TOR
H DOCTOR
FORMER
ARTIST
DAVE TAYLOR
COLORIST
HI-FI WITH DAVE TAYLOR

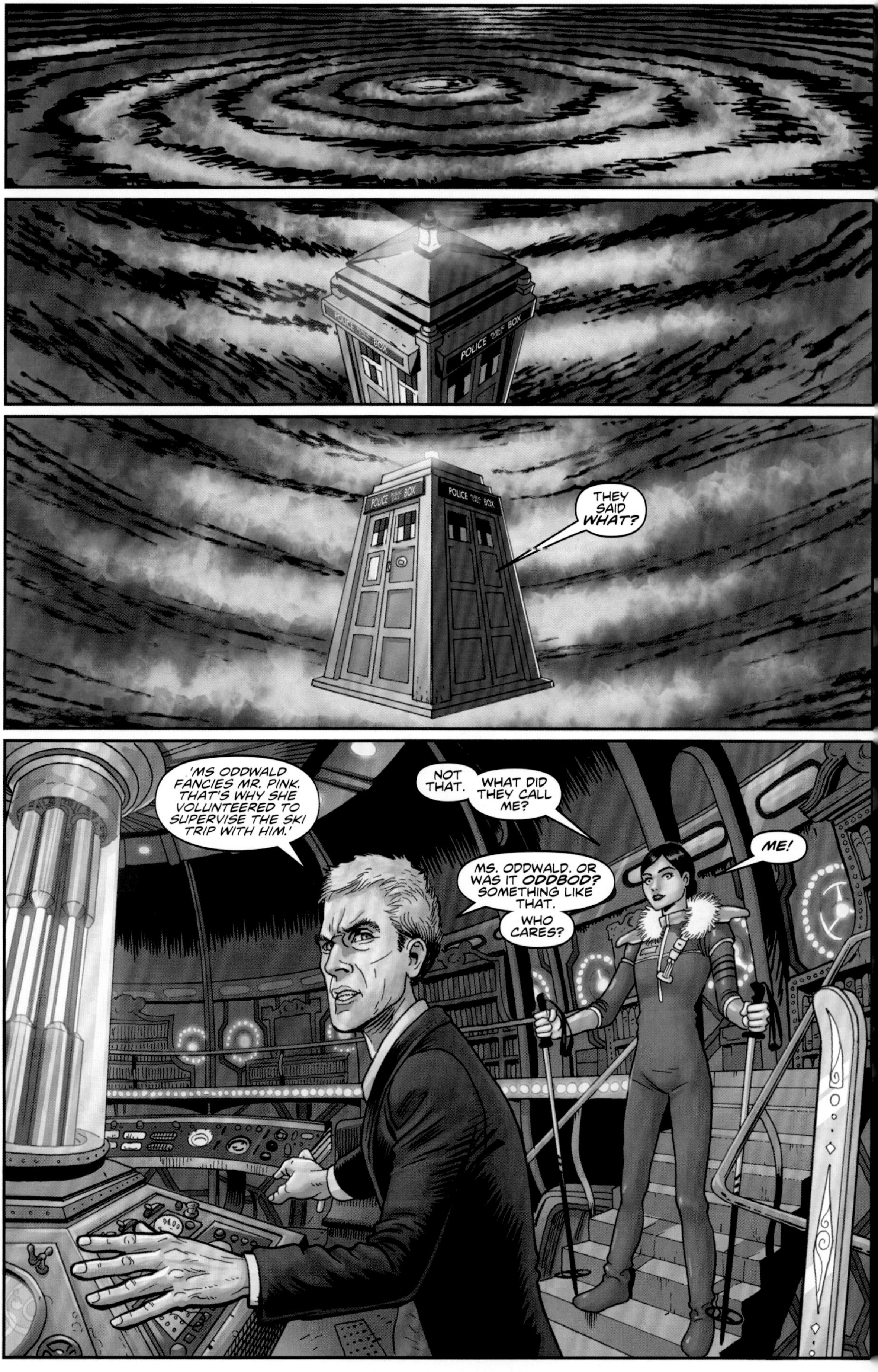
POLICE PUBLIC CALL BOX
THEY SAID WHAT?
'MS ODDWALD FANCIES MR. PINK. THAT'S WHY SHE VOLUNTEERED TO SUPERVISE THE SKI TRIP WITH HIM.'
NOT THAT.
WHAT DID THEY CALL ME?
MS. ODDWALD. OR WAS IT ODDBOD? SOMETHING LIKE THAT.
WHO CARES?
ME!

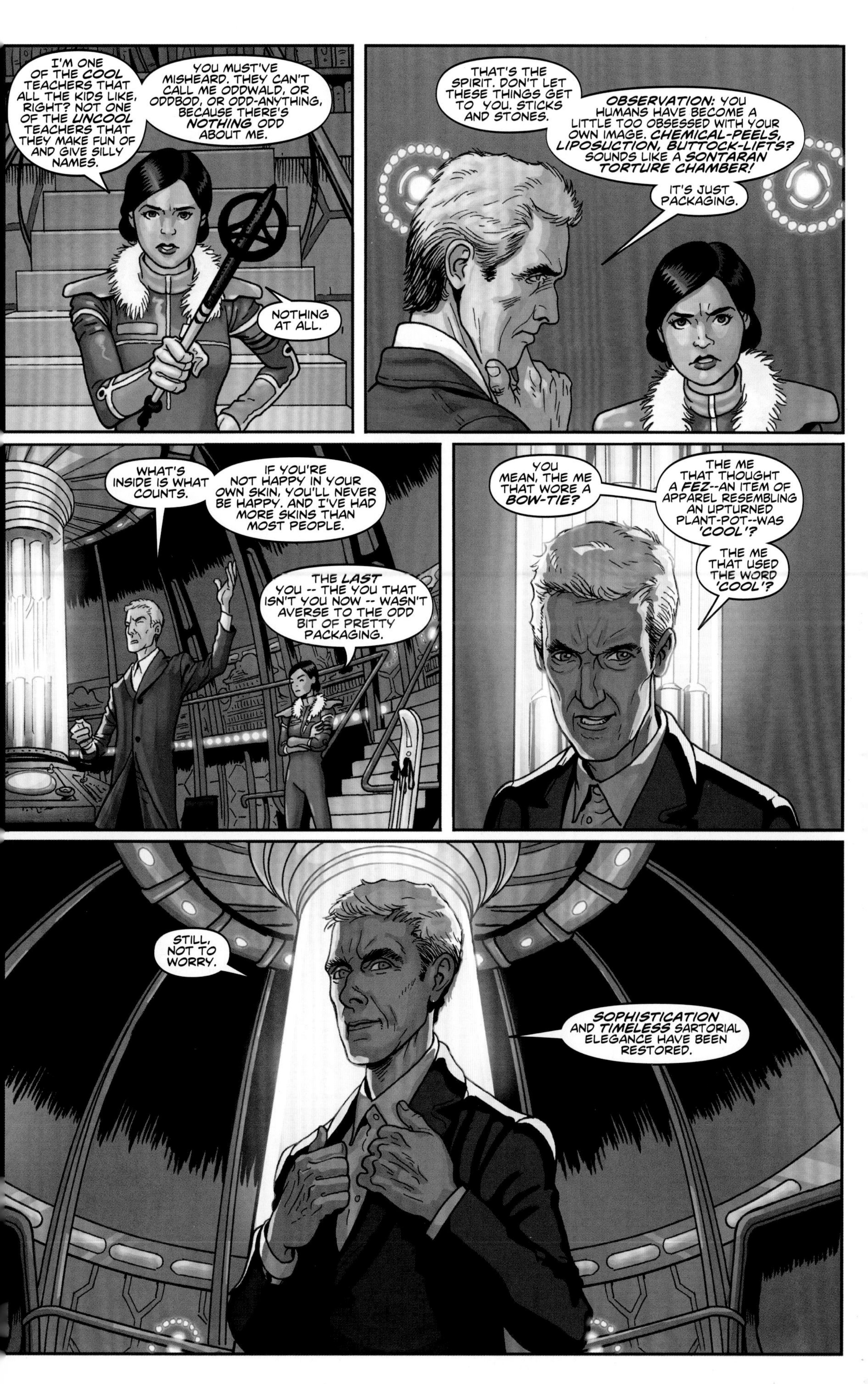
I'M ONE OF THE COOL TEACHERS THAT ALL THE KIDS LIKE, RIGHT? NOT ONE OF THE UNCOOL TEACHERS THAT THEY MAKE FUN OF AND GIVE SILLY NAMES.
YOU MUST'VE MISHEARD. THEY CAN'T CALL ME ODDWALD, OR ODDBOD, OR ODD-ANYTHING, BECAUSE THERE'S NOTHING ODD ABOUT ME.
NOTHING AT ALL.
THAT'S THE SPIRIT. DON'T LET THESE THINGS GET TO YOU. STICKS AND STONES.
OBSERVATION: YOU HUMANS HAVE BECOME A LITTLE TOO OBSESSED WITH YOUR OWN IMAGE. CHEMICAL-PEELS, LIPOSUCTION, BUTTOCK-LIFTS? SOUNDS LIKE A SONTARAN TORTURE CHAMBER!
IT'S JUST PACKAGING.
WHAT'S INSIDE IS WHAT COUNTS.
IF YOU'RE NOT HAPPY IN YOUR OWN SKIN, YOU'LL NEVER BE HAPPY. AND I'VE HAD MORE SKINS THAN MOST PEOPLE.
THE LAST YOU -- THE YOU THAT ISN'T YOU NOW -- WASN'T AVERSE TO THE ODD BIT OF PRETTY PACKAGING.
YOU MEAN, THE ME THAT WORE A BOW-TIE?
THE ME THAT THOUGHT A FEZ--AN ITEM OF APPAREL RESEMBLING AN UPTURNED PLANT-POT--WAS 'COOL'?
THE ME THAT USED THE WORD 'COOL'?
STILL, NOT TO WORRY.
SOPHISTICATION AND TIMELESS SARTORIAL ELEGANCE HAVE BEEN RESTORED.

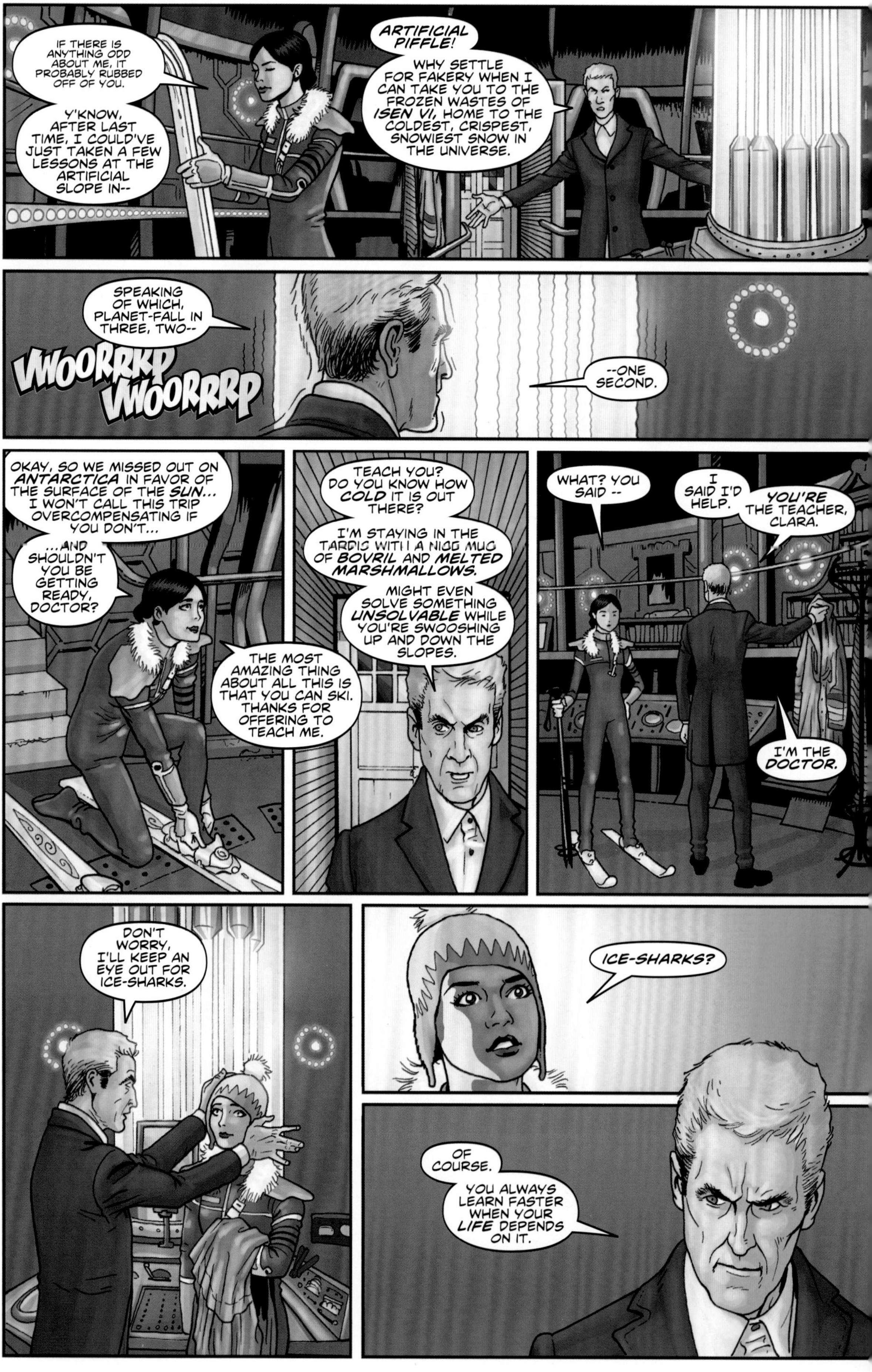

IF THERE IS ANYTHING ODD ABOUT ME, IT PROBABLY RUBBED OFF OF YOU.
Y'KNOW, AFTER LAST TIME, I COULD'VE JUST TAKEN A FEW LESSONS AT THE ARTIFICIAL SLOPE IN--
ARTIFICIAL PIFFLE!
WHY SETTLE FOR FAKERY WHEN I CAN TAKE YOU TO THE FROZEN WASTES OF ISEN VI, HOME TO THE COLDEST, CRISPEST, SNOWIEST SNOW IN THE UNIVERSE.
SPEAKING OF WHICH, PLANET-FALL IN THREE, TWO--
VWOORRRP VWOORRRP
--ONE SECOND.
OKAY, SO WE MISSED OUT ON ANTARCTICA IN FAVOR OF THE SURFACE OF THE SUN... I WON'T CALL THIS TRIP OVERCOMPENSATING IF YOU DON'T...
...AND SHOULDN'T YOU BE GETTING READY, DOCTOR?
THE MOST AMAZING THING ABOUT ALL THIS IS THAT YOU CAN SKI. THANKS FOR OFFERING TO TEACH ME.
TEACH YOU? DO YOU KNOW HOW COLD IT IS OUT THERE?
I'M STAYING IN THE TARDIS WITH A NICE MUG OF BOVRIL AND MELTED MARSHMALLOWS.
MIGHT EVEN SOLVE SOMETHING UNSOLVABLE WHILE YOU'RE SWOOSHING UP AND DOWN THE SLOPES.
WHAT? YOU SAID --
I SAID I'D HELP.
YOU'RE THE TEACHER, CLARA.
I'M THE DOCTOR.
DON'T WORRY, I'LL KEEP AN EYE OUT FOR ICE-SHARKS.
ICE-SHARKS?
OF COURSE.
YOU ALWAYS LEARN FASTER WHEN YOUR LIFE DEPENDS ON IT.

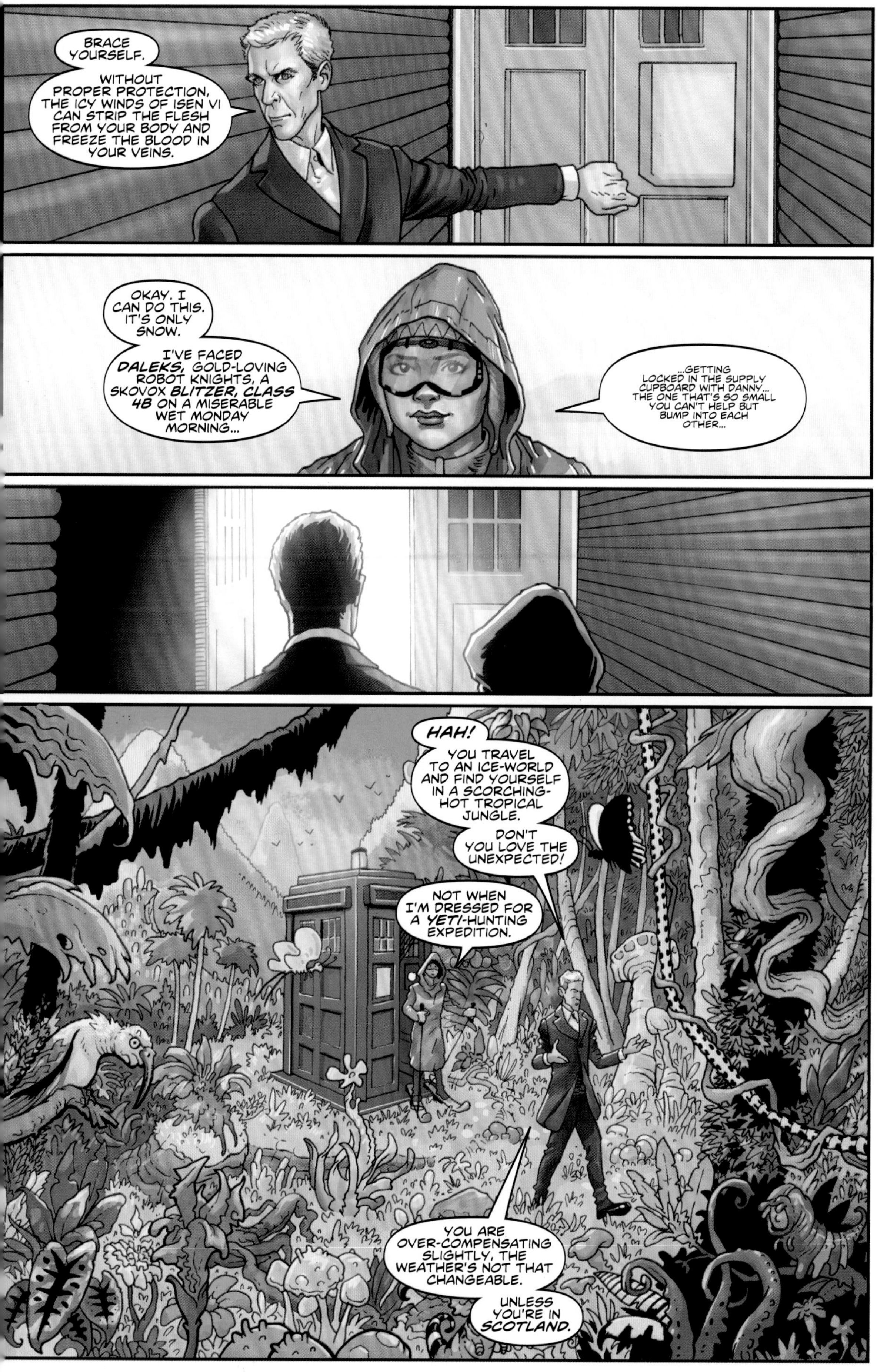
BRACE YOURSELF.
WITHOUT PROPER PROTECTION, THE ICY WINDS OF ISEN VI CAN STRIP THE FLESH FROM YOUR BODY AND FREEZE THE BLOOD IN YOUR VEINS.
OKAY. I CAN DO THIS. IT'S ONLY SNOW.
I'VE FACED DALEKS, GOLD-LOVING ROBOT KNIGHTS, A SKOVOX BLITZER, CLASS 4B ON A MISERABLE WET MONDAY MORNING...
...GETTING LOCKED IN THE SUPPLY CUPBOARD WITH DANNY... THE ONE THAT'S SO SMALL YOU CAN'T HELP BUT BUMP INTO EACH OTHER...
HAH!
YOU TRAVEL TO AN ICE-WORLD AND FIND YOURSELF IN A SCORCHING-HOT TROPICAL JUNGLE.
DON'T YOU LOVE THE UNEXPECTED!
NOT WHEN I'M DRESSED FOR A YETI-HUNTING EXPEDITION.
YOU ARE OVER-COMPENSATING SLIGHTLY, THE WEATHER'S NOT THAT CHANGEABLE.
UNLESS YOU'RE IN SCOTLAND.

ARE YOU SURE WE'RE IN THE RIGHT PLACE?

NO DOUBT ABOUT IT. SPATIAL AND TEMPORAL CO-ORDINATES ALL CO-ORDINATE NICELY.

CURIOUS. THE LAST PLANETARY SURVEY OF THIS SYSTEM WAS ONLY A FEW DECADES AGO -- AND ISEN VI WAS STILL A GIANT SNOWBALL THEN.

QUESTION: WHAT NATURAL PHENOMENA COULD TRANSFORM A WORLD SO RADICALLY IN SUCH A SHORT SPACE OF TIME?

A REALLY HOT METEOR --?

ANSWER: NONE.

WHICH MEANS OUTSIDE INTERFERENCE.

I HATE OUTSIDE INTERFERENCE.

INTERESTING, BECAUSE ALL YOU DO IS INTERFERE.

NONSENSE, THINGS JUST SEEM TO HAPPEN WHENEVER I'M AROUND.

I'M A MAGNET FOR ADVENTURE.

DOCTOR, YOU SEEM PRETTY WELL-PREPARED FOR ALL THIS. DID YOU HAVE ANY OTHER REASON FOR COMING HERE, APART FROM NOT TEACHING ME TO SKI?

AN ULTERIOR MOTIVE?

NO! HOW COULD YOU THINK SUCH A THING?

ALTHOUGH, THERE WAS A SIGNAL...

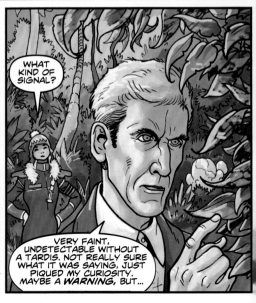

WHAT KIND OF SIGNAL?

VERY FAINT, UNDETECTABLE WITHOUT A TARDIS. NOT REALLY SURE WHAT IT WAS SAYING, JUST PIQUED MY CURIOSITY. MAYBE A WARNING, BUT...

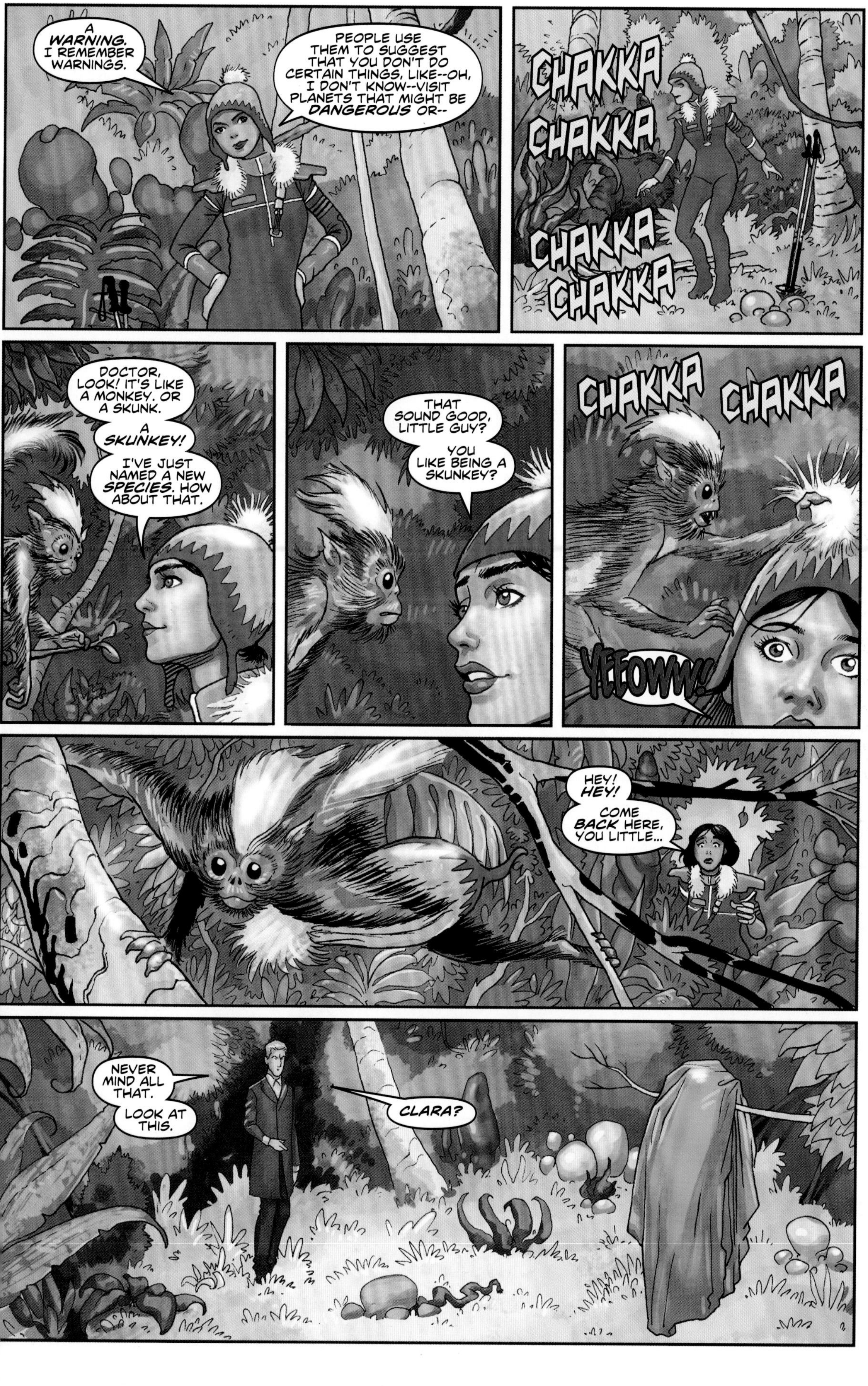

A WARNING. I REMEMBER WARNINGS.
PEOPLE USE THEM TO SUGGEST THAT YOU DON'T DO CERTAIN THINGS, LIKE--OH, I DON'T KNOW--VISIT PLANETS THAT MIGHT BE DANGEROUS OR--
CHAKKA CHAKKA
CHAKKA CHAKKA
DOCTOR, LOOK! IT'S LIKE A MONKEY. OR A SKUNK.
A SKUNKEY!
I'VE JUST NAMED A NEW SPECIES. HOW ABOUT THAT.
THAT SOUND GOOD, LITTLE GUY?
YOU LIKE BEING A SKUNKEY?
CHAKKA CHAKKA
YEEOWW!
HEY! HEY!
COME BACK HERE, YOU LITTLE...
NEVER MIND ALL THAT.
LOOK AT THIS.
CLARA?

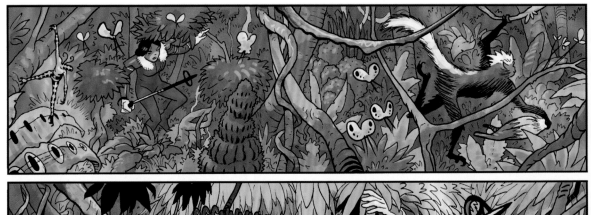

RIGHT...

YOU AND WHOSE *ARMY,* HUH?

HAT! NOW!

SHAKKA

SHAKKA

SHAKKA

SHAKKA

DOCTOR!

FFDDMMPH

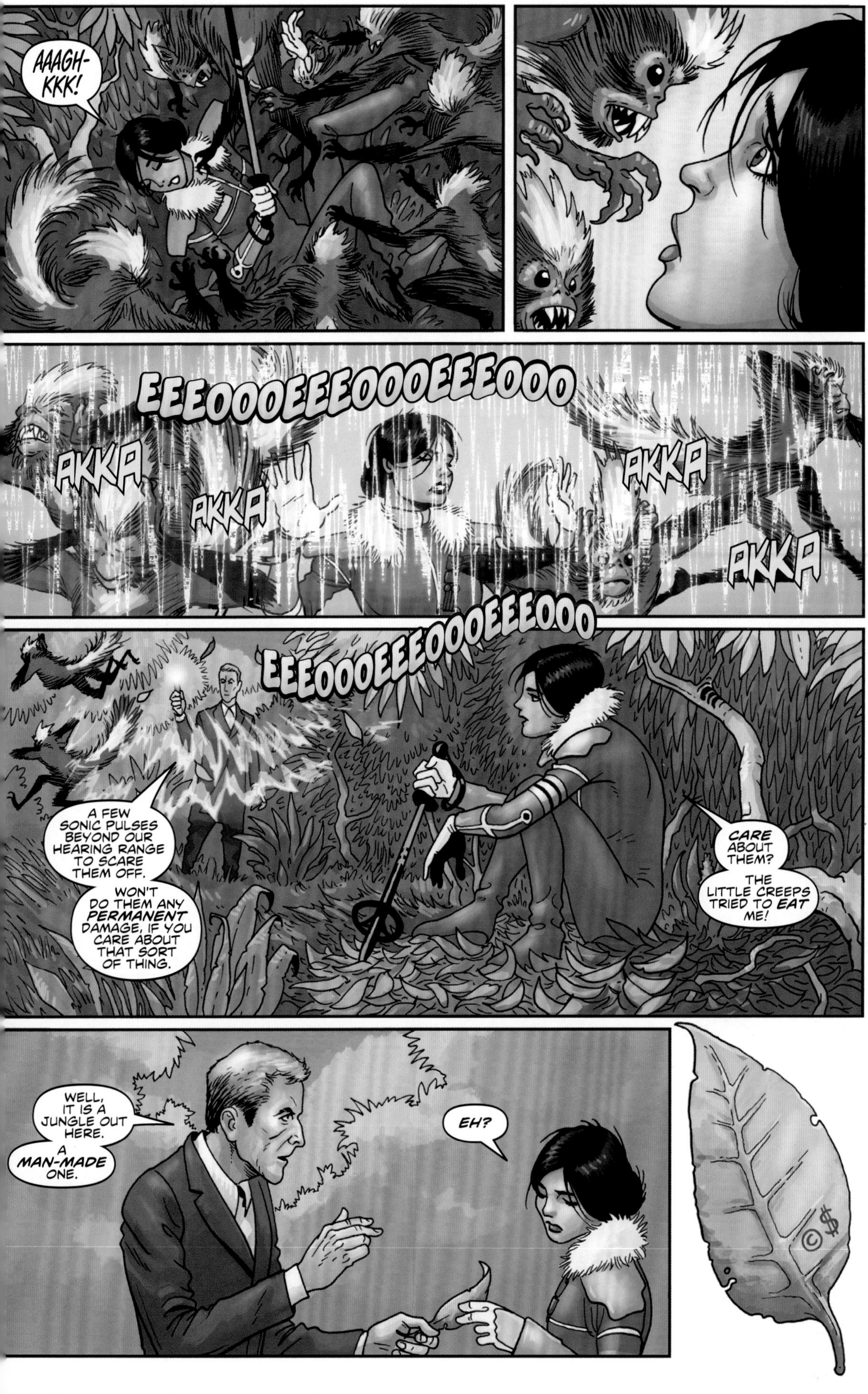

AAAGH-KKK!
EEEOOOEEEOOOEEEOOO
AKKA
AKKA
AKKA
AKKA
EEEOOOEEEOOOEEEOOO
A FEW SONIC PULSES BEYOND OUR HEARING RANGE TO SCARE THEM OFF.
WON'T DO THEM ANY PERMANENT DAMAGE, IF YOU CARE ABOUT THAT SORT OF THING.
CARE ABOUT THEM?
THE LITTLE CREEPS TRIED TO EAT ME!
WELL, IT IS A JUNGLE OUT HERE.
A MAN-MADE ONE.
EH?

A COPYRIGHT NOTICE AND A *DOLLAR* SIGN? I DON'T...

ARE YOU SAYING SOMEONE *MADE* THIS PLACE?

MORE LIKE RE-MADE. WHAT YOU'D PROBABLY CALL A MAKEOVER.

IN FACT, IF YOU SHAVED ONE OF YOUR LITTLE PALS BACK THERE, I SUSPECT YOU'D FIND THE SAME MARKINGS.

YUCK!

AND WHAT DOES THE DOLLAR SIGN MEAN?

MONEY, CLARA! *OBSCENE* AMOUNTS OF MONEY. MORE MONEY THAN SENSE, BECAUSE YOU MESS WITH NATURAL EVOLUTION AT YOUR OWN PERIL.

I *HATE* MONEY!

EXPLAINS WHY YOU NEVER HAVE ANY.

OR AT LEAST WHY IT TAKES YOU SO LONG TO GET THE COFFEE --

ATTENTION!

THIS WORLD IS PRIVATE PROPERTY. YOU ARE TRESPASSING.

YOUR SPACECRAFT IS ALREADY IN OUR CUSTODY. SURRENDER AND YOU WILL NOT BE HARMED.

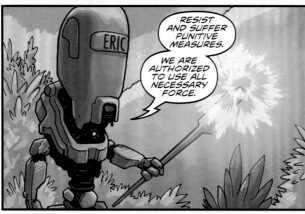

RESIST AND SUFFER PUNITIVE MEASURES.

WE ARE AUTHORIZED TO USE ALL NECESSARY FORCE.

OH, YOU *ARE*, ARE YOU?

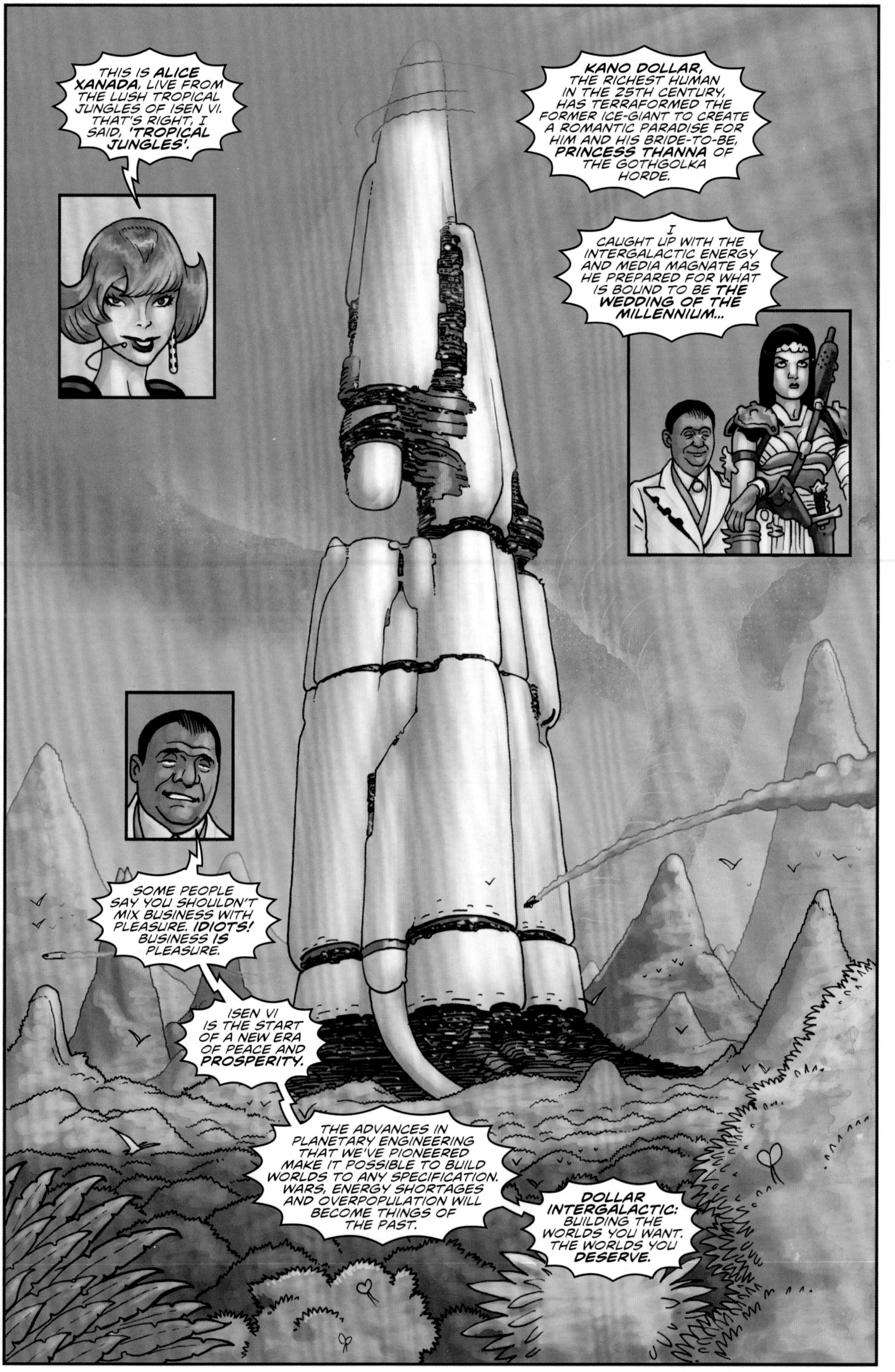
THIS IS ALICE XANADA, LIVE FROM THE LUSH TROPICAL JUNGLES OF ISEN VI. THAT'S RIGHT, I SAID, 'TROPICAL JUNGLES'.
KANO DOLLAR, THE RICHEST HUMAN IN THE 25TH CENTURY, HAS TERRAFORMED THE FORMER ICE-GIANT TO CREATE A ROMANTIC PARADISE FOR HIM AND HIS BRIDE-TO-BE, PRINCESS THANNA OF THE GOTHGOLKA HORDE.
I CAUGHT UP WITH THE INTERGALACTIC ENERGY AND MEDIA MAGNATE AS HE PREPARED FOR WHAT IS BOUND TO BE THE WEDDING OF THE MILLENNIUM...
SOME PEOPLE SAY YOU SHOULDN'T MIX BUSINESS WITH PLEASURE. IDIOTS! BUSINESS IS PLEASURE.
ISEN VI IS THE START OF A NEW ERA OF PEACE AND PROSPERITY.
THE ADVANCES IN PLANETARY ENGINEERING THAT WE'VE PIONEERED MAKE IT POSSIBLE TO BUILD WORLDS TO ANY SPECIFICATION. WARS, ENERGY SHORTAGES AND OVERPOPULATION WILL BECOME THINGS OF THE PAST.
DOLLAR INTERGALACTIC: BUILDING THE WORLDS YOU WANT. THE WORLDS YOU DESERVE.

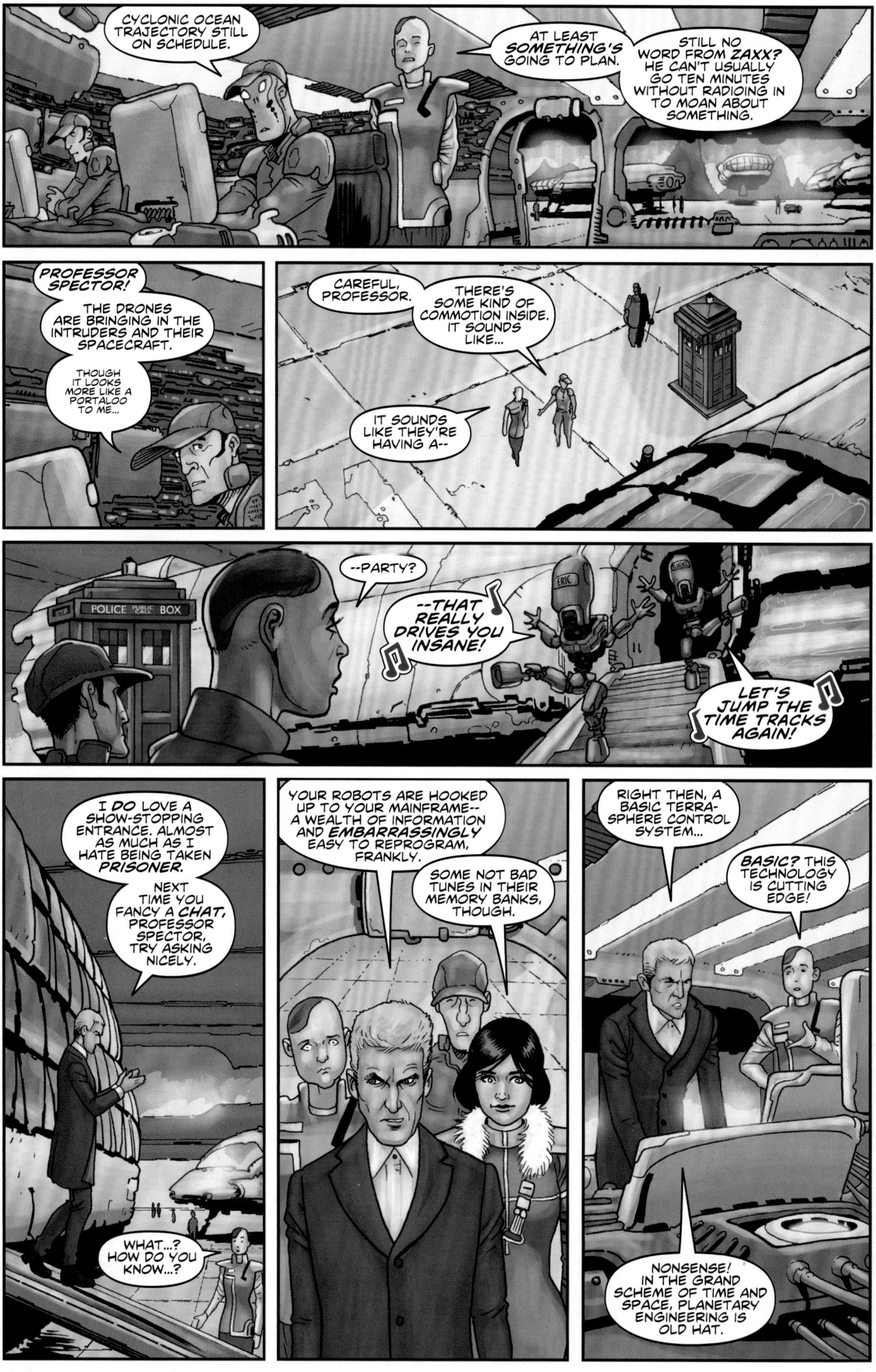
CYCLONIC OCEAN TRAJECTORY STILL ON SCHEDULE.
AT LEAST SOMETHING'S GOING TO PLAN.
STILL NO WORD FROM ZAXX? HE CAN'T USUALLY GO TEN MINUTES WITHOUT RADIOING IN TO MOAN ABOUT SOMETHING.
PROFESSOR SPECTOR!
THE DRONES ARE BRINGING IN THE INTRUDERS AND THEIR SPACECRAFT.
THOUGH IT LOOKS MORE LIKE A PORTALOO TO ME...
CAREFUL, PROFESSOR.
THERE'S SOME KIND OF COMMOTION INSIDE. IT SOUNDS LIKE...
IT SOUNDS LIKE THEY'RE HAVING A--
POLICE PUBLIC CALL BOX
--PARTY?
--THAT REALLY DRIVES YOU INSANE!
ERIC
LET'S JUMP THE TIME TRACKS AGAIN!
I DO LOVE A SHOW-STOPPING ENTRANCE. ALMOST AS MUCH AS I HATE BEING TAKEN PRISONER.
NEXT TIME YOU FANCY A CHAT, PROFESSOR SPECTOR, TRY ASKING NICELY.
WHAT...? HOW DO YOU KNOW...?
YOUR ROBOTS ARE HOOKED UP TO YOUR MAINFRAME-- A WEALTH OF INFORMATION AND EMBARRASSINGLY EASY TO REPROGRAM, FRANKLY.
SOME NOT BAD TUNES IN THEIR MEMORY BANKS, THOUGH.
RIGHT THEN, A BASIC TERRA-SPHERE CONTROL SYSTEM...
BASIC? THIS TECHNOLOGY IS CUTTING EDGE!
NONSENSE! IN THE GRAND SCHEME OF TIME AND SPACE, PLANETARY ENGINEERING IS OLD HAT.

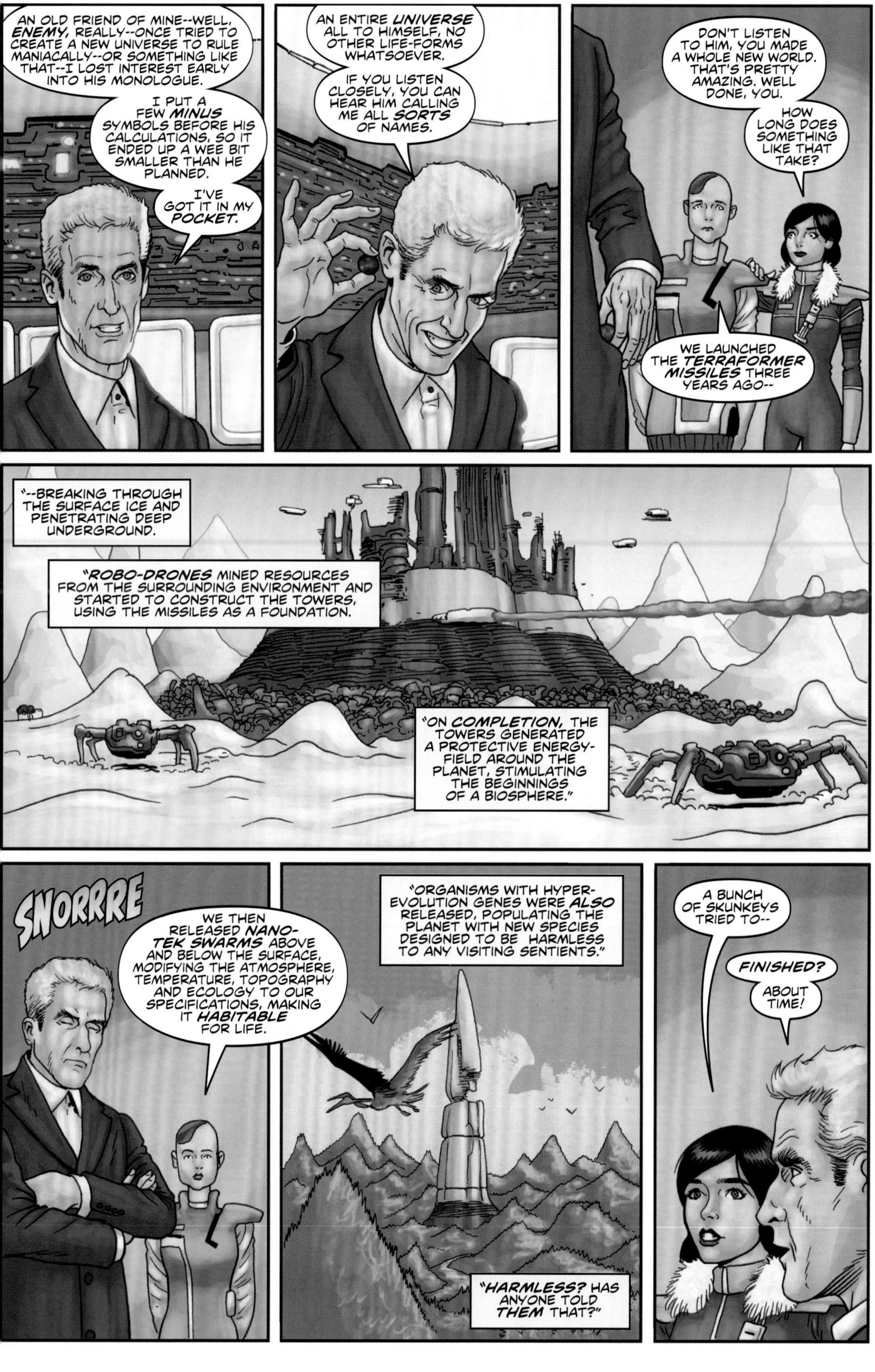
AN OLD FRIEND OF MINE--WELL, ENEMY, REALLY--ONCE TRIED TO CREATE A NEW UNIVERSE TO RULE MANIACALLY--OR SOMETHING LIKE THAT--I LOST INTEREST EARLY INTO HIS MONOLOGUE.
I PUT A FEW MINUS SYMBOLS BEFORE HIS CALCULATIONS, SO IT ENDED UP A WEE BIT SMALLER THAN HE PLANNED.
I'VE GOT IT IN MY POCKET.
AN ENTIRE UNIVERSE ALL TO HIMSELF, NO OTHER LIFE-FORMS WHATSOEVER.
IF YOU LISTEN CLOSELY, YOU CAN HEAR HIM CALLING ME ALL SORTS OF NAMES.
DON'T LISTEN TO HIM, YOU MADE A WHOLE NEW WORLD. THAT'S PRETTY AMAZING. WELL DONE, YOU.
HOW LONG DOES SOMETHING LIKE THAT TAKE?
WE LAUNCHED THE TERRAFORMER MISSILES THREE YEARS AGO--
"--BREAKING THROUGH THE SURFACE ICE AND PENETRATING DEEP UNDERGROUND.
"ROBO-DRONES MINED RESOURCES FROM THE SURROUNDING ENVIRONMENT AND STARTED TO CONSTRUCT THE TOWERS, USING THE MISSILES AS A FOUNDATION.
"ON COMPLETION, THE TOWERS GENERATED A PROTECTIVE ENERGY-FIELD AROUND THE PLANET, STIMULATING THE BEGINNINGS OF A BIOSPHERE."
SNORRRE
WE THEN RELEASED NANO-TEK SWARMS ABOVE AND BELOW THE SURFACE, MODIFYING THE ATMOSPHERE, TEMPERATURE, TOPOGRAPHY AND ECOLOGY TO OUR SPECIFICATIONS, MAKING IT HABITABLE FOR LIFE.
"ORGANISMS WITH HYPER-EVOLUTION GENES WERE ALSO RELEASED, POPULATING THE PLANET WITH NEW SPECIES DESIGNED TO BE HARMLESS TO ANY VISITING SENTIENTS."
"HARMLESS? HAS ANYONE TOLD THEM THAT?"
A BUNCH OF SKUNKEYS TRIED TO--
FINISHED?
ABOUT TIME!

TEMPERATURES ESCALATING AT BOTH POLES. GLACIERS MELTING AT A QUITE TERRIFYING RATE.

SEISMIC ACTIVITY OFF THE SCALE ON EVERY CONTINENT.

YOU'RE HEADING FOR A *GLOBAL CATACLYSM*, PROFESSOR. I'D RUN AWAY IF I WERE YOU. VERY FAST.

MY WORLD. *NO ONE* LEAVES WITHOUT MY PERMISSION.

SOME OF THE MOST POWERFUL AND INFLUENTIAL BEINGS IN THE GALAXY ARE HERE, AND RIGHT NOW I NEED *ALL* THAT POWER AND INFLUENCE ON MY SIDE.

I'VE INDULGED YOUR *SO-CALLED* GENIUS FOR TOO LONG, PROFESSOR.

STABILIZE ISEN VI OR I'LL SHOW YOU EXACTLY HOW *CUTTHROAT* A BUSINESSMAN I CAN BE.

THE COMPANY YOU KEEP LEAVES *MUCH* TO BE DESIRED.

FUNDING'S HARD TO COME BY.

SO'S INTEGRITY.

WHO THE HELL ARE YOU? WHAT ARE YOU DOING HERE?

HE'S THE DOCTOR.

DOCTOR WHO?

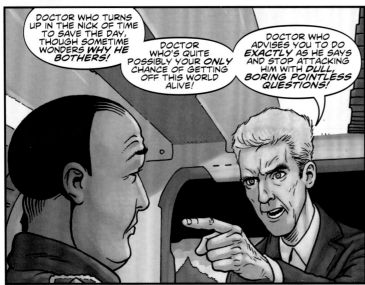

DOCTOR WHO TURNS UP IN THE NICK OF TIME TO SAVE THE DAY, THOUGH SOMETIME WONDERS *WHY HE BOTHERS!*

DOCTOR WHO'S QUITE POSSIBLY YOUR *ONLY* CHANCE OF GETTING OFF THIS WORLD ALIVE!

DOCTOR WHO ADVISES YOU TO DO *EXACTLY* AS HE SAYS AND STOP ATTACKING HIM WITH *DULL, BORING POINTLESS QUESTIONS!*

AND THE DOCTOR WHO'S JUST REMEMBERED THAT HE KNOWS *VENUSIAN KARATE*, SO IF ANYONE ELSE ASKS ANOTHER DULL --

ER, HELLO?

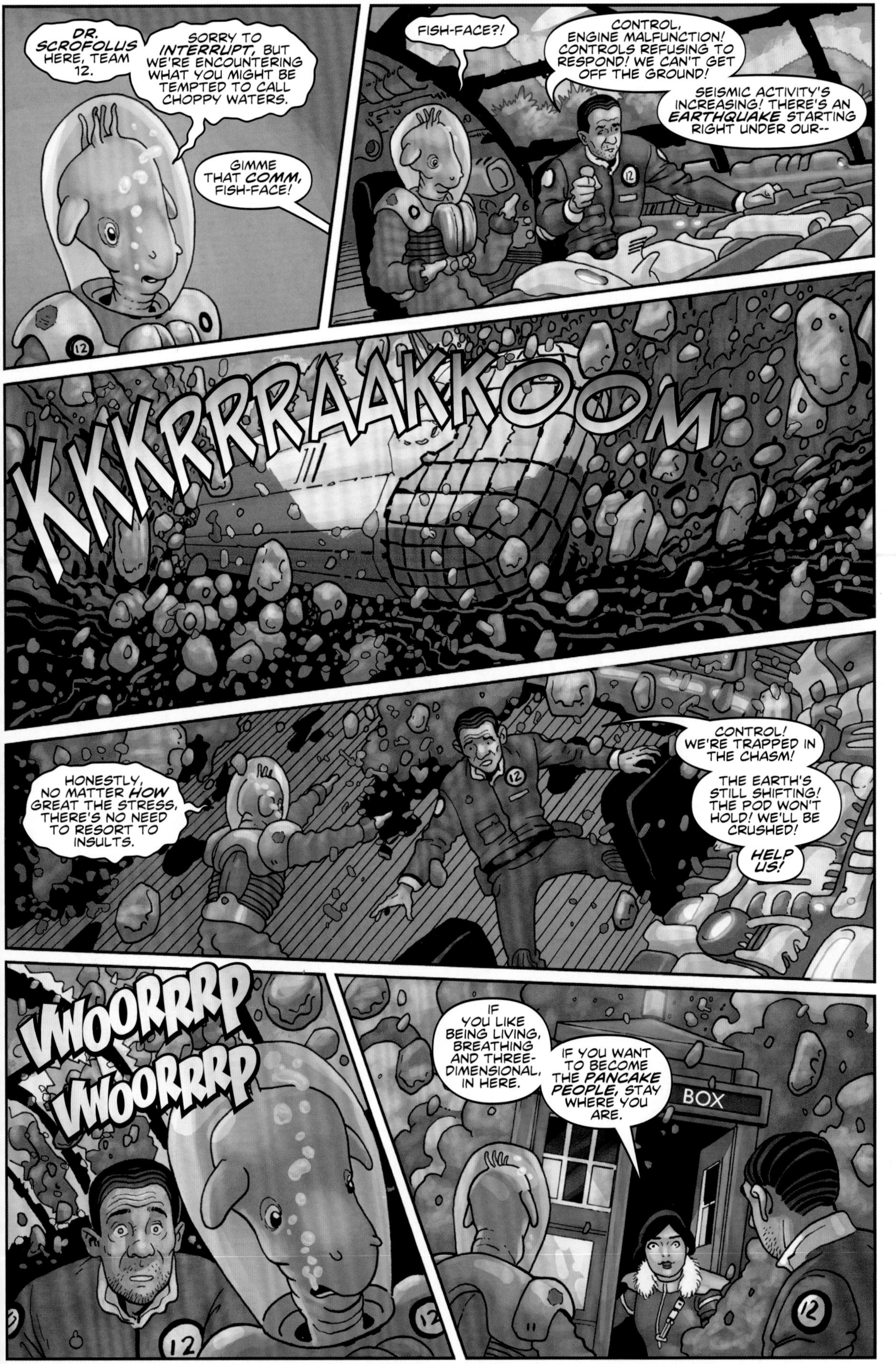
DR. SCROFOLUS HERE, TEAM 12.
SORRY TO INTERRUPT, BUT WE'RE ENCOUNTERING WHAT YOU MIGHT BE TEMPTED TO CALL CHOPPY WATERS.
GIMME THAT COMM, FISH-FACE!
FISH-FACE?!
CONTROL, ENGINE MALFUNCTION! CONTROLS REFUSING TO RESPOND! WE CAN'T GET OFF THE GROUND!
SEISMIC ACTIVITY'S INCREASING! THERE'S AN EARTHQUAKE STARTING RIGHT UNDER OUR--
KKKRRRAAKKOOOM
HONESTLY, NO MATTER HOW GREAT THE STRESS, THERE'S NO NEED TO RESORT TO INSULTS.
CONTROL! WE'RE TRAPPED IN THE CHASM!
THE EARTH'S STILL SHIFTING! THE POD WON'T HOLD! WE'LL BE CRUSHED!
HELP US!
VWOORRRP VWOORRRP
IF YOU LIKE BEING LIVING, BREATHING AND THREE-DIMENSIONAL, IN HERE.
IF YOU WANT TO BECOME THE PANCAKE PEOPLE, STAY WHERE YOU ARE.
BOX

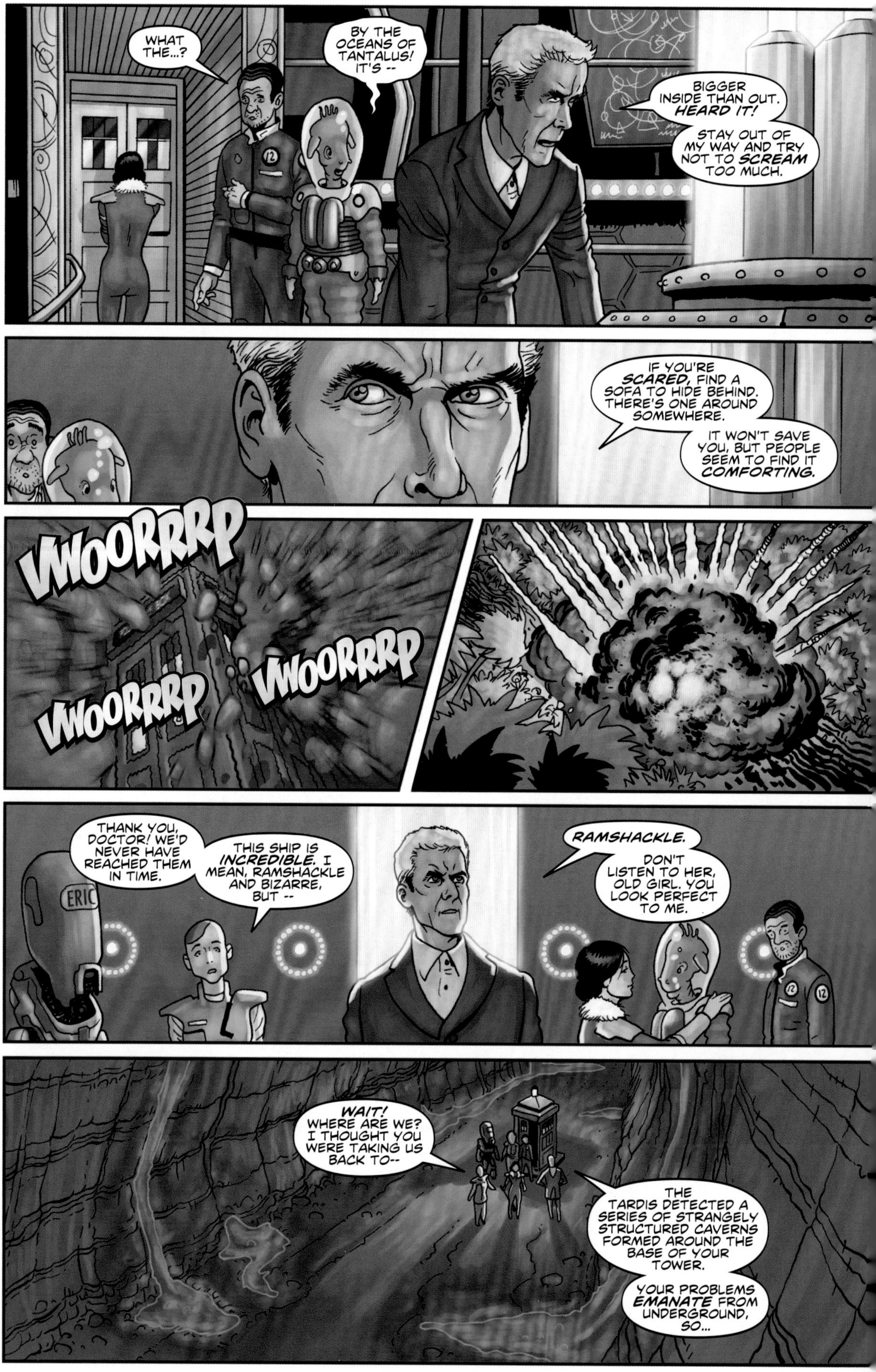

WHAT THE...?
BY THE OCEANS OF TANTALUS! IT'S --
BIGGER INSIDE THAN OUT. HEARD IT!
STAY OUT OF MY WAY AND TRY NOT TO SCREAM TOO MUCH.
IF YOU'RE SCARED, FIND A SOFA TO HIDE BEHIND. THERE'S ONE AROUND SOMEWHERE.
IT WON'T SAVE YOU, BUT PEOPLE SEEM TO FIND IT COMFORTING.
VWOORRRP
VWOORRRP
VWOORRRP
THANK YOU, DOCTOR! WE'D NEVER HAVE REACHED THEM IN TIME.
THIS SHIP IS INCREDIBLE. I MEAN, RAMSHACKLE AND BIZARRE, BUT --
RAMSHACKLE.
DON'T LISTEN TO HER, OLD GIRL. YOU LOOK PERFECT TO ME.
ERIC
WAIT! WHERE ARE WE? I THOUGHT YOU WERE TAKING US BACK TO--
THE TARDIS DETECTED A SERIES OF STRANGELY STRUCTURED CAVERNS FORMED AROUND THE BASE OF YOUR TOWER.
YOUR PROBLEMS EMANATE FROM UNDERGROUND, SO...

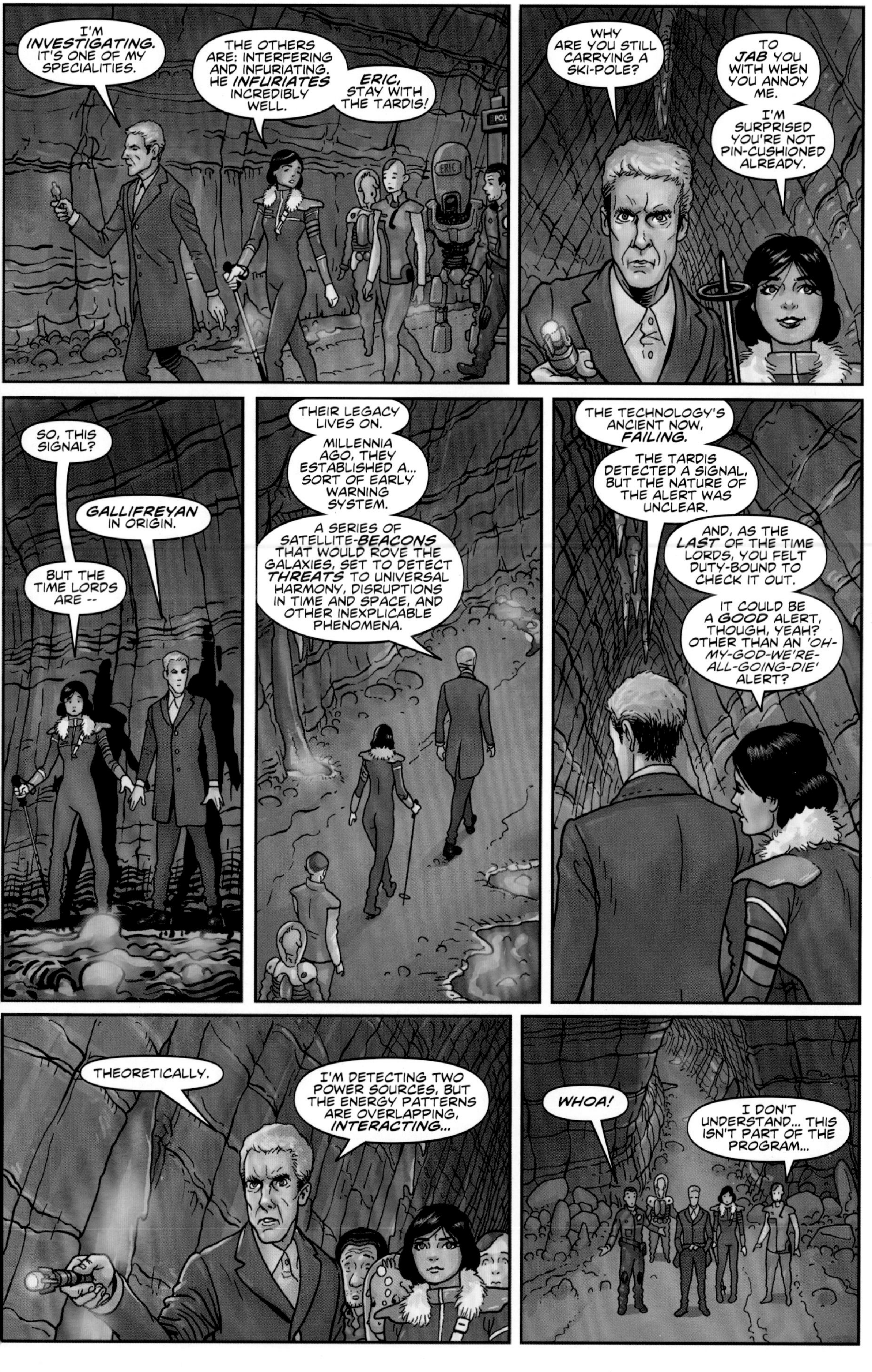
I'M INVESTIGATING. IT'S ONE OF MY SPECIALITIES.
THE OTHERS ARE: INTERFERING AND INFURIATING. HE INFURIATES INCREDIBLY WELL.
ERIC, STAY WITH THE TARDIS!
ERIC
POL
WHY ARE YOU STILL CARRYING A SKI-POLE?
TO JAB YOU WITH WHEN YOU ANNOY ME.
I'M SURPRISED YOU'RE NOT PIN-CUSHIONED ALREADY.
SO, THIS SIGNAL?
GALLIFREYAN IN ORIGIN.
BUT THE TIME LORDS ARE --
THEIR LEGACY LIVES ON.
MILLENNIA AGO, THEY ESTABLISHED A... SORT OF EARLY WARNING SYSTEM.
A SERIES OF SATELLITE-BEACONS THAT WOULD ROVE THE GALAXIES, SET TO DETECT THREATS TO UNIVERSAL HARMONY, DISRUPTIONS IN TIME AND SPACE, AND OTHER INEXPLICABLE PHENOMENA.
THE TECHNOLOGY'S ANCIENT NOW, FAILING.
THE TARDIS DETECTED A SIGNAL, BUT THE NATURE OF THE ALERT WAS UNCLEAR.
AND, AS THE LAST OF THE TIME LORDS, YOU FELT DUTY-BOUND TO CHECK IT OUT.
IT COULD BE A GOOD ALERT, THOUGH, YEAH? OTHER THAN AN 'OH-MY-GOD-WE'RE-ALL-GOING-DIE' ALERT?
THEORETICALLY.
I'M DETECTING TWO POWER SOURCES, BUT THE ENERGY PATTERNS ARE OVERLAPPING, INTERACTING...
WHOA!
I DON'T UNDERSTAND... THIS ISN'T PART OF THE PROGRAM...

AMAZING HOW OFTEN PLANS DON'T QUITE GO TO PLAN.

WHEN YOU LAUNCHED THE TERRAFORMER AT ISEN VI, IT PENETRATED MORE THAN JUST THE PLANET.

IMPOSSIBLE! WE SCANNED EXTENSIVELY. EVERYTHING WAS CLEAR.

SOMETHING THAT'S GONE TO THE BOTHER OF CONCEALING ITSELF MILES UNDERGROUND JUST *MIGHT* EMPLOY SENSOR-SHIELDS.

WHAT IS IT, DOCTOR? A SHIP?

AT ONE TIME, MAYBE, BUT NOW...

IT'S FUSED WITH THE TERRA-SPHERE, CREATING A SINGLE ENTITY. *THIS* IS WHAT'S IN EVOLUTIONARY CONTROL OF ISEN VI, PROFESSOR.

NOT YOU.

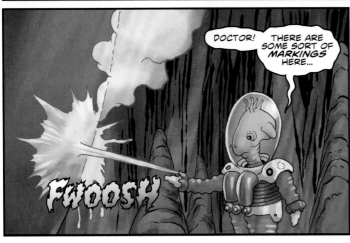

DOCTOR! THERE ARE SOME SORT OF *MARKINGS* HERE...

FWOOSH

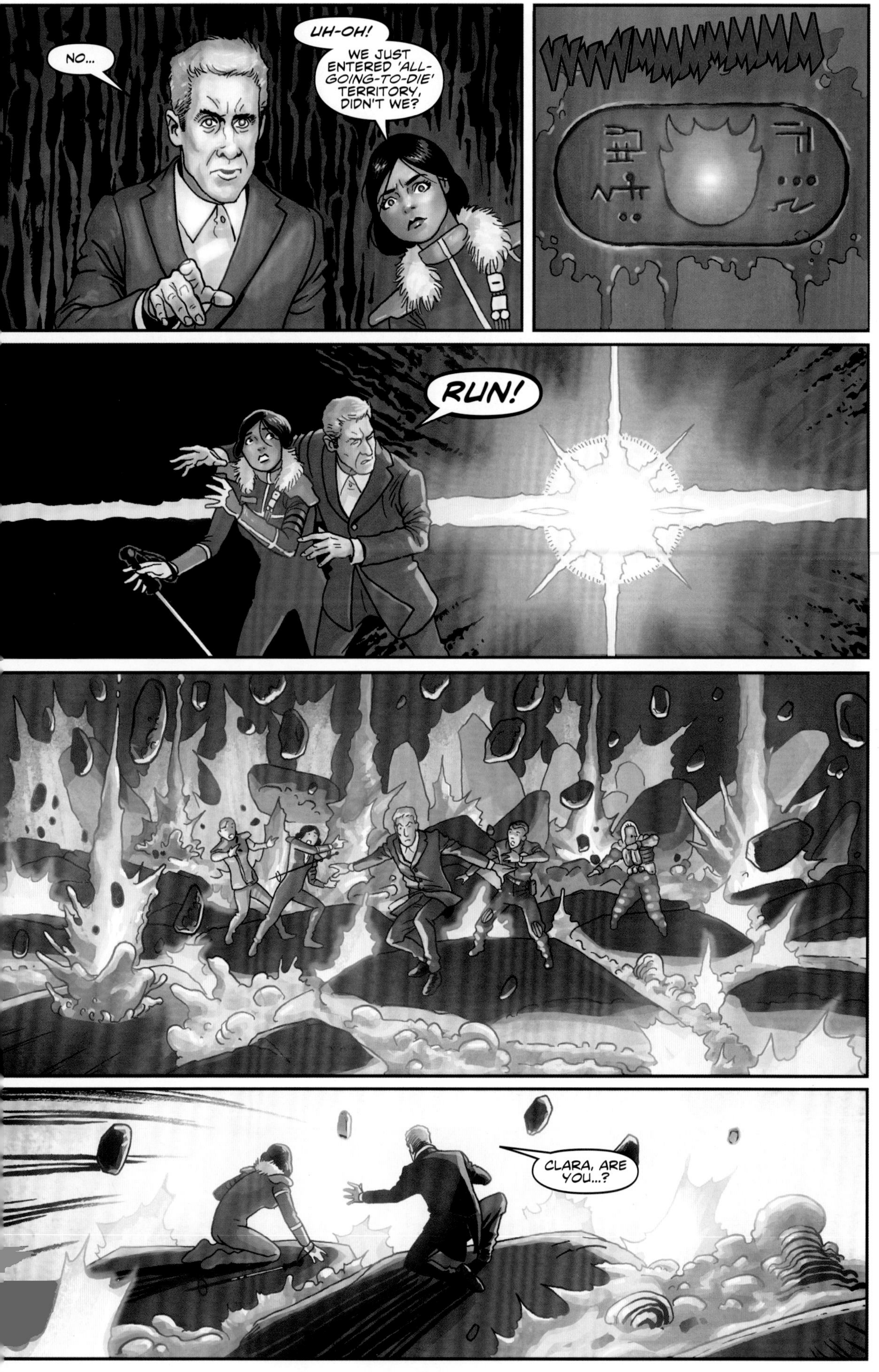
NO...
UH-OH!
WE JUST ENTERED 'ALL-GOING-TO-DIE' TERRITORY, DIDN'T WE?
VWWMMMMMMM
RUN!
CLARA, ARE YOU...?

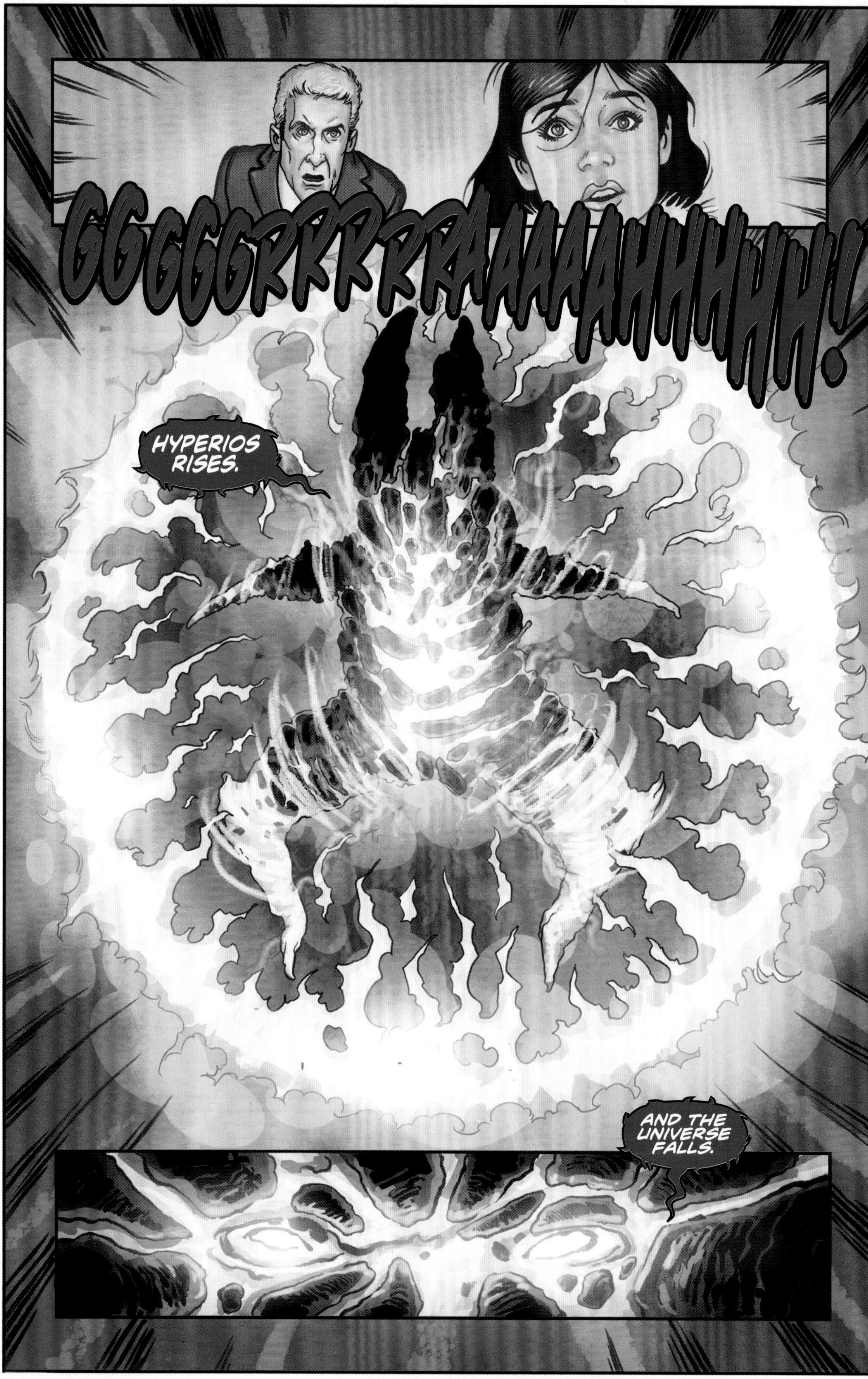
GGGGGRRRRRRAAAAAAHHHHHH!
HYPERIOS RISES.
AND THE UNIVERSE FALLS.

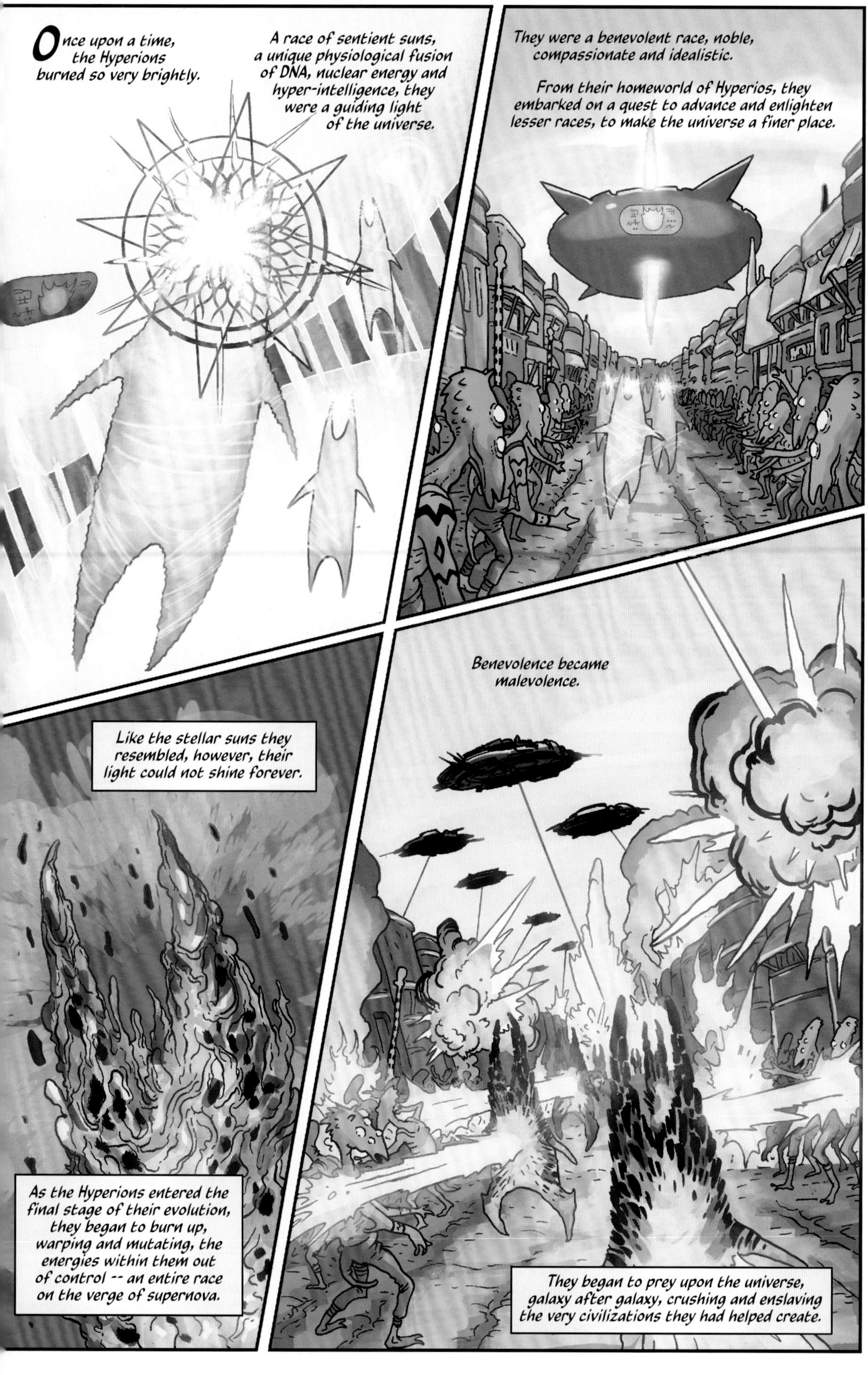
Once upon a time, the Hyperions burned so very brightly.
A race of sentient suns, a unique physiological fusion of DNA, nuclear energy and hyper-intelligence, they were a guiding light of the universe.
They were a benevolent race, noble, compassionate and idealistic.
From their homeworld of Hyperios, they embarked on a quest to advance and enlighten lesser races, to make the universe a finer place.
Like the stellar suns they resembled, however, their light could not shine forever.
As the Hyperions entered the final stage of their evolution, they began to burn up, warping and mutating, the energies within them out of control -- an entire race on the verge of supernova.
Benevolence became malevolence.
They began to prey upon the universe, galaxy after galaxy, crushing and enslaving the very civilizations they had helped create.

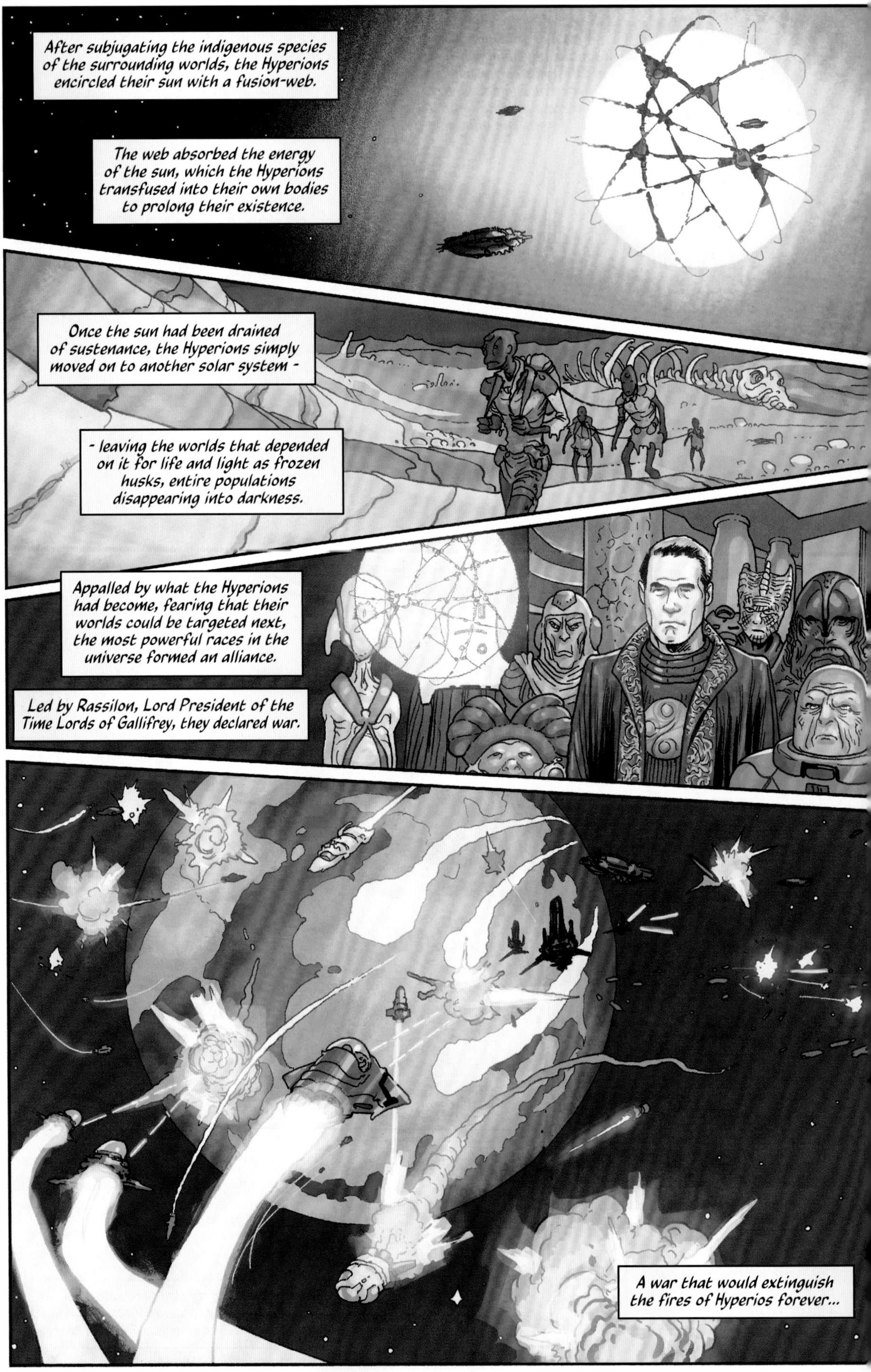
After subjugating the indigenous species of the surrounding worlds, the Hyperions encircled their sun with a fusion-web.
The web absorbed the energy of the sun, which the Hyperions transfused into their own bodies to prolong their existence.
Once the sun had been drained of sustenance, the Hyperions simply moved on to another solar system -
- leaving the worlds that depended on it for life and light as frozen husks, entire populations disappearing into darkness.
Appalled by what the Hyperions had become, fearing that their worlds could be targeted next, the most powerful races in the universe formed an alliance.
Led by Rassilon, Lord President of the Time Lords of Gallifrey, they declared war.
A war that would extinguish the fires of Hyperios forever...

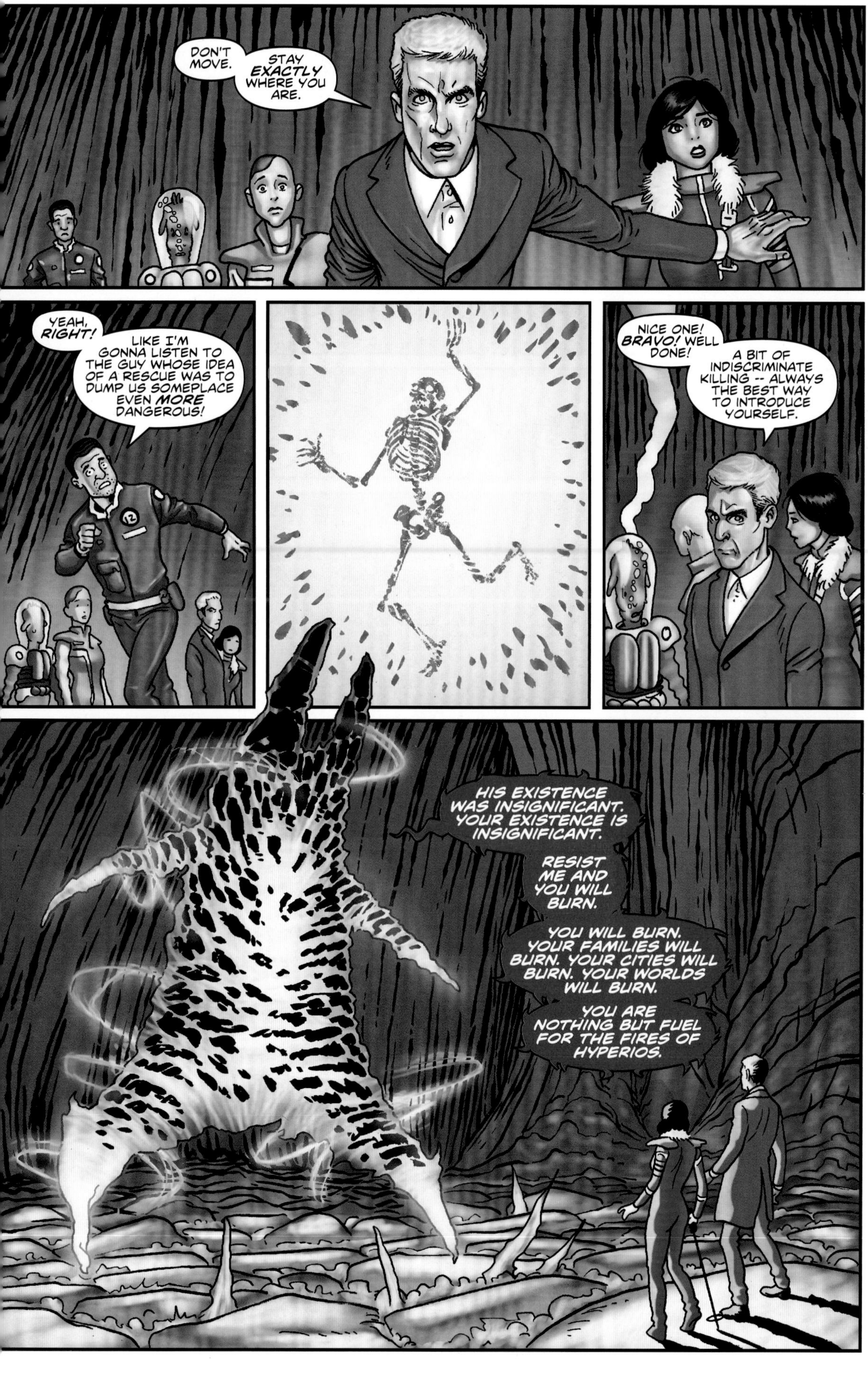
DON'T MOVE.
STAY EXACTLY WHERE YOU ARE.
YEAH, RIGHT!
LIKE I'M GONNA LISTEN TO THE GUY WHOSE IDEA OF A RESCUE WAS TO DUMP US SOMEPLACE EVEN MORE DANGEROUS!
NICE ONE! BRAVO! WELL DONE!
A BIT OF INDISCRIMINATE KILLING -- ALWAYS THE BEST WAY TO INTRODUCE YOURSELF.
HIS EXISTENCE WAS INSIGNIFICANT. YOUR EXISTENCE IS INSIGNIFICANT.
RESIST ME AND YOU WILL BURN.
YOU WILL BURN. YOUR FAMILIES WILL BURN. YOUR CITIES WILL BURN. YOUR WORLDS WILL BURN.
YOU ARE NOTHING BUT FUEL FOR THE FIRES OF HYPERIOS.

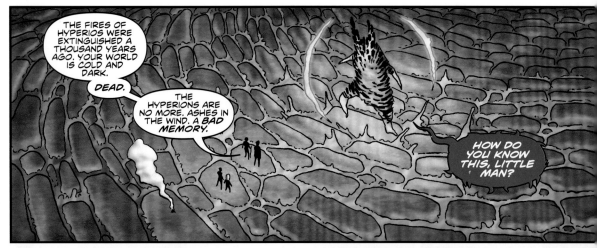

THE FIRES OF HYPERIOS WERE EXTINGUISHED A THOUSAND YEARS AGO. YOUR WORLD IS COLD AND DARK.

DEAD.

THE HYPERIONS ARE NO MORE. ASHES IN THE WIND. A *BAD MEMORY*.

HOW DO YOU KNOW THIS, LITTLE MAN?

BECAUSE WE DESTROYED THEM.

OH, VERY DIPLOMATIC. THAT'LL GO DOWN WELL.

TIME LORD.

MY APOLOGIES, YOU ARE FAR FROM INSIGNIFICANT. KILLING TIME LORDS IS OF THE GREATEST IMPORTANCE. THE GREATEST PLEASURE.

WHERE IS YOUR ARMY? SURELY NOT EVEN A TIME LORD WOULD HAVE THE HUBRIS TO FACE ME ALONE?

I'M THE DOCTOR. I DON'T NEED AN ARMY.

I HAVE PLANS, PLANS WITHIN PLANS. A HUNDRED DIFFERENT WAYS TO DESTROY YOU.

AND THAT IS THE ONE YOU CHOOSE FIRST?

WHAT IS THIS TERRIFYING INSTRUMENT, MAY I ASK?

SONIC SCREWDRIVER.

IT SCANS AND ANALYSES TO A SUB-ATOMIC LEVEL, ACCESSES ALL KNOWN COMPUTER SYSTEMS, CRACKS EVERY LOCK IN THE UNIVERSE--

APART FROM MY *FLAT* THAT TIME I GOT LOCKED OUT. DEAD LOSS AGAINST DEAD-BOLTS.

--AND--

--IT UNSCREWS!

WEEOOO WEEOOO WEEOOO WEEOOO

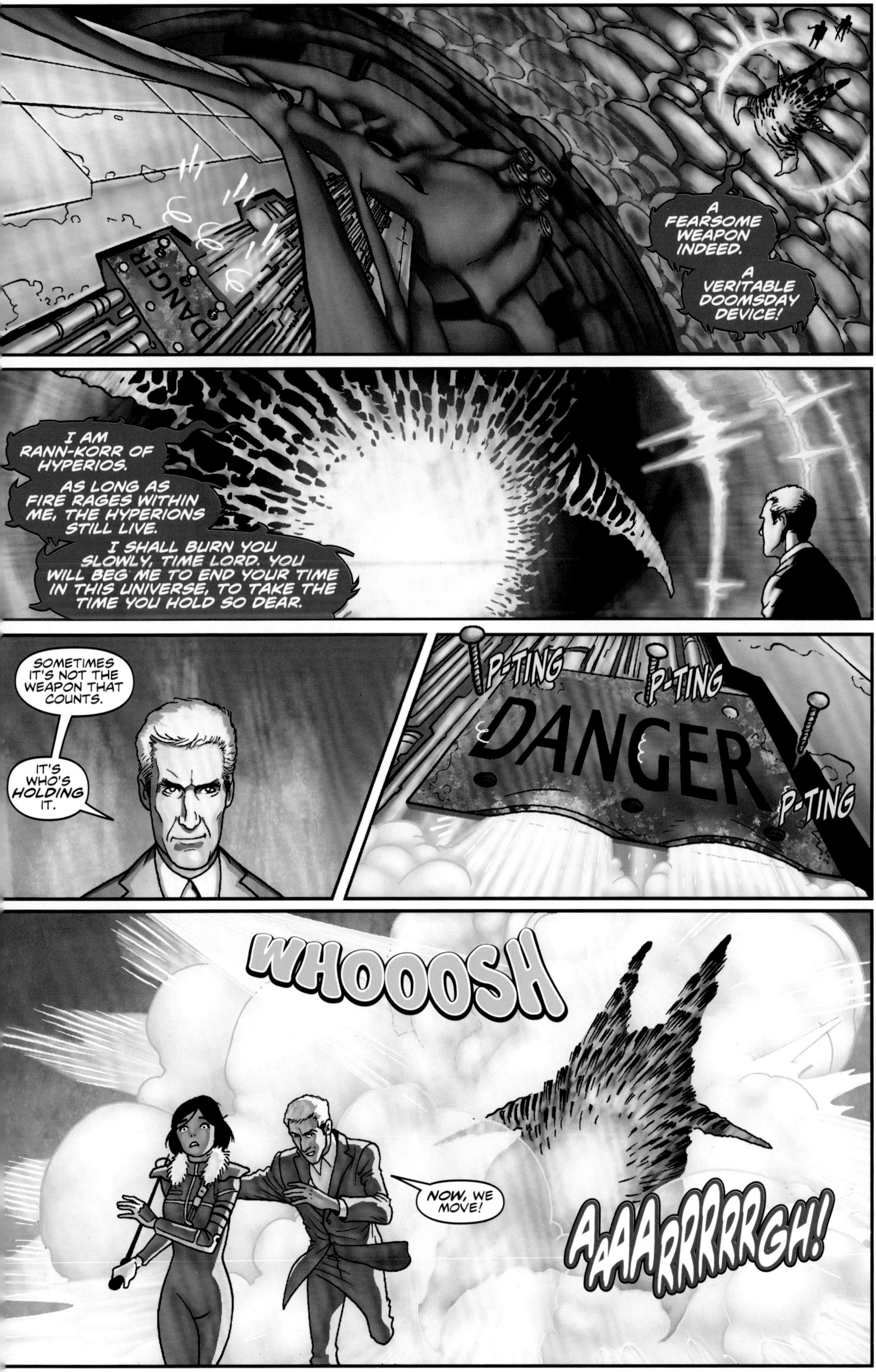
DANGER
A FEARSOME WEAPON INDEED.
A VERITABLE DOOMSDAY DEVICE!
I AM RANN-KORR OF HYPERIOS.
AS LONG AS FIRE RAGES WITHIN ME, THE HYPERIONS STILL LIVE.
I SHALL BURN YOU SLOWLY, TIME LORD. YOU WILL BEG ME TO END YOUR TIME IN THIS UNIVERSE, TO TAKE THE TIME YOU HOLD SO DEAR.
SOMETIMES IT'S NOT THE WEAPON THAT COUNTS.
IT'S WHO'S HOLDING IT.
P-TING
P-TING
DANGER
P-TING
WHOOOSH
NOW, WE MOVE!
AAAARRRRRGH!

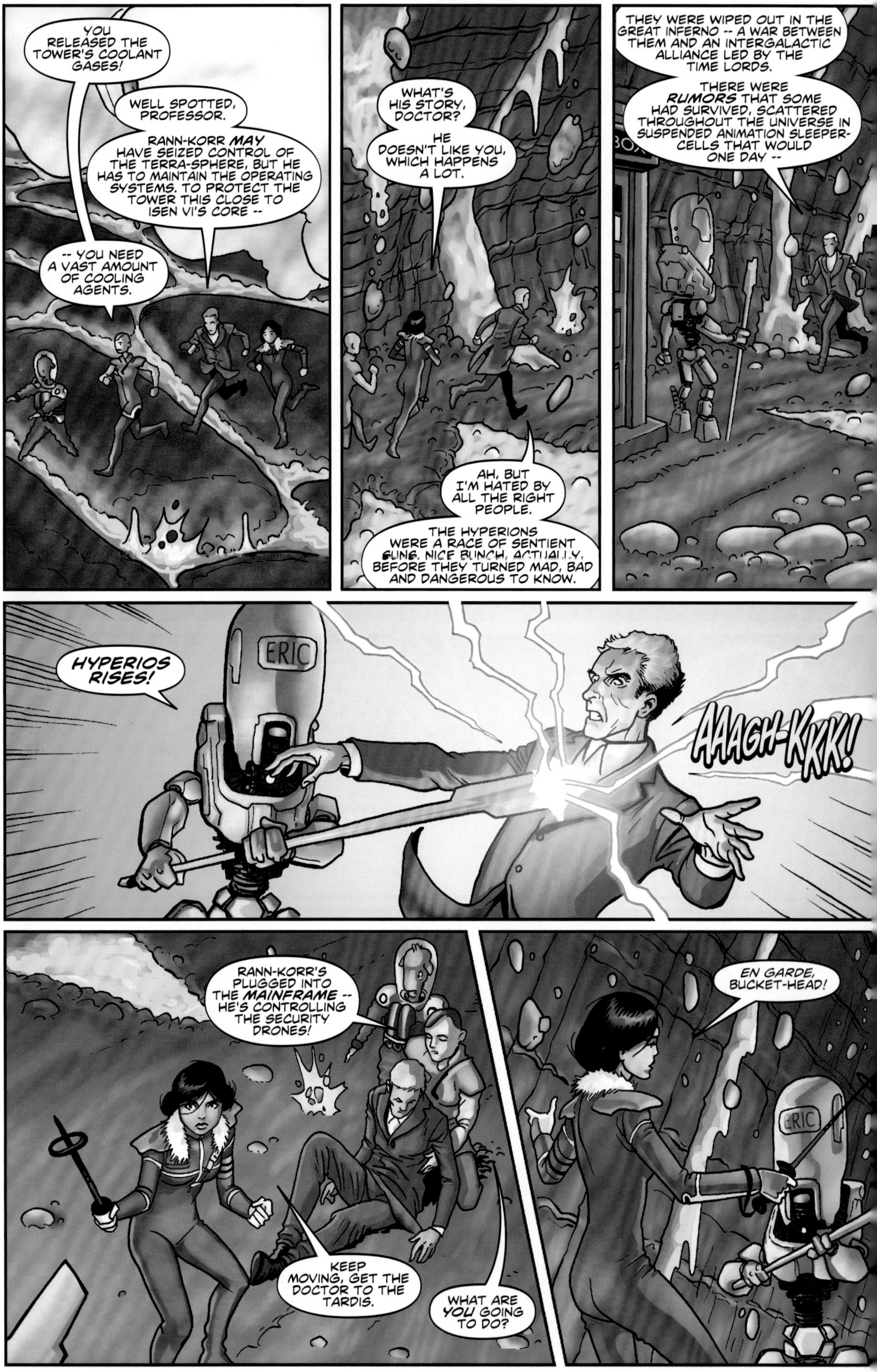
YOU RELEASED THE TOWER'S COOLANT GASES!
WELL SPOTTED, PROFESSOR.
RANN-KORR *MAY* HAVE SEIZED CONTROL OF THE TERRA-SPHERE, BUT HE HAS TO MAINTAIN THE OPERATING SYSTEMS. TO PROTECT THE TOWER THIS CLOSE TO ISEN VI'S CORE --
-- YOU NEED A VAST AMOUNT OF COOLING AGENTS.
WHAT'S HIS STORY, DOCTOR?
HE DOESN'T LIKE YOU, WHICH HAPPENS A LOT.
AH, BUT I'M HATED BY ALL THE RIGHT PEOPLE.
THE HYPERIONS WERE A RACE OF SENTIENT SUNS. NICE BUNCH, ACTUALLY. BEFORE THEY TURNED MAD, BAD AND DANGEROUS TO KNOW.
THEY WERE WIPED OUT IN THE GREAT INFERNO -- A WAR BETWEEN THEM AND AN INTERGALACTIC ALLIANCE LED BY THE TIME LORDS.
THERE WERE *RUMORS* THAT SOME HAD SURVIVED, SCATTERED THROUGHOUT THE UNIVERSE IN SUSPENDED ANIMATION SLEEPER-CELLS THAT WOULD ONE DAY --
BOX
ERIC
HYPERIOS RISES!
AAAGH-KKK!
RANN-KORR'S PLUGGED INTO THE *MAINFRAME* -- HE'S CONTROLLING THE SECURITY DRONES!
KEEP MOVING, GET THE DOCTOR TO THE TARDIS.
WHAT ARE *YOU* GOING TO DO?
EN GARDE, BUCKET-HEAD!
ERIC

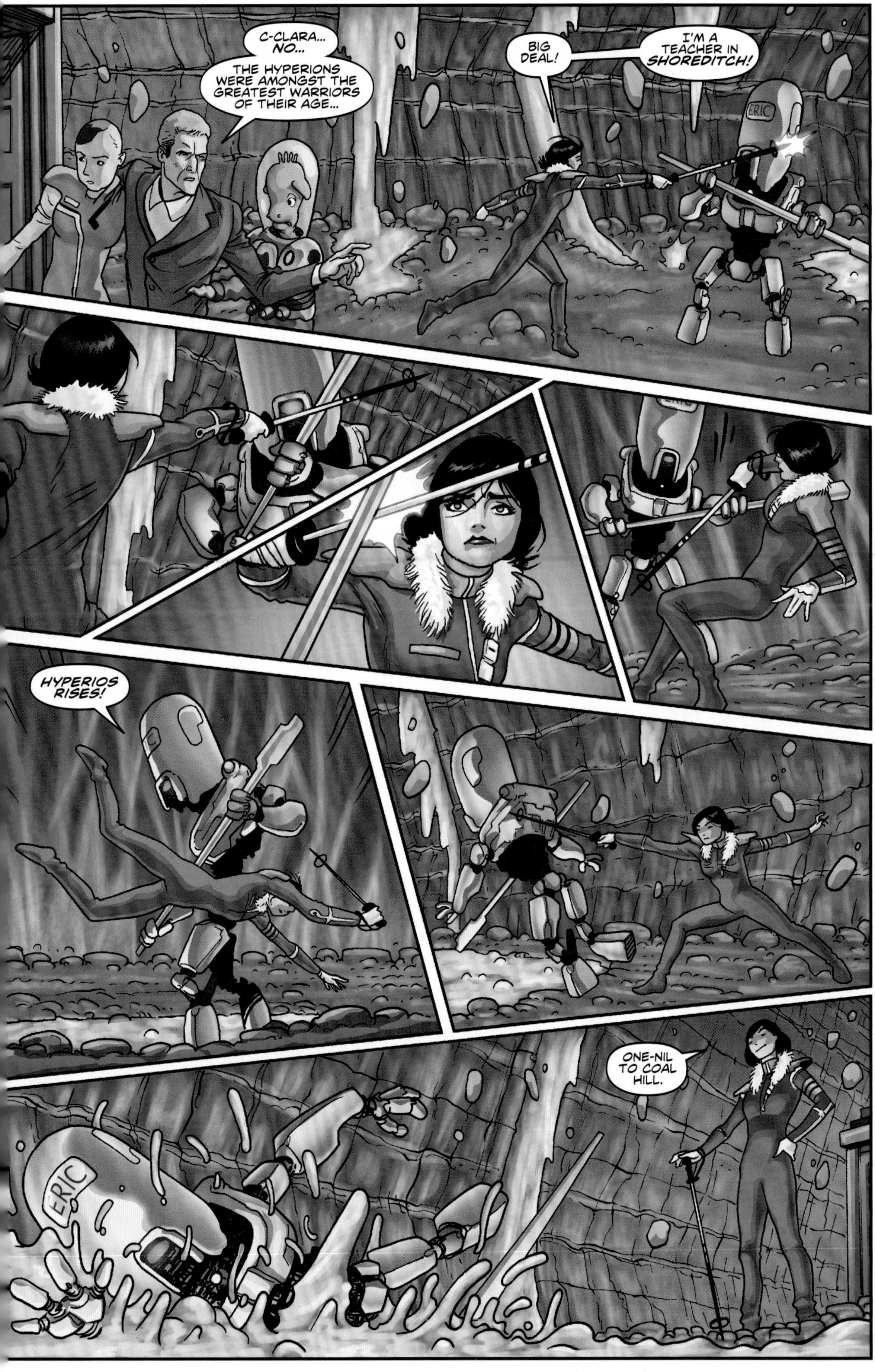
C-CLARA... NO...
THE HYPERIONS WERE AMONGST THE GREATEST WARRIORS OF THEIR AGE...
BIG DEAL!
I'M A TEACHER IN SHOREDITCH!
ERIC
HYPERIOS RISES!
ONE-NIL TO COAL HILL.
ERIC

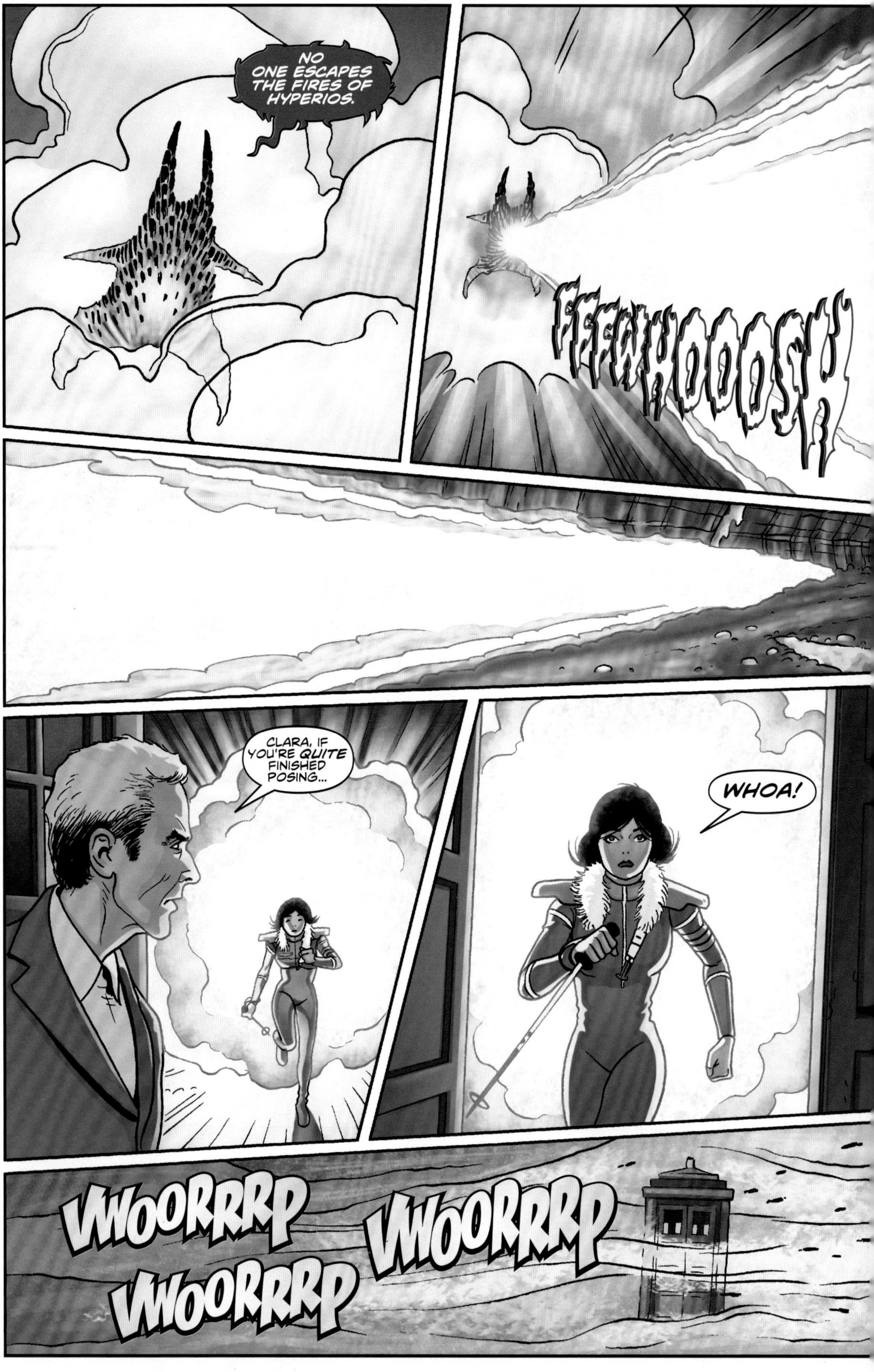

NO ONE ESCAPES THE FIRES OF HYPERIOS.
FFFWHOOOOSH
CLARA, IF YOU'RE *QUITE* FINISHED POSING...
WHOA!
VWOORRRP
VWOORRRP
VWOORRRP

HMM. WE'LL START THE FENCING LESSONS ONCE YOU'VE MASTERED THE SKIING.

FOR A RACE THAT WAS *WIPED OUT*, HE LOOKED VERY MUCH ALIVE.

AND POSITIVELY LIVID. TEMPER LIKE A MEGA-TSUNAMI.

RANN-KORR'S REANIMATION SEQUENCE WOULD HAVE BEEN TRIGGERED WHEN YOUR TERRAFORMER STRUCK HIS CRAFT.

HYPERION SHIPS ARE SEMI-SENTIENT, DESIGNED TO EVOLVE AND ADAPT. IT SUPERCEDED YOUR CONTROL AND MANIPULATED THE TERRAFORMING OF ISEN VI IN RANN-KORR'S FAVOR.

THAT'S WHY YOU'RE SUFFERING COAST-TO-COAST ENVIRONMENTAL UPHEAVAL. AND WHY YOUR 'HARMLESS' NEW SPECIES TRIED TO DEVOUR CLARA.

HE'S TURNING YOUR OWN WORLD AGAINST YOU.

CLEVER.

MIGHT EVEN DO THE SAME MYSELF, IF I WAS AN INTERGALACTIC MASS-MURDERER.

WELL, 'LEAST WE HAVE A PLAN TO BEAT HIM.

WE DO? *GREAT!*

WHAT'S THE PLAN?

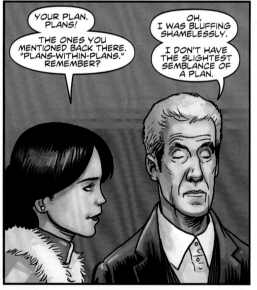

YOUR PLAN. PLANS!

THE ONES YOU MENTIONED BACK THERE. "PLANS-WITHIN-PLANS." REMEMBER?

OH, I WAS BLUFFING SHAMELESSLY. I DON'T HAVE THE SLIGHTEST SEMBLANCE OF A PLAN.

YET.

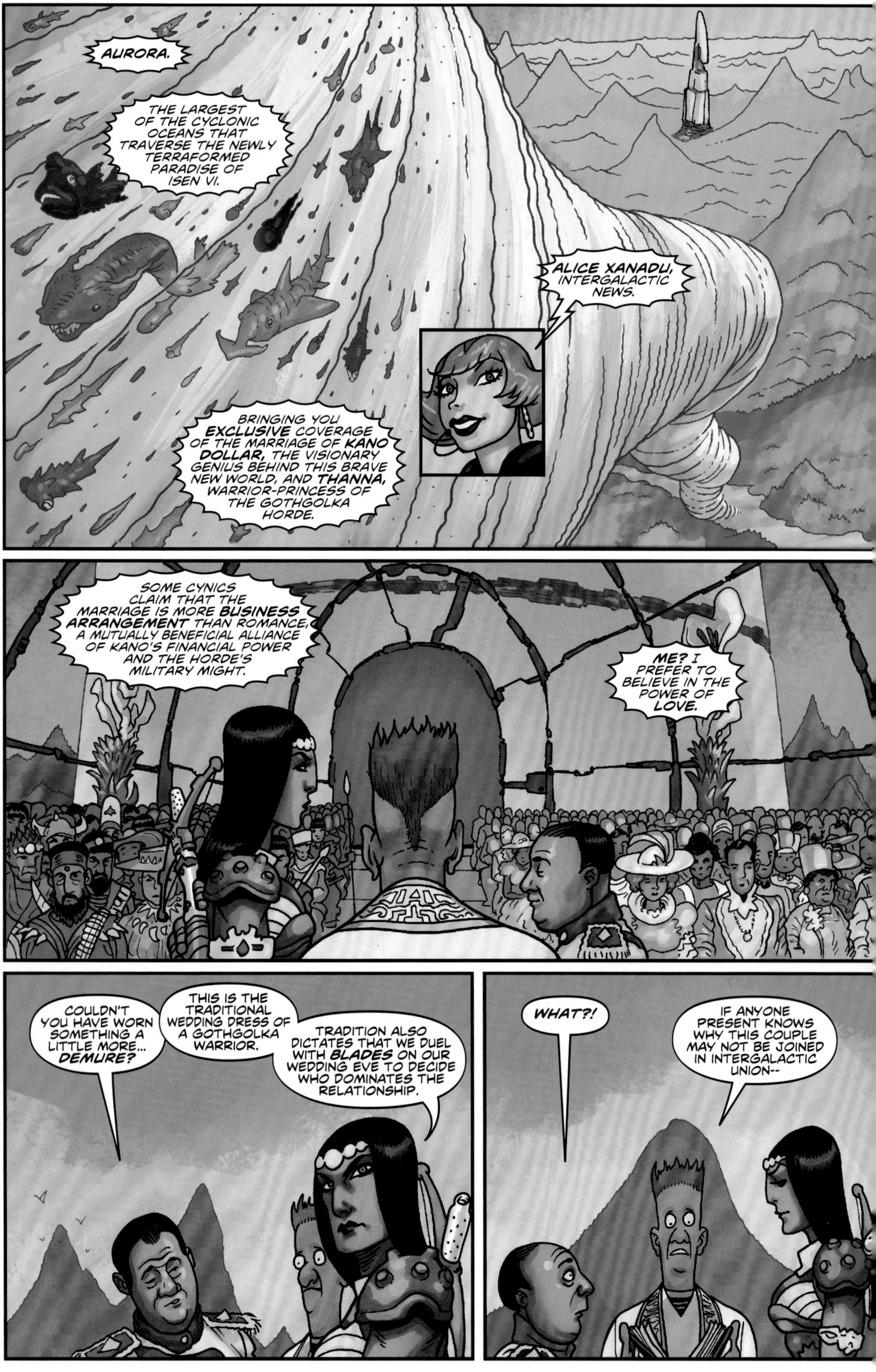
AURORA.
THE LARGEST OF THE CYCLONIC OCEANS THAT TRAVERSE THE NEWLY TERRAFORMED PARADISE OF ISEN VI.
ALICE XANADU, INTERGALACTIC NEWS.
BRINGING YOU EXCLUSIVE COVERAGE OF THE MARRIAGE OF KANO DOLLAR, THE VISIONARY GENIUS BEHIND THIS BRAVE NEW WORLD, AND THANNA, WARRIOR-PRINCESS OF THE GOTHGOLKA HORDE.
SOME CYNICS CLAIM THAT THE MARRIAGE IS MORE BUSINESS ARRANGEMENT THAN ROMANCE, A MUTUALLY BENEFICIAL ALLIANCE OF KANO'S FINANCIAL POWER AND THE HORDE'S MILITARY MIGHT.
ME? I PREFER TO BELIEVE IN THE POWER OF LOVE.
COULDN'T YOU HAVE WORN SOMETHING A LITTLE MORE... DEMURE?
THIS IS THE TRADITIONAL WEDDING DRESS OF A GOTHGOLKA WARRIOR.
TRADITION ALSO DICTATES THAT WE DUEL WITH BLADES ON OUR WEDDING EVE TO DECIDE WHO DOMINATES THE RELATIONSHIP.
WHAT?!
IF ANYONE PRESENT KNOWS WHY THIS COUPLE MAY NOT BE JOINED IN INTERGALACTIC UNION--

VVOORRRP VVOORRRP

-- LET THEM SPEAK NOW OR FOREVER HOLD THEIR --

EXCUSE ME!

DID I INADVERTENTLY STEP BACK IN TIME, OR ARE YOU ALL JUST *DAFT?*

WHEN I WARN PEOPLE ABOUT AN *IMPENDING GLOBAL CATACLYSM,* I DON'T EXPECT THEM TO SWAN ABOUT IN THEIR SUNDAY BEST, WAITING FOR IT TO HAPPEN.

YOU DARE ATTEMPT TO BREAK UP THIS UNION, LITTLE MAN?

THANNAGRRR, EMPEROR OF THE HORDE, WILL *SPLIT* YOUR SKULL AND SUP ON YOUR--

SORRY, *NO OFFENCE,* BUT YOUR SCARY FACE IS POSITIVELY CUTE COMPARED TO THE PIT OF HELL WE'VE JUST BEEN STARING INTO.

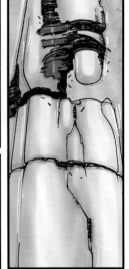

KKKRROOOMM

HYPERIOS RISES.

AND THE UNIVERSE FALLS.

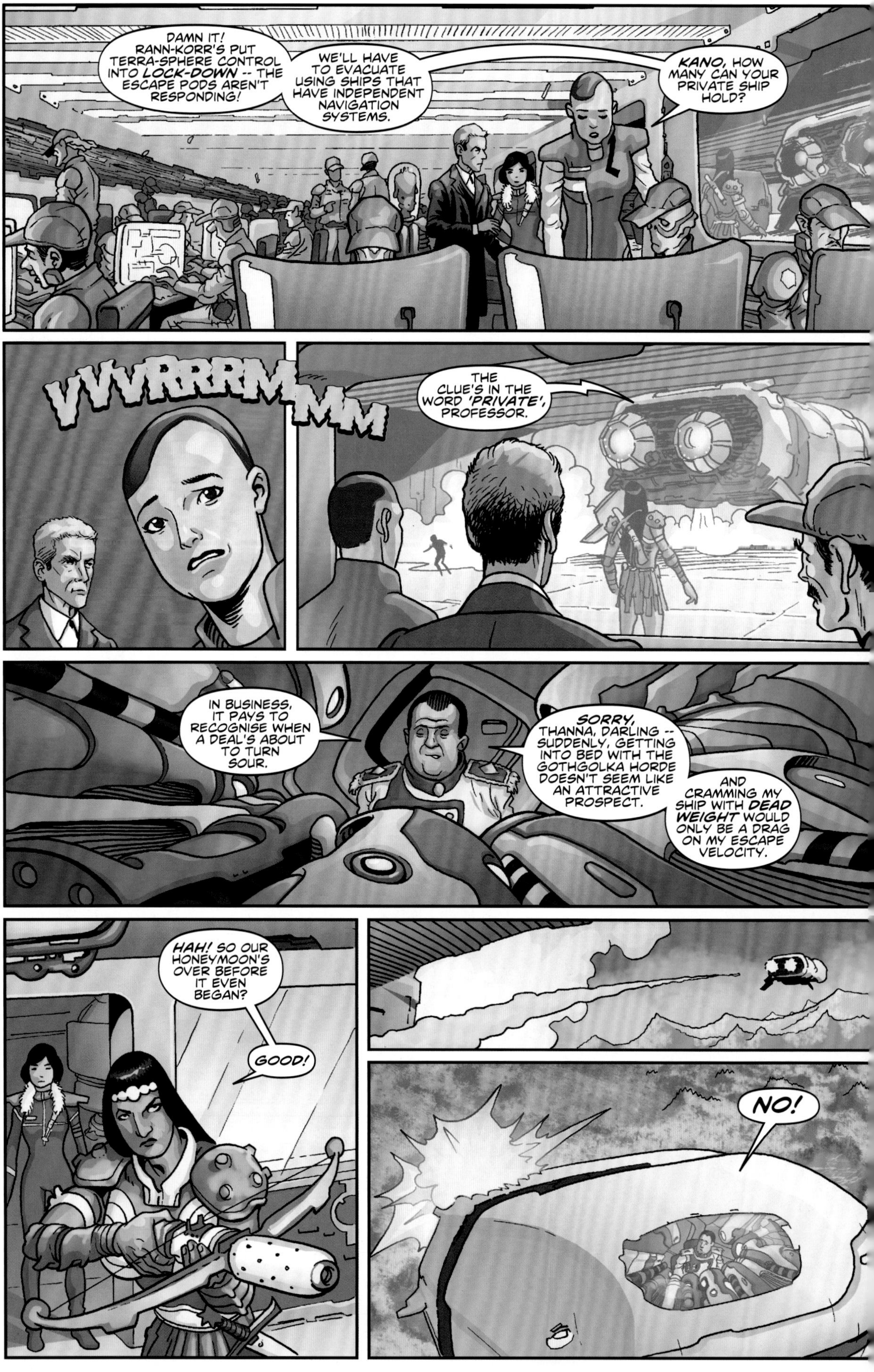
DAMN IT! RANN-KORR'S PUT TERRA-SPHERE CONTROL INTO LOCK-DOWN -- THE ESCAPE PODS AREN'T RESPONDING!
WE'LL HAVE TO EVACUATE USING SHIPS THAT HAVE INDEPENDENT NAVIGATION SYSTEMS.
KANO, HOW MANY CAN YOUR PRIVATE SHIP HOLD?
VVVRRRMMMM
THE CLUE'S IN THE WORD 'PRIVATE', PROFESSOR.
IN BUSINESS, IT PAYS TO RECOGNISE WHEN A DEAL'S ABOUT TO TURN SOUR.
SORRY, THANNA, DARLING -- SUDDENLY, GETTING INTO BED WITH THE GOTHGOLKA HORDE DOESN'T SEEM LIKE AN ATTRACTIVE PROSPECT.
AND CRAMMING MY SHIP WITH DEAD WEIGHT WOULD ONLY BE A DRAG ON MY ESCAPE VELOCITY.
HAH! SO OUR HONEYMOON'S OVER BEFORE IT EVEN BEGAN?
GOOD!
NO!

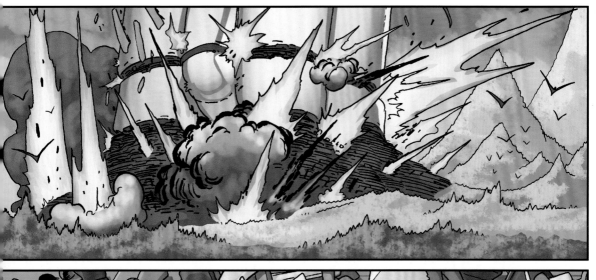

AAAAAAAHHHHH!

KKKRRRAAASSHH

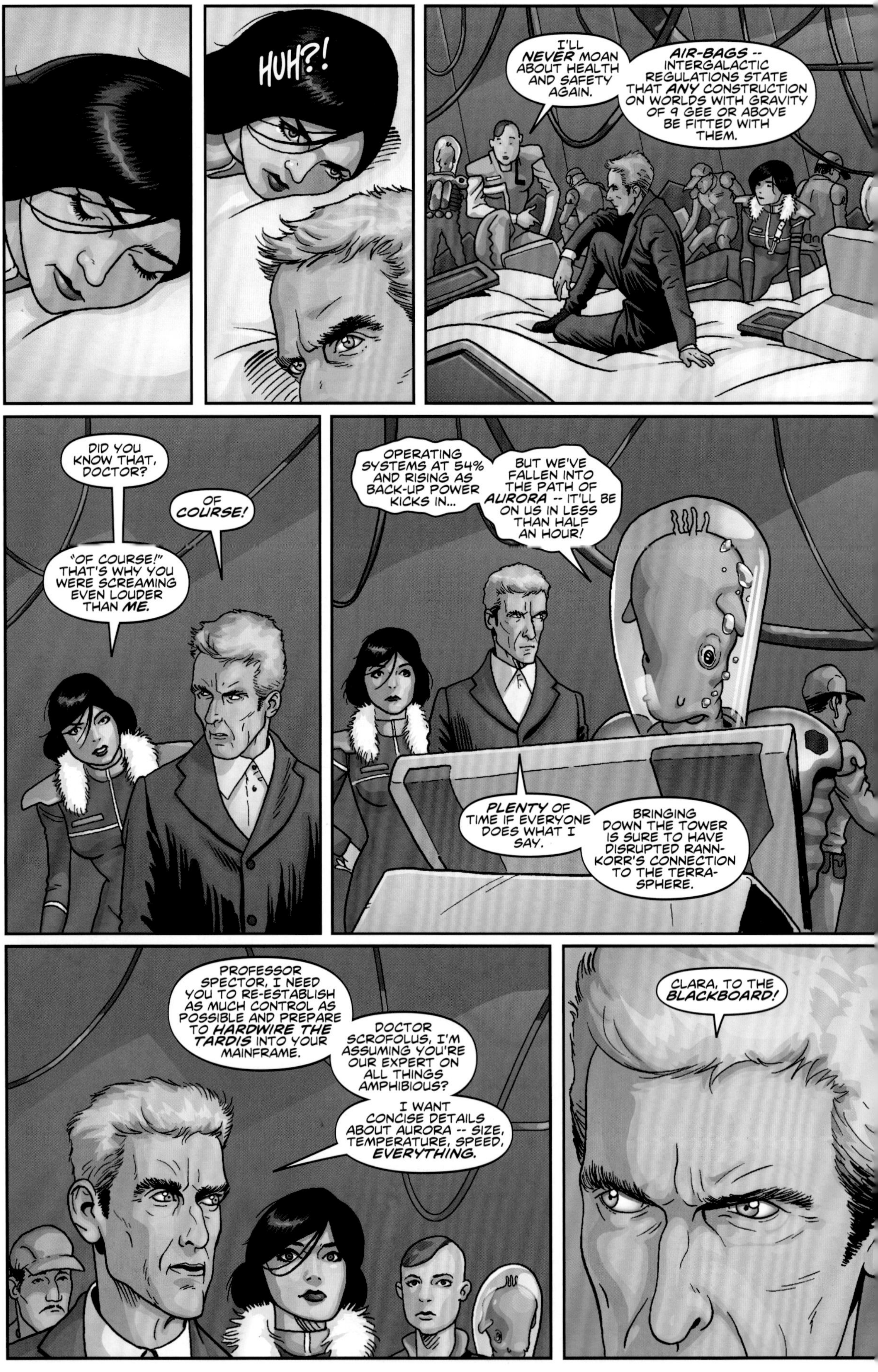
HUH?!
I'LL NEVER MOAN ABOUT HEALTH AND SAFETY AGAIN.
AIR-BAGS -- INTERGALACTIC REGULATIONS STATE THAT ANY CONSTRUCTION ON WORLDS WITH GRAVITY OF 9 GEE OR ABOVE BE FITTED WITH THEM.
DID YOU KNOW THAT, DOCTOR?
OF COURSE!
"OF COURSE!" THAT'S WHY YOU WERE SCREAMING EVEN LOUDER THAN ME.
OPERATING SYSTEMS AT 54% AND RISING AS BACK-UP POWER KICKS IN...
BUT WE'VE FALLEN INTO THE PATH OF AURORA -- IT'LL BE ON US IN LESS THAN HALF AN HOUR!
PLENTY OF TIME IF EVERYONE DOES WHAT I SAY.
BRINGING DOWN THE TOWER IS SURE TO HAVE DISRUPTED RANN-KORR'S CONNECTION TO THE TERRA-SPHERE.
PROFESSOR SPECTOR, I NEED YOU TO RE-ESTABLISH AS MUCH CONTROL AS POSSIBLE AND PREPARE TO HARDWIRE THE TARDIS INTO YOUR MAINFRAME.
DOCTOR SCROFOLUS, I'M ASSUMING YOU'RE OUR EXPERT ON ALL THINGS AMPHIBIOUS?
I WANT CONCISE DETAILS ABOUT AURORA -- SIZE, TEMPERATURE, SPEED, EVERYTHING.
CLARA, TO THE BLACKBOARD!

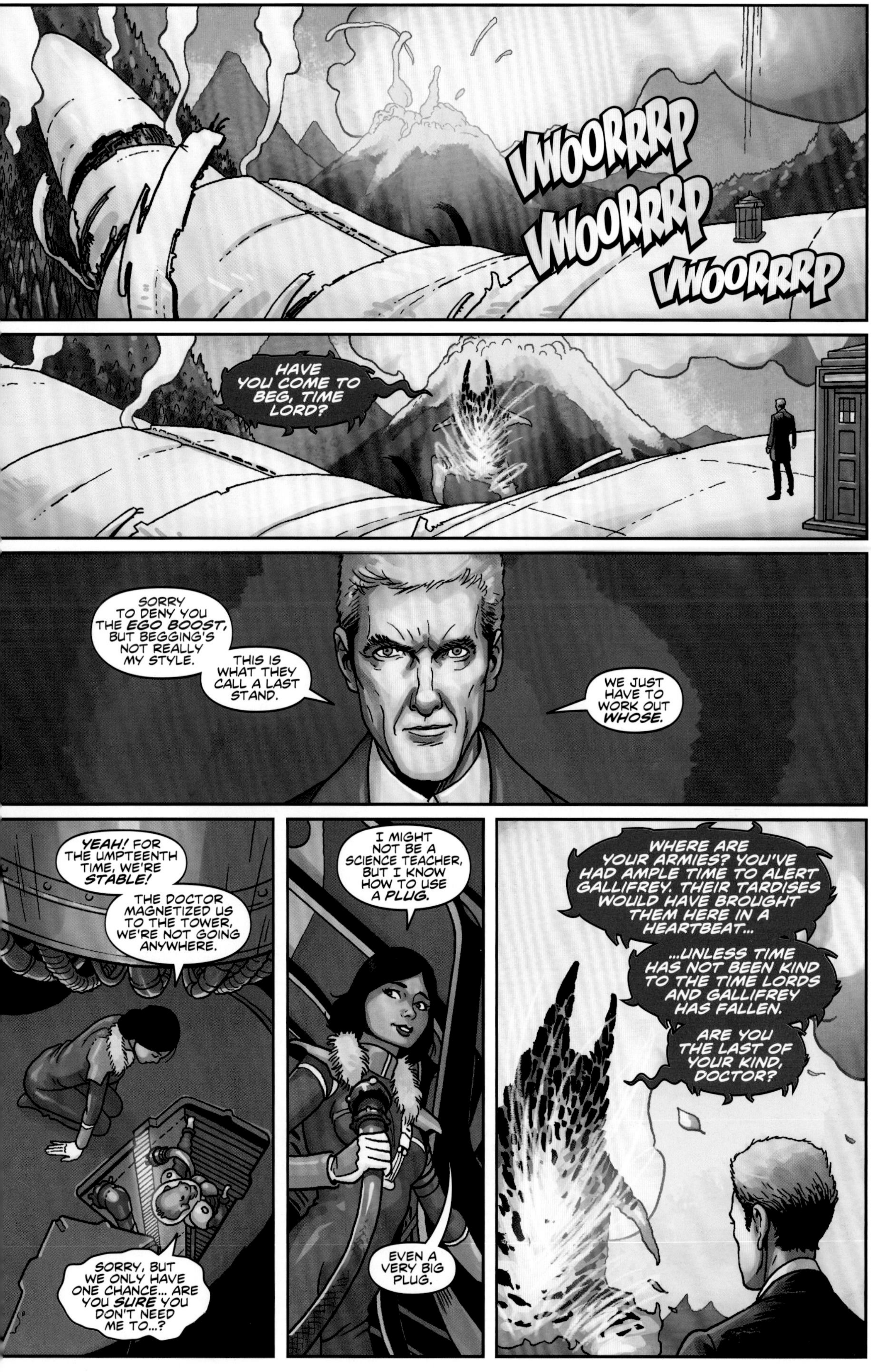

VWOORRRP
VWOORRRP
VWOORRRP
HAVE YOU COME TO BEG, TIME LORD?
SORRY TO DENY YOU THE EGO BOOST, BUT BEGGING'S NOT REALLY MY STYLE.
THIS IS WHAT THEY CALL A LAST STAND.
WE JUST HAVE TO WORK OUT WHOSE.
YEAH! FOR THE UMPTEENTH TIME, WE'RE STABLE!
THE DOCTOR MAGNETIZED US TO THE TOWER, WE'RE NOT GOING ANYWHERE.
SORRY, BUT WE ONLY HAVE ONE CHANCE... ARE YOU SURE YOU DON'T NEED ME TO...?
I MIGHT NOT BE A SCIENCE TEACHER, BUT I KNOW HOW TO USE A PLUG.
EVEN A VERY BIG PLUG.
WHERE ARE YOUR ARMIES? YOU'VE HAD AMPLE TIME TO ALERT GALLIFREY. THEIR TARDISES WOULD HAVE BROUGHT THEM HERE IN A HEARTBEAT...
...UNLESS TIME HAS NOT BEEN KIND TO THE TIME LORDS AND GALLIFREY HAS FALLEN.
ARE YOU THE LAST OF YOUR KIND, DOCTOR?

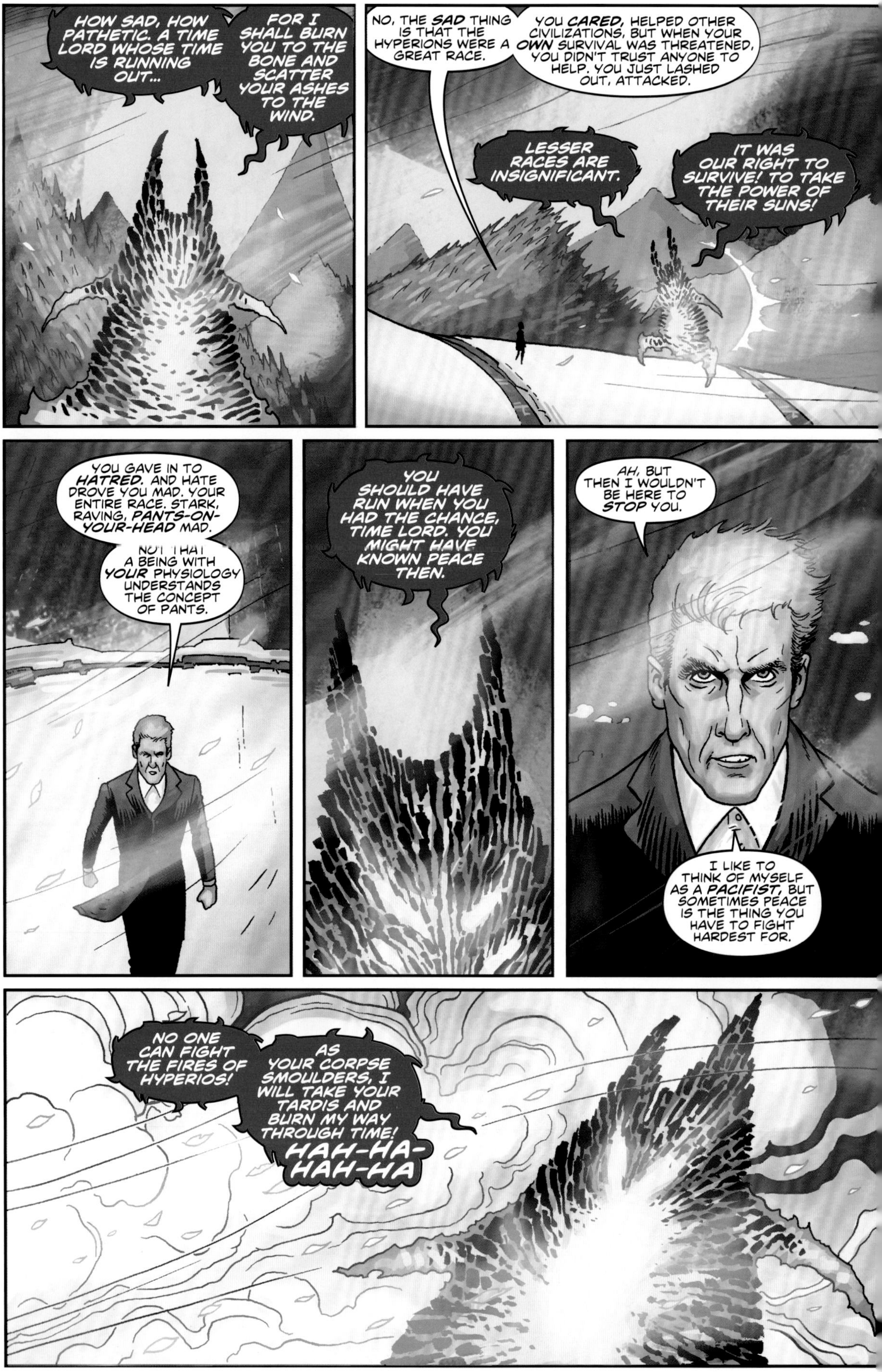
HOW SAD, HOW PATHETIC. A TIME LORD WHOSE TIME IS RUNNING OUT...
FOR I SHALL BURN YOU TO THE BONE AND SCATTER YOUR ASHES TO THE WIND.
NO, THE SAD THING IS THAT THE HYPERIONS WERE A GREAT RACE.
YOU CARED, HELPED OTHER CIVILIZATIONS, BUT WHEN YOUR OWN SURVIVAL WAS THREATENED, YOU DIDN'T TRUST ANYONE TO HELP. YOU JUST LASHED OUT, ATTACKED.
LESSER RACES ARE INSIGNIFICANT.
IT WAS OUR RIGHT TO SURVIVE! TO TAKE THE POWER OF THEIR SUNS!
YOU GAVE IN TO HATRED. AND HATE DROVE YOU MAD. YOUR ENTIRE RACE. STARK, RAVING, PANTS-ON-YOUR-HEAD MAD.
NOT THAT A BEING WITH YOUR PHYSIOLOGY UNDERSTANDS THE CONCEPT OF PANTS.
YOU SHOULD HAVE RUN WHEN YOU HAD THE CHANCE, TIME LORD. YOU MIGHT HAVE KNOWN PEACE THEN.
AH, BUT THEN I WOULDN'T BE HERE TO STOP YOU.
I LIKE TO THINK OF MYSELF AS A PACIFIST, BUT SOMETIMES PEACE IS THE THING YOU HAVE TO FIGHT HARDEST FOR.
NO ONE CAN FIGHT THE FIRES OF HYPERIOS!
AS YOUR CORPSE SMOULDERS, I WILL TAKE YOUR TARDIS AND BURN MY WAY THROUGH TIME!
HAH-HA-HAH-HA

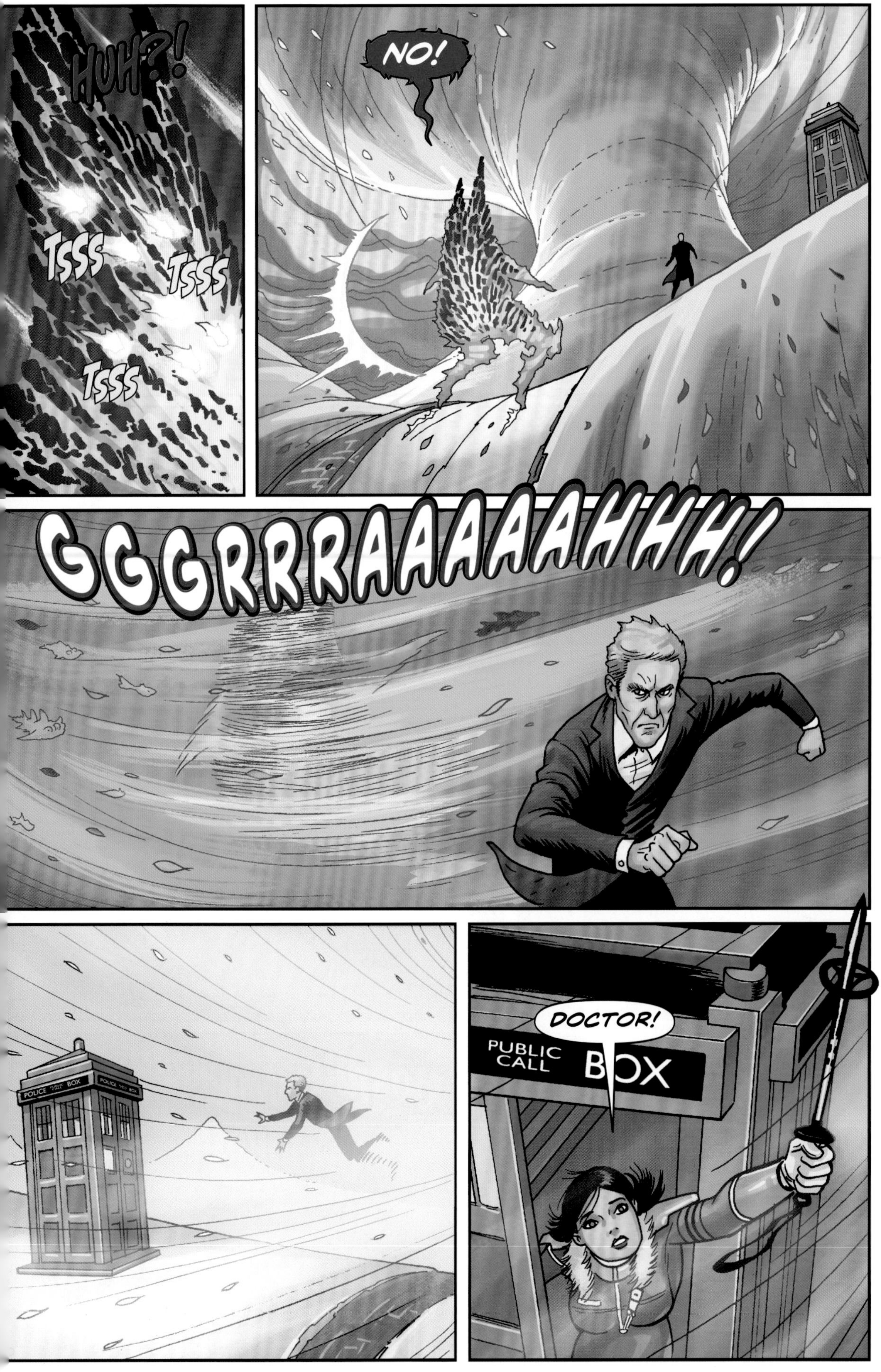
HUH?!
TSSS
TSSS
TSSS
NO!
GGGRRRAAAAAAHHH!
DOCTOR!
PUBLIC CALL BOX
POLICE BOX

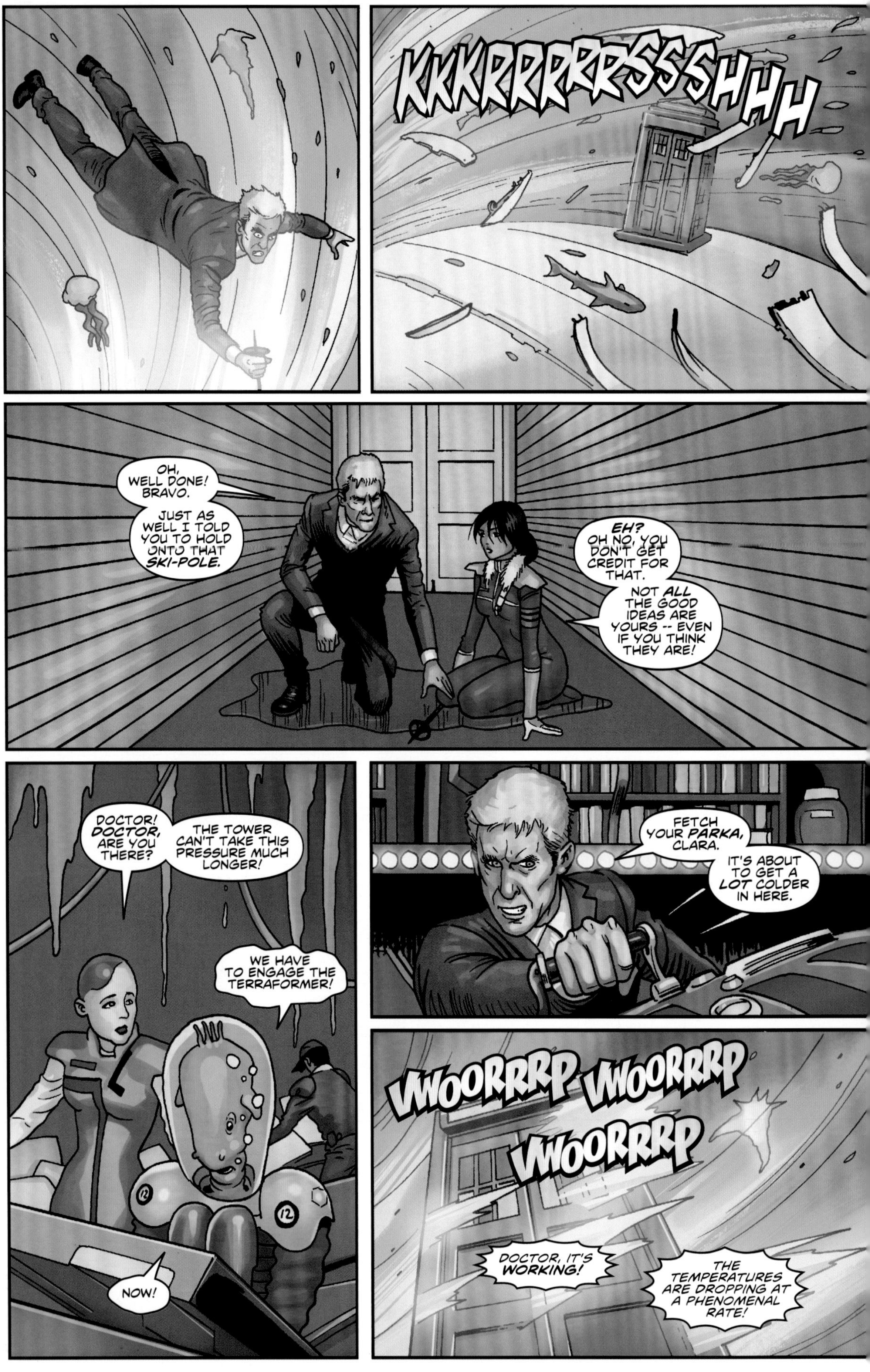
KKKRRRRRSSSHHH
OH, WELL DONE! BRAVO.
JUST AS WELL I TOLD YOU TO HOLD ONTO THAT SKI-POLE.
EH? OH NO, YOU DON'T GET CREDIT FOR THAT.
NOT ALL THE GOOD IDEAS ARE YOURS -- EVEN IF YOU THINK THEY ARE!
DOCTOR! DOCTOR, ARE YOU THERE?
THE TOWER CAN'T TAKE THIS PRESSURE MUCH LONGER!
WE HAVE TO ENGAGE THE TERRAFORMER!
NOW!
FETCH YOUR PARKA, CLARA.
IT'S ABOUT TO GET A LOT COLDER IN HERE.
VWOORRRP VWOORRRP VWOORRRP
DOCTOR, IT'S WORKING!
THE TEMPERATURES ARE DROPPING AT A PHENOMENAL RATE!

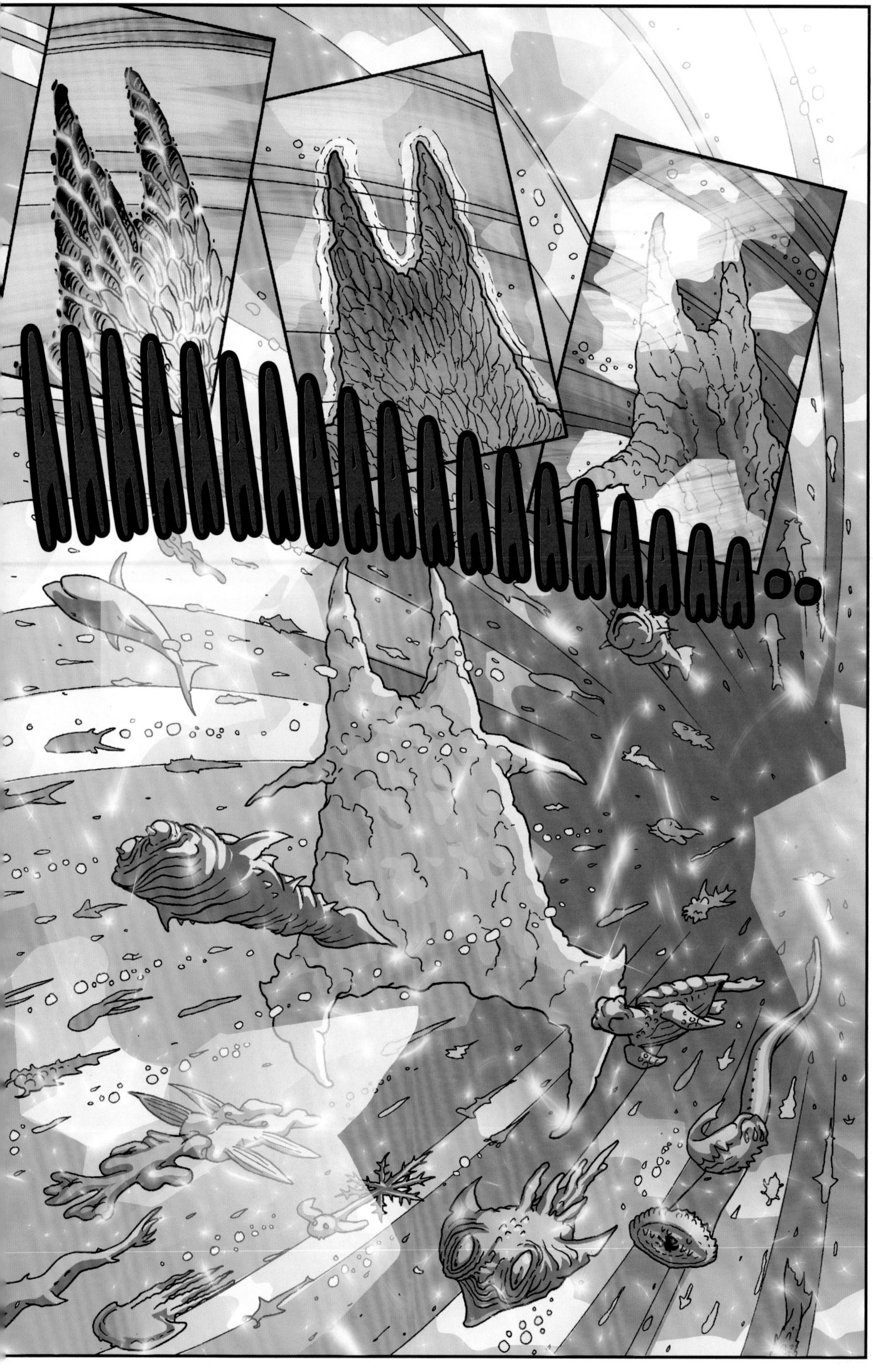
AAAAAAAAAAAAAAAAAAA..

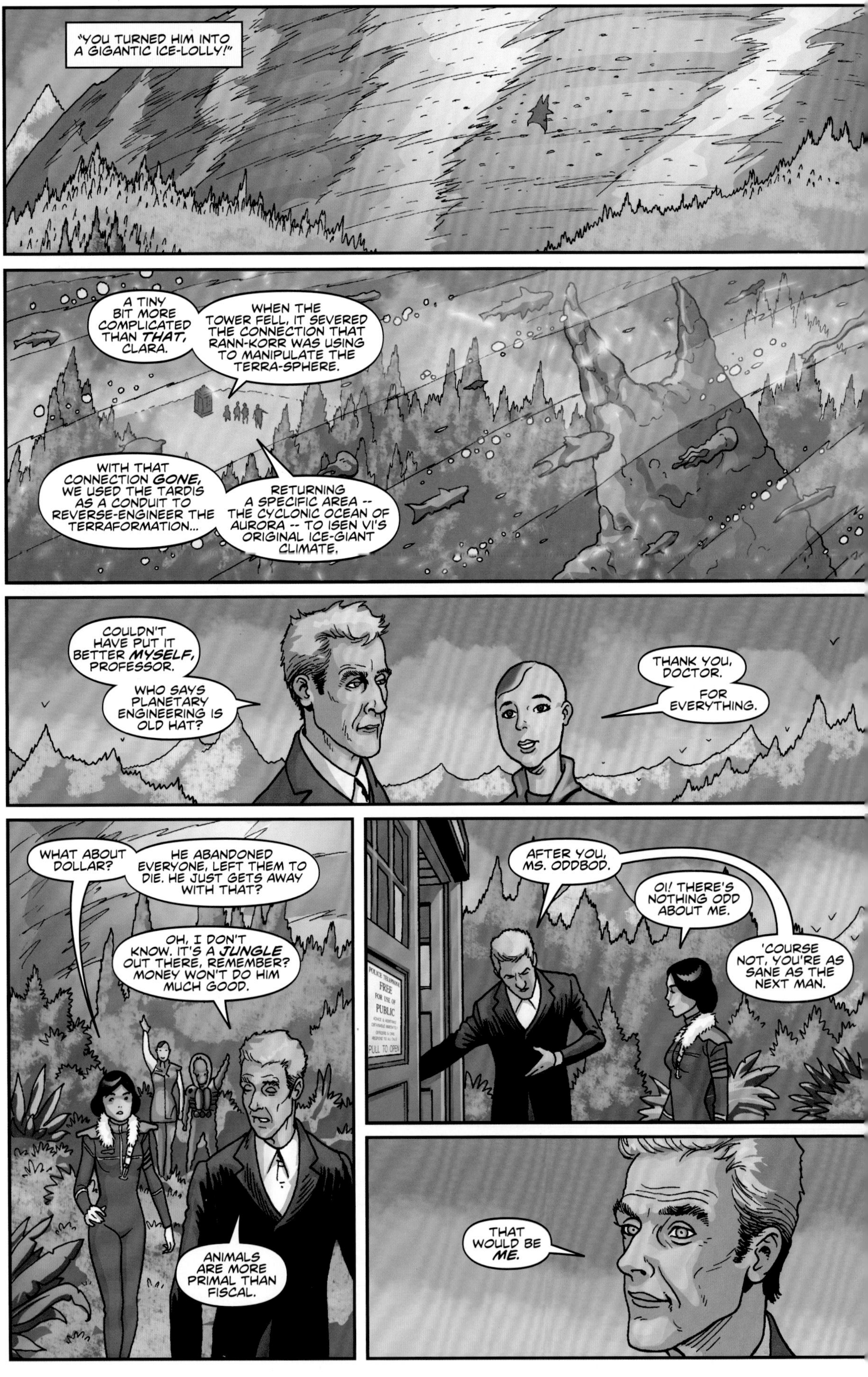
"YOU TURNED HIM INTO A GIGANTIC ICE-LOLLY!"
A TINY BIT MORE COMPLICATED THAN *THAT*, CLARA.
WHEN THE TOWER FELL, IT SEVERED THE CONNECTION THAT RANN-KORR WAS USING TO MANIPULATE THE TERRA-SPHERE.
WITH THAT CONNECTION **GONE**, WE USED THE TARDIS AS A CONDUIT TO REVERSE-ENGINEER THE TERRAFORMATION...
RETURNING A SPECIFIC AREA -- THE CYCLONIC OCEAN OF AURORA -- TO ISEN VI'S ORIGINAL ICE-GIANT CLIMATE.
COULDN'T HAVE PUT IT BETTER ***MYSELF***, PROFESSOR.
WHO SAYS PLANETARY ENGINEERING IS OLD HAT?
THANK YOU, DOCTOR.
FOR EVERYTHING.
WHAT ABOUT DOLLAR?
HE ABANDONED EVERYONE, LEFT THEM TO DIE. HE JUST GETS AWAY WITH THAT?
OH, I DON'T KNOW. IT'S A ***JUNGLE*** OUT THERE, REMEMBER? MONEY WON'T DO HIM MUCH GOOD.
ANIMALS ARE MORE PRIMAL THAN FISCAL.
AFTER YOU, MS. ODDBOD.
OI! THERE'S NOTHING ODD ABOUT ME.
'COURSE NOT, YOU'RE AS SANE AS THE NEXT MAN.
POLICE TELEPHONE FREE FOR USE OF PUBLIC
PULL TO OPEN
THAT WOULD BE ***ME.***

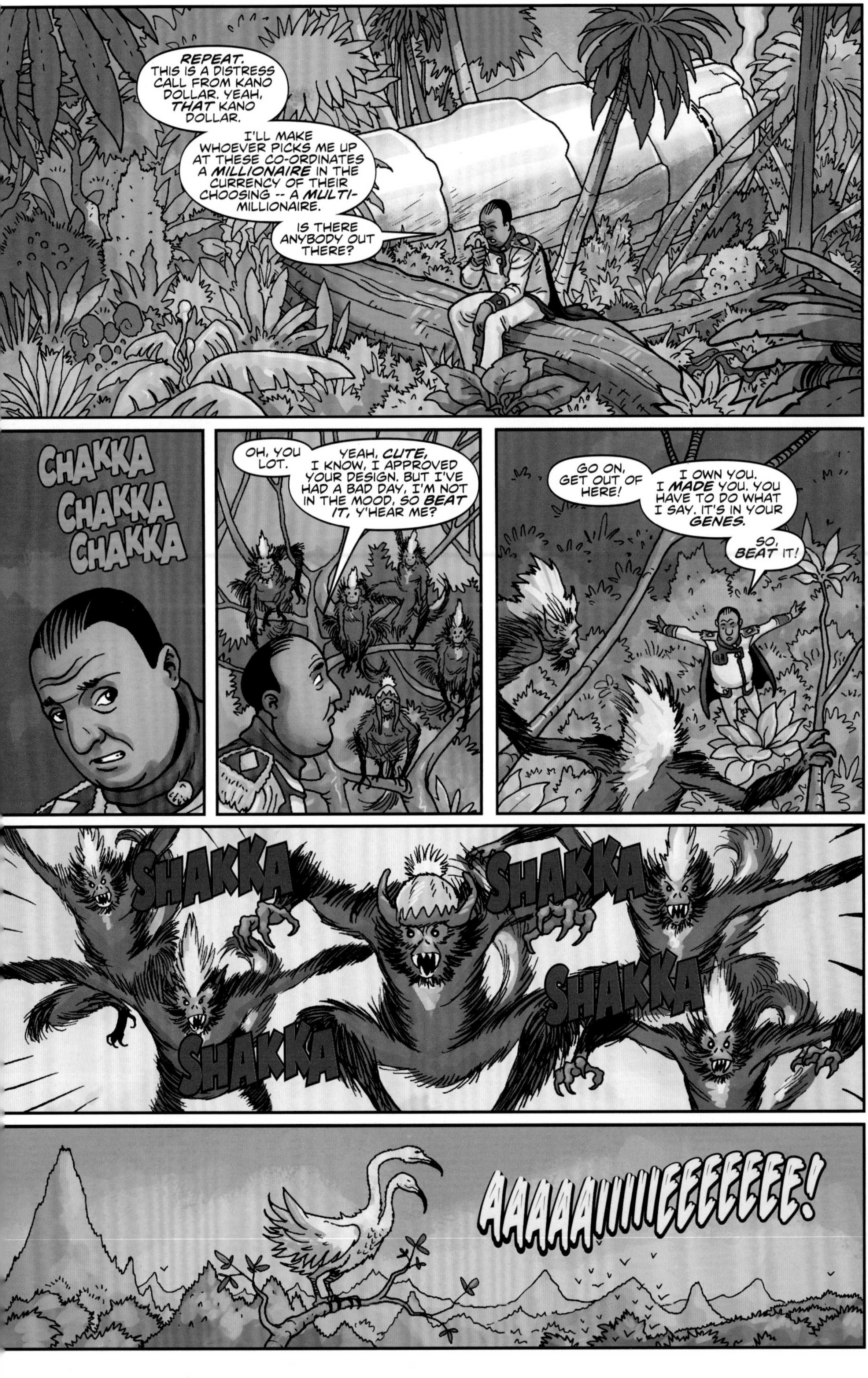
REPEAT. THIS IS A DISTRESS CALL FROM KANO DOLLAR. YEAH, THAT KANO DOLLAR.
I'LL MAKE WHOEVER PICKS ME UP AT THESE CO-ORDINATES A MILLIONAIRE IN THE CURRENCY OF THEIR CHOOSING -- A MULTI-MILLIONAIRE.
IS THERE ANYBODY OUT THERE?
CHAKKA CHAKKA CHAKKA
OH, YOU LOT.
YEAH, CUTE, I KNOW, I APPROVED YOUR DESIGN. BUT I'VE HAD A BAD DAY, I'M NOT IN THE MOOD, SO BEAT IT, Y'HEAR ME?
GO ON, GET OUT OF HERE!
I OWN YOU. I MADE YOU. YOU HAVE TO DO WHAT I SAY. IT'S IN YOUR GENES.
SO, BEAT IT!
SHAKKA
SHAKKA
SHAKKA
SHAKKA
AAAAAIIIIIEEEEEEE!

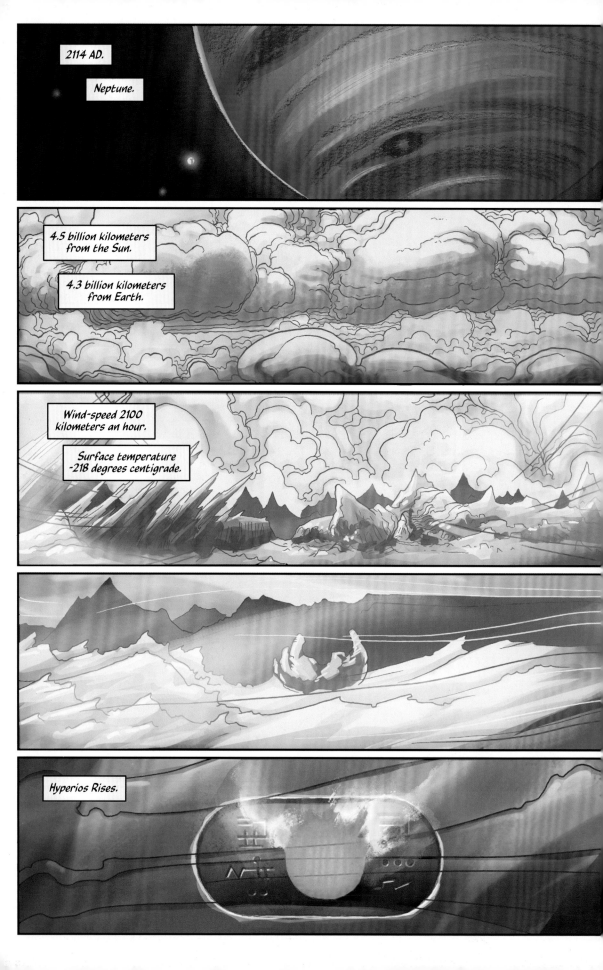

2114 AD.

Neptune.

4.5 billion kilometers from the Sun.

4.3 billion kilometers from Earth.

Wind-speed 2100 kilometers an hour.

Surface temperature -218 degrees centigrade.

Hyperios Rises.

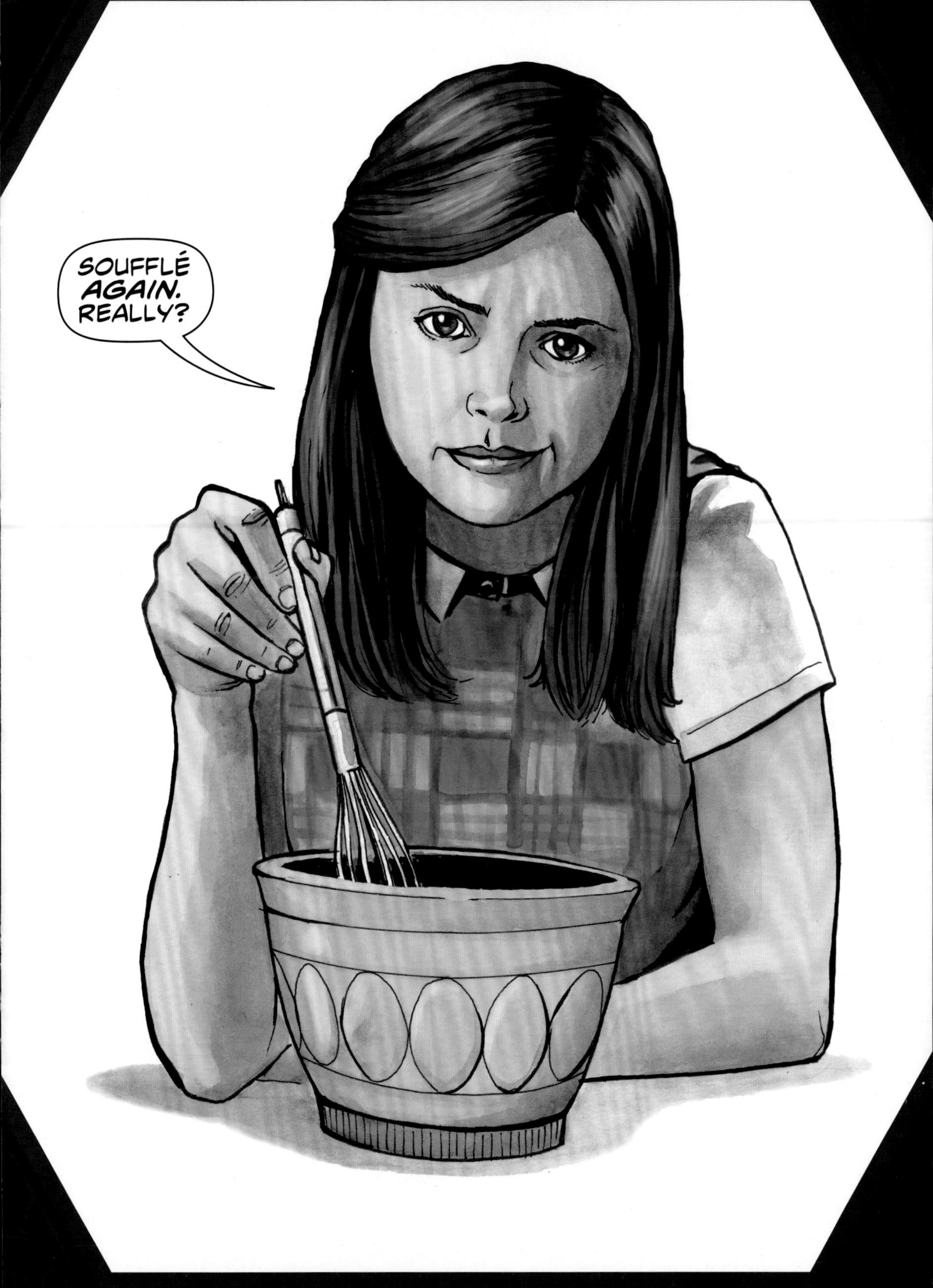
SOUFFLÉ AGAIN. REALLY?

12D #1 Cover Art by Mariano Laclaustra

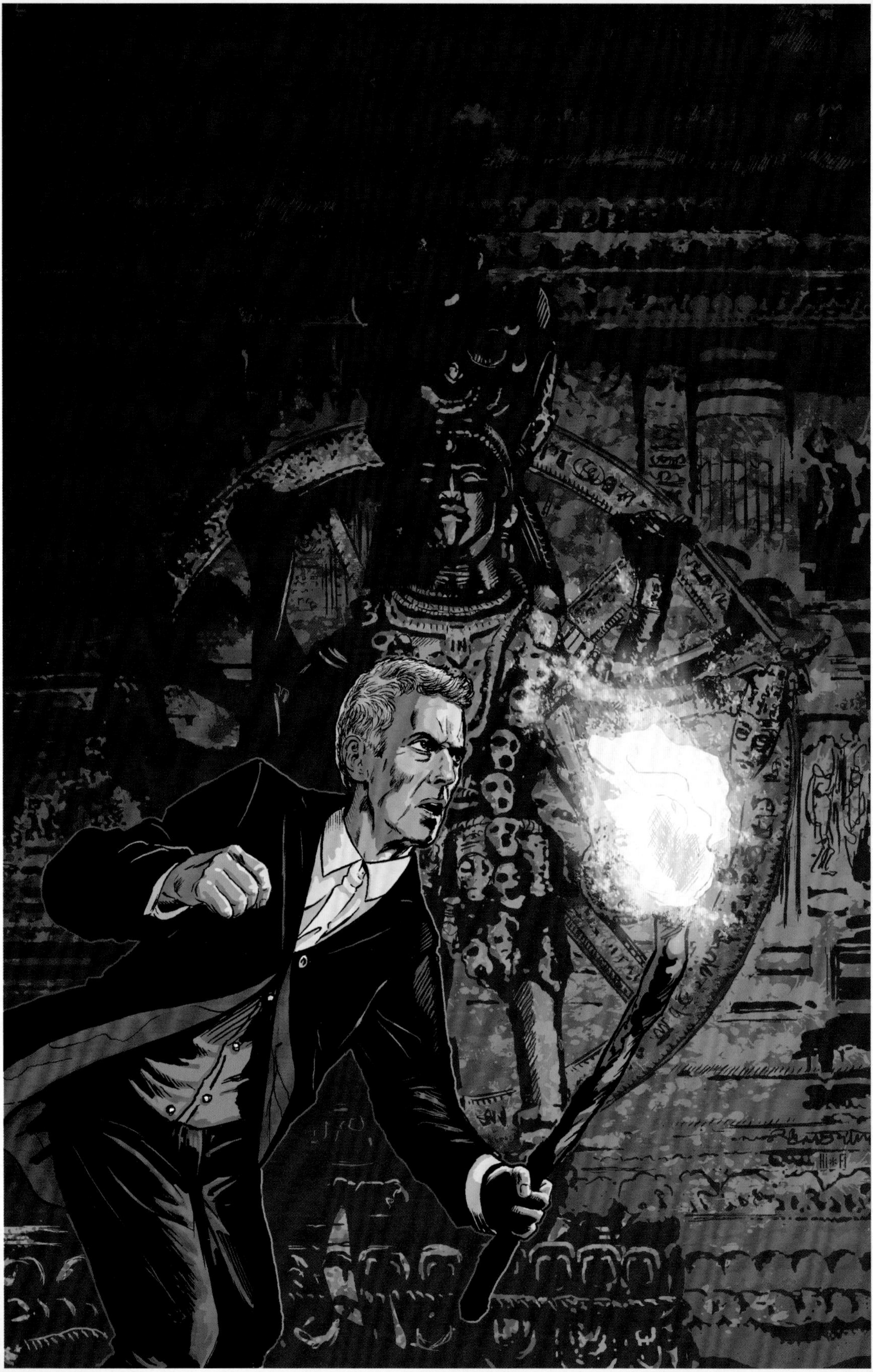
Hi*Fi

CHAPTER 3

Cover A: Brian Williamson & Hi-Fi

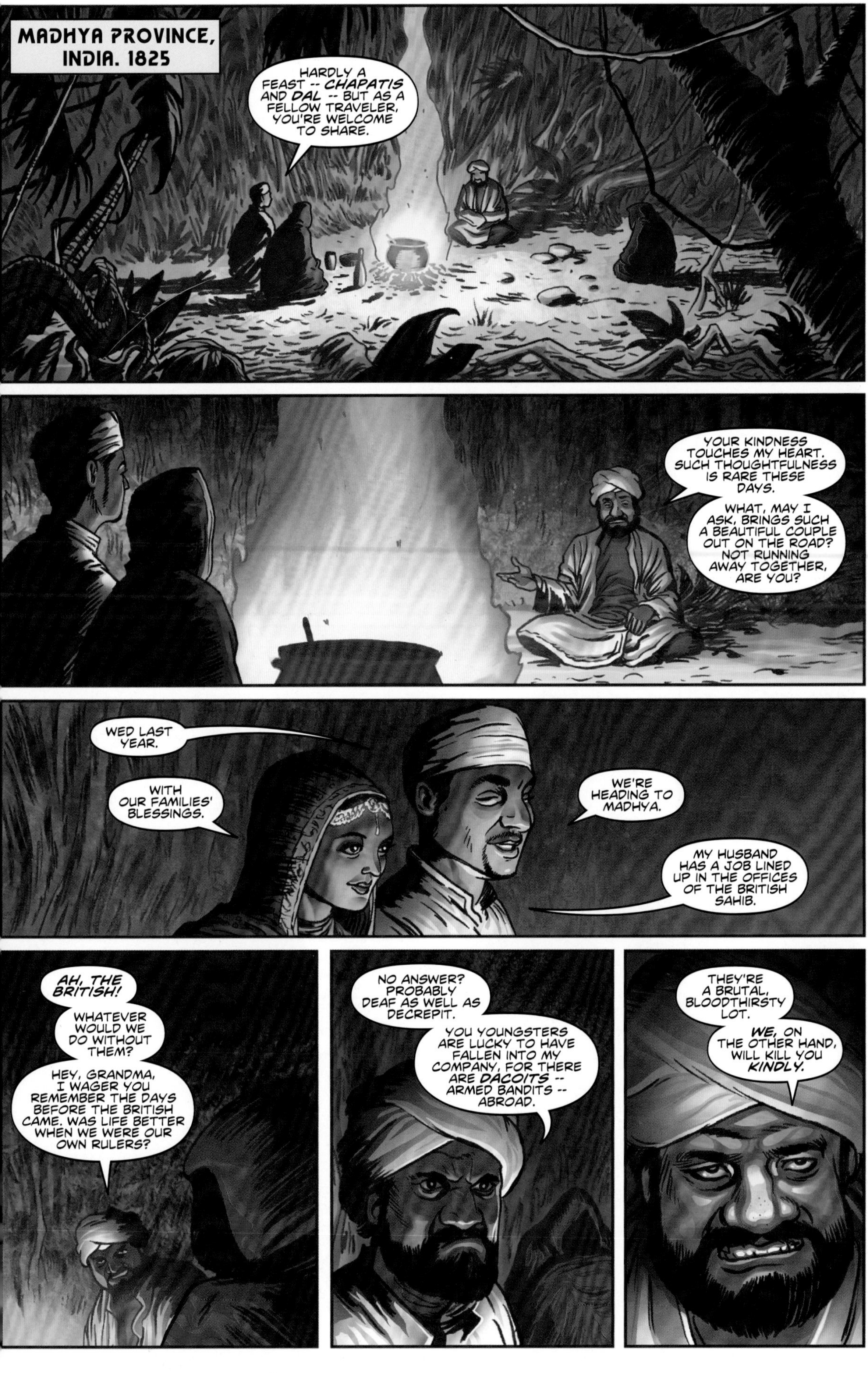
MADHYA PROVINCE, INDIA. 1825
HARDLY A FEAST -- CHAPATIS AND DAL -- BUT AS A FELLOW TRAVELER, YOU'RE WELCOME TO SHARE.
YOUR KINDNESS TOUCHES MY HEART. SUCH THOUGHTFULNESS IS RARE THESE DAYS.
WHAT, MAY I ASK, BRINGS SUCH A BEAUTIFUL COUPLE OUT ON THE ROAD? NOT RUNNING AWAY TOGETHER, ARE YOU?
WED LAST YEAR.
WITH OUR FAMILIES' BLESSINGS.
WE'RE HEADING TO MADHYA.
MY HUSBAND HAS A JOB LINED UP IN THE OFFICES OF THE BRITISH SAHIB.
AH, THE BRITISH!
WHATEVER WOULD WE DO WITHOUT THEM?
HEY, GRANDMA, I WAGER YOU REMEMBER THE DAYS BEFORE THE BRITISH CAME. WAS LIFE BETTER WHEN WE WERE OUR OWN RULERS?
NO ANSWER? PROBABLY DEAF AS WELL AS DECREPIT.
YOU YOUNGSTERS ARE LUCKY TO HAVE FALLEN INTO MY COMPANY, FOR THERE ARE DACOITS -- ARMED BANDITS -- ABROAD.
THEY'RE A BRUTAL, BLOODTHIRSTY LOT.
WE, ON THE OTHER HAND, WILL KILL YOU KINDLY.

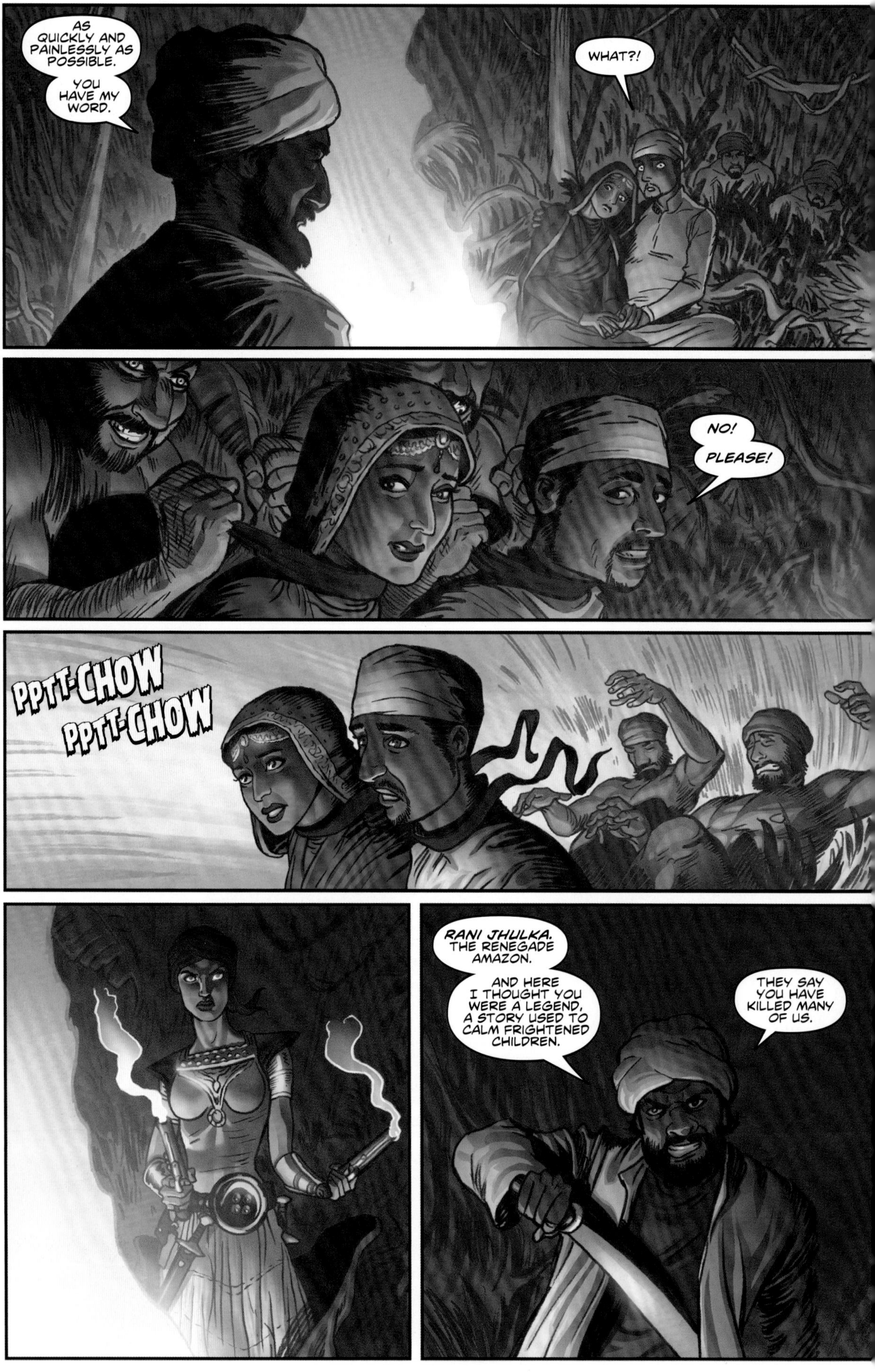
AS QUICKLY AND PAINLESSLY AS POSSIBLE.
YOU HAVE MY WORD.
WHAT?!
NO!
PLEASE!
PPTT-CHOW
PPTT-CHOW
RANI JHULKA. THE RENEGADE AMAZON.
AND HERE I THOUGHT YOU WERE A LEGEND, A STORY USED TO CALM FRIGHTENED CHILDREN.
THEY SAY YOU HAVE KILLED MANY OF US.

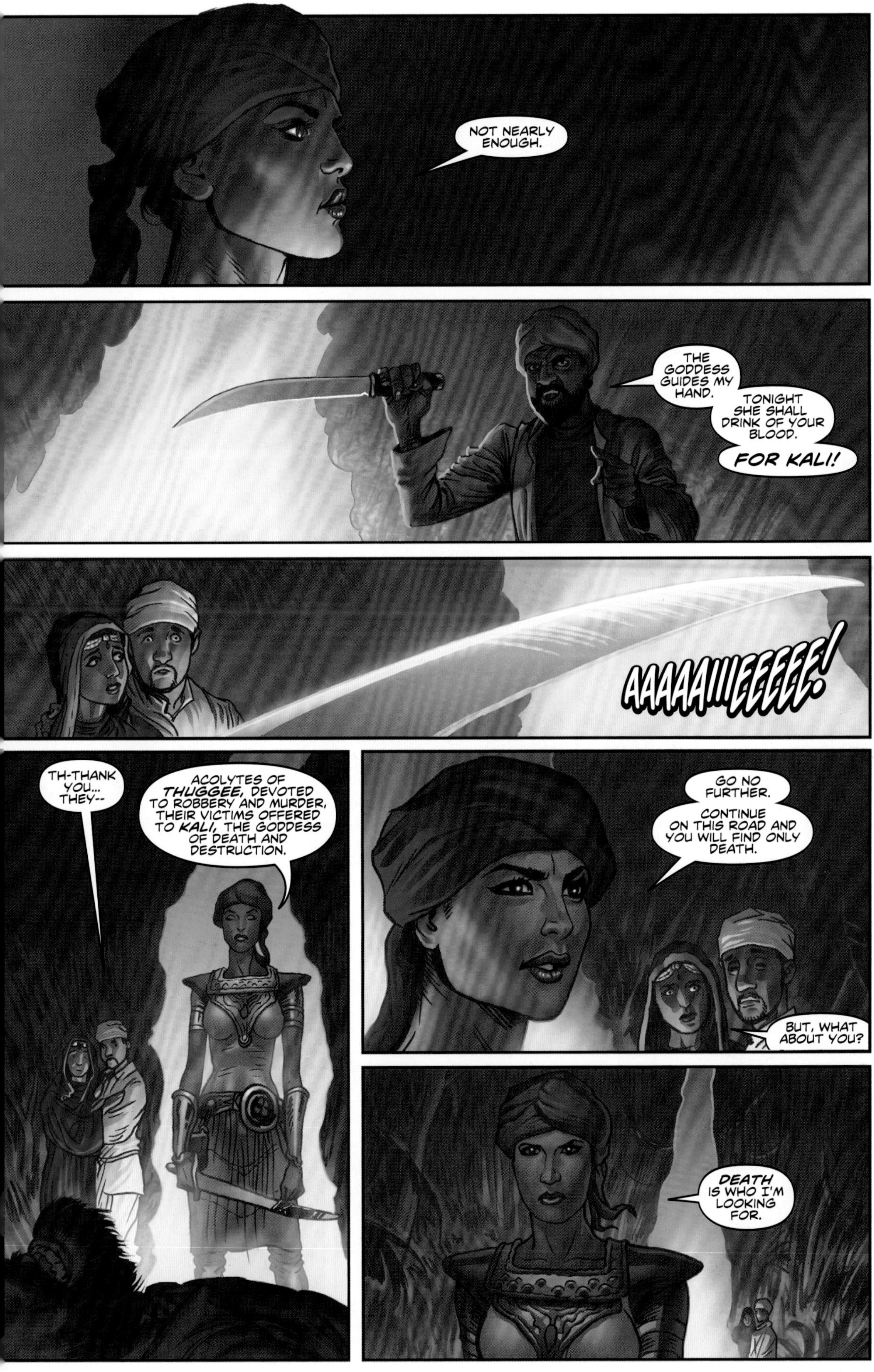

NOT NEARLY ENOUGH.
THE GODDESS GUIDES MY HAND.
TONIGHT SHE SHALL DRINK OF YOUR BLOOD.
FOR KALI!
AAAAAIIIIEEEEE!
TH-THANK YOU... THEY--
ACOLYTES OF THUGGEE, DEVOTED TO ROBBERY AND MURDER, THEIR VICTIMS OFFERED TO KALI, THE GODDESS OF DEATH AND DESTRUCTION.
GO NO FURTHER.
CONTINUE ON THIS ROAD AND YOU WILL FIND ONLY DEATH.
BUT, WHAT ABOUT YOU?
DEATH IS WHO I'M LOOKING FOR.

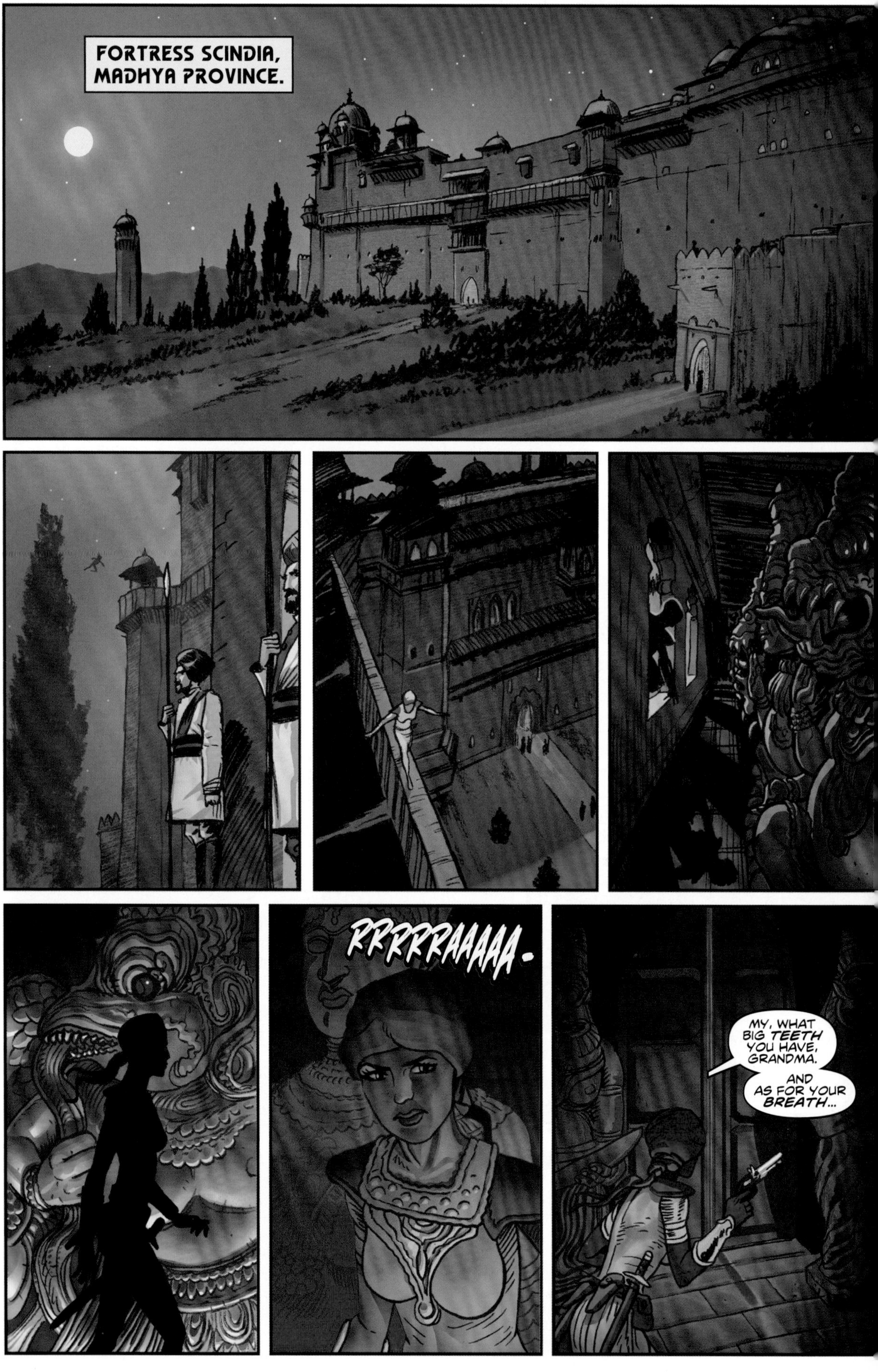
FORTRESS SCINDIA, MADHYA PROVINCE.
RRRRRAAAAAA-
MY, WHAT BIG TEETH YOU HAVE, GRANDMA.
AND AS FOR YOUR BREATH...

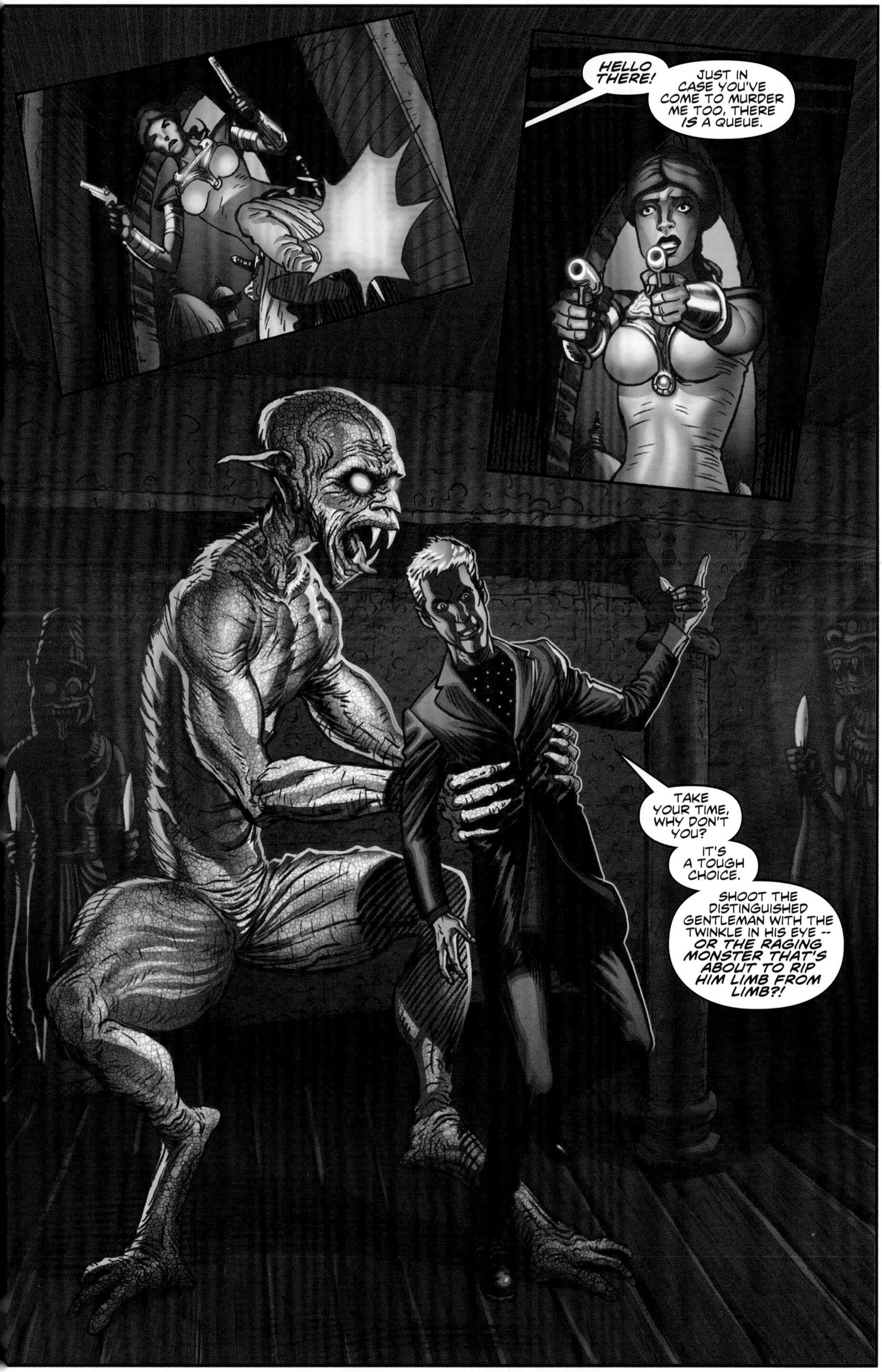
HELLO THERE!
JUST IN CASE YOU'VE COME TO MURDER ME TOO, THERE *IS* A QUEUE.
TAKE YOUR TIME, WHY DON'T YOU?
IT'S A TOUGH CHOICE.
SHOOT THE DISTINGUISHED GENTLEMAN WITH THE TWINKLE IN HIS EYE -- ***OR THE RAGING MONSTER THAT'S ABOUT TO RIP HIM LIMB FROM LIMB?!***

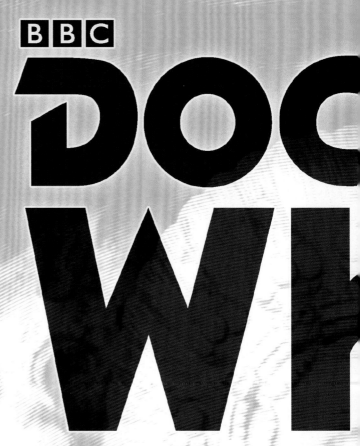

DOC
WH
THE TWELFT
THE SWOR

WRITER
ROBBIE MORRISON

LETTERER
RICHARD STARKINGS AND
COMICRAFT'S JIMMY BETANCOURT

TOR
10
H DOCTOR
DS OF KALI

ARTIST
DAVE TAYLOR
WITH MARIANO LACLAUSTRA

COLORIST
LUIS GUERRERO

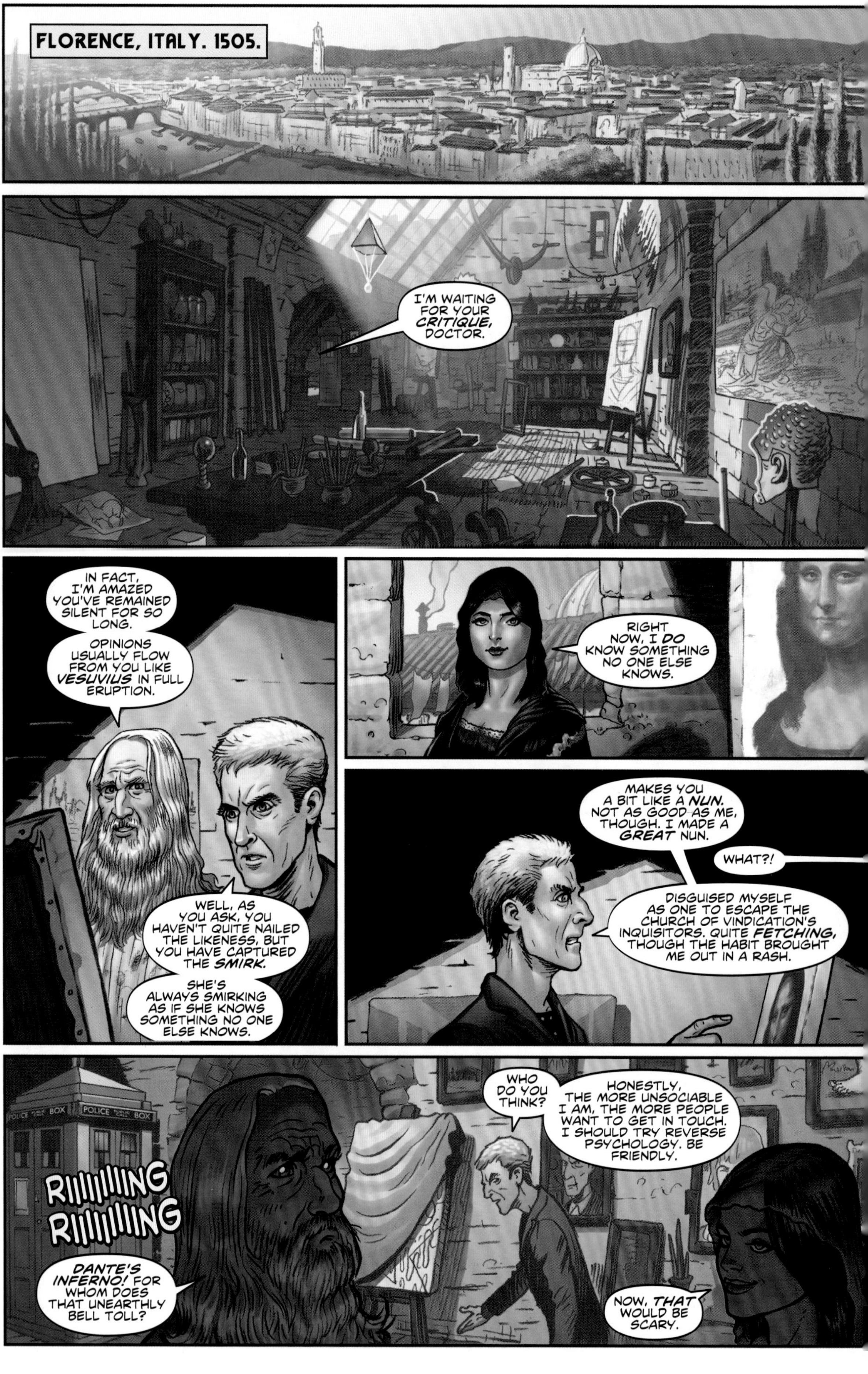
FLORENCE, ITALY. 1505.
I'M WAITING FOR YOUR CRITIQUE, DOCTOR.
IN FACT, I'M AMAZED YOU'VE REMAINED SILENT FOR SO LONG.
OPINIONS USUALLY FLOW FROM YOU LIKE VESUVIUS IN FULL ERUPTION.
WELL, AS YOU ASK, YOU HAVEN'T QUITE NAILED THE LIKENESS, BUT YOU HAVE CAPTURED THE SMIRK.
SHE'S ALWAYS SMIRKING AS IF SHE KNOWS SOMETHING NO ONE ELSE KNOWS.
RIGHT NOW, I DO KNOW SOMETHING NO ONE ELSE KNOWS.
MAKES YOU A BIT LIKE A NUN. NOT AS GOOD AS ME, THOUGH. I MADE A GREAT NUN.
WHAT?!
DISGUISED MYSELF AS ONE TO ESCAPE THE CHURCH OF VINDICATION'S INQUISITORS. QUITE FETCHING, THOUGH THE HABIT BROUGHT ME OUT IN A RASH.
RIIIIIIING RIIIIIIING
DANTE'S INFERNO! FOR WHOM DOES THAT UNEARTHLY BELL TOLL?
WHO DO YOU THINK?
HONESTLY, THE MORE UNSOCIABLE I AM, THE MORE PEOPLE WANT TO GET IN TOUCH. I SHOULD TRY REVERSE PSYCHOLOGY. BE FRIENDLY.
NOW, THAT WOULD BE SCARY.

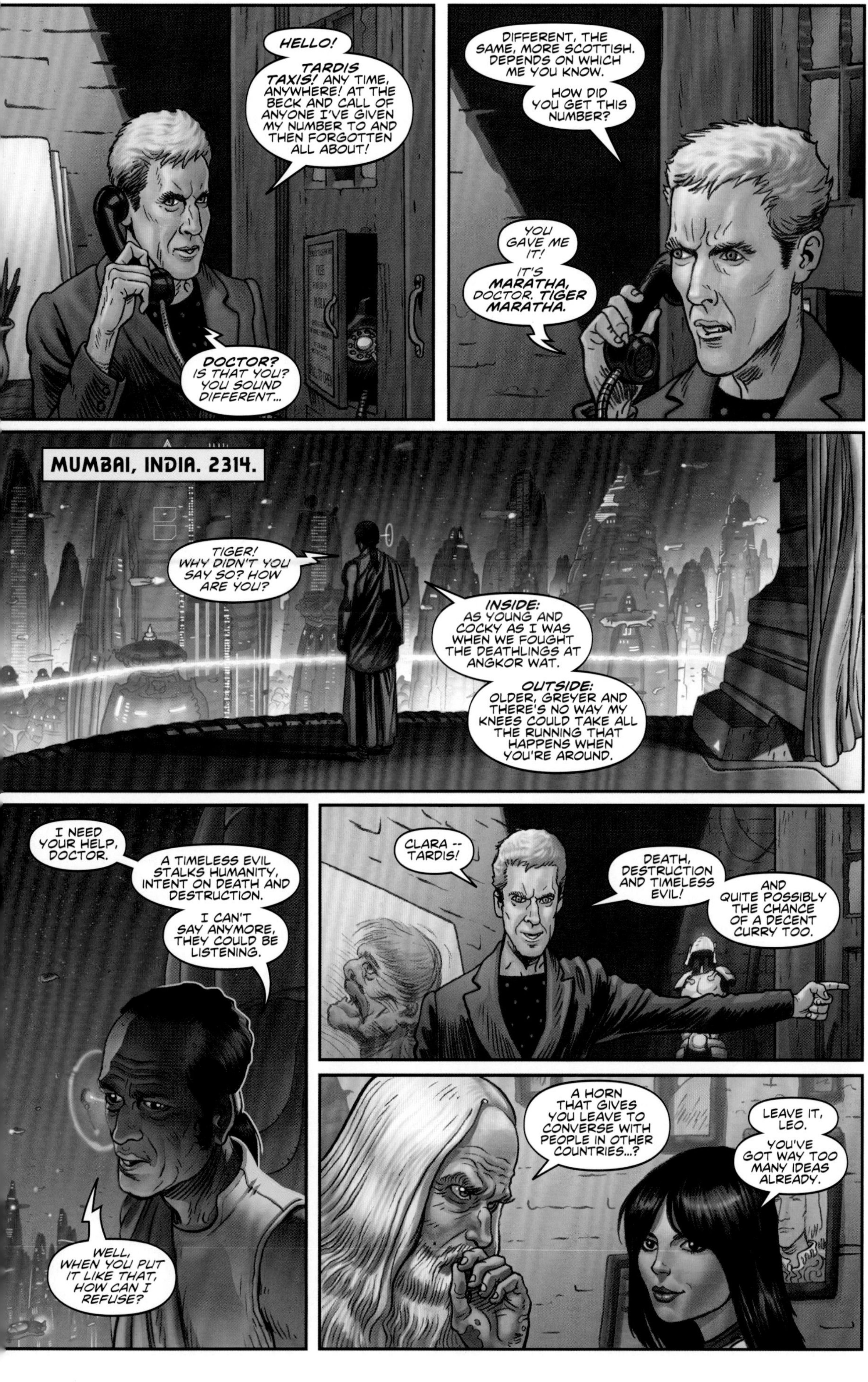
HELLO!
TARDIS TAXIS! ANY TIME, ANYWHERE! AT THE BECK AND CALL OF ANYONE I'VE GIVEN MY NUMBER TO AND THEN FORGOTTEN ALL ABOUT!
DOCTOR? IS THAT YOU? YOU SOUND DIFFERENT...
DIFFERENT, THE SAME, MORE SCOTTISH. DEPENDS ON WHICH ME YOU KNOW.
HOW DID YOU GET THIS NUMBER?
YOU GAVE ME IT!
IT'S MARATHA, DOCTOR. TIGER MARATHA.
MUMBAI, INDIA. 2314.
TIGER! WHY DIDN'T YOU SAY SO? HOW ARE YOU?
INSIDE: AS YOUNG AND COCKY AS I WAS WHEN WE FOUGHT THE DEATHLINGS AT ANGKOR WAT.
OUTSIDE: OLDER, GREYER AND THERE'S NO WAY MY KNEES COULD TAKE ALL THE RUNNING THAT HAPPENS WHEN YOU'RE AROUND.
I NEED YOUR HELP, DOCTOR.
A TIMELESS EVIL STALKS HUMANITY, INTENT ON DEATH AND DESTRUCTION.
I CAN'T SAY ANYMORE, THEY COULD BE LISTENING.
WELL, WHEN YOU PUT IT LIKE THAT, HOW CAN I REFUSE?
CLARA -- TARDIS!
DEATH, DESTRUCTION AND TIMELESS EVIL!
AND QUITE POSSIBLY THE CHANCE OF A DECENT CURRY TOO.
A HORN THAT GIVES YOU LEAVE TO CONVERSE WITH PEOPLE IN OTHER COUNTRIES...?
LEAVE IT, LEO.
YOU'VE GOT WAY TOO MANY IDEAS ALREADY.

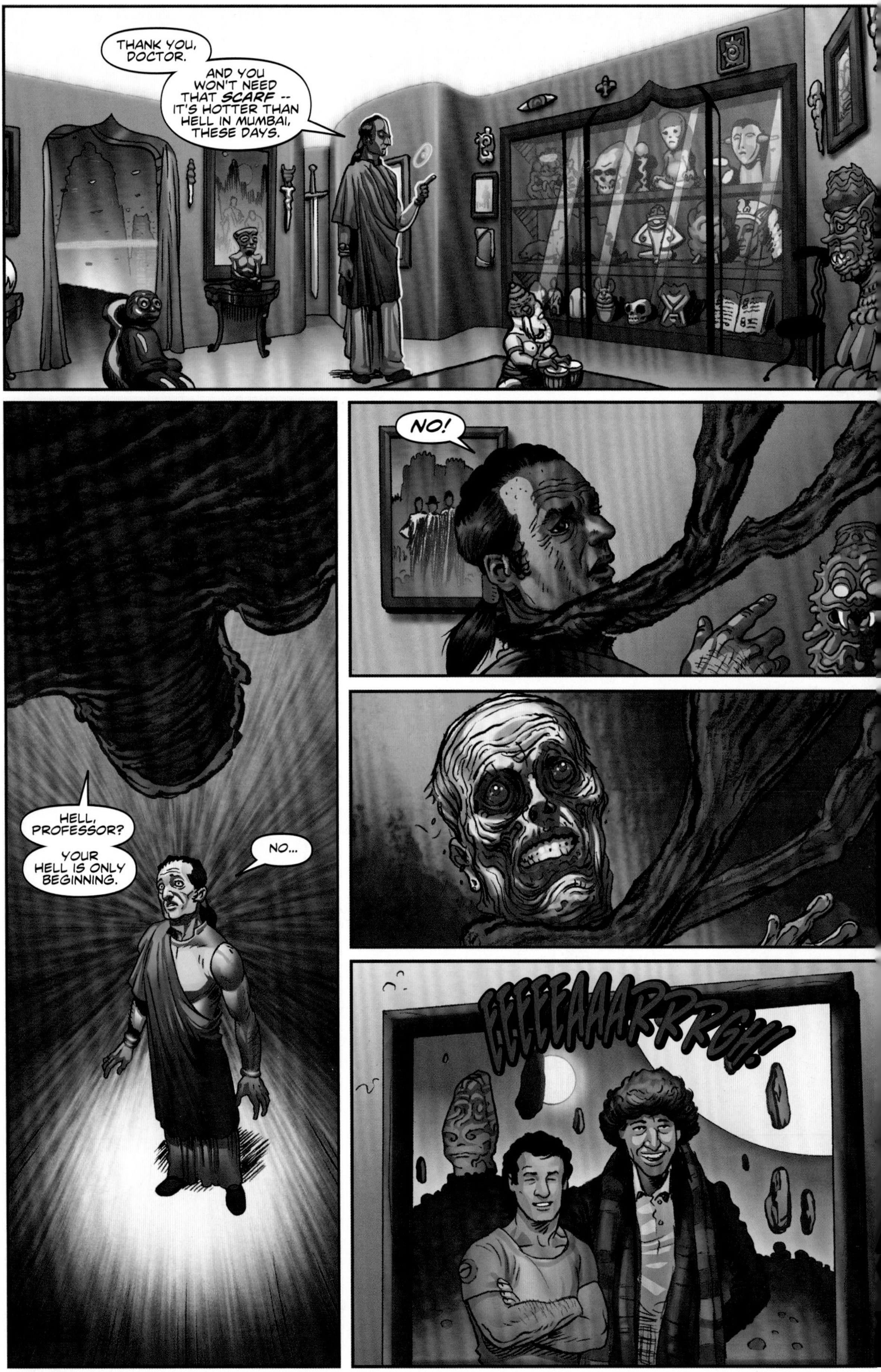
THANK YOU, DOCTOR.
AND YOU WON'T NEED THAT SCARF -- IT'S HOTTER THAN HELL IN MUMBAI, THESE DAYS.
HELL, PROFESSOR?
YOUR HELL IS ONLY BEGINNING.
NO...
NO!
EEEEEAAARRRGH!!

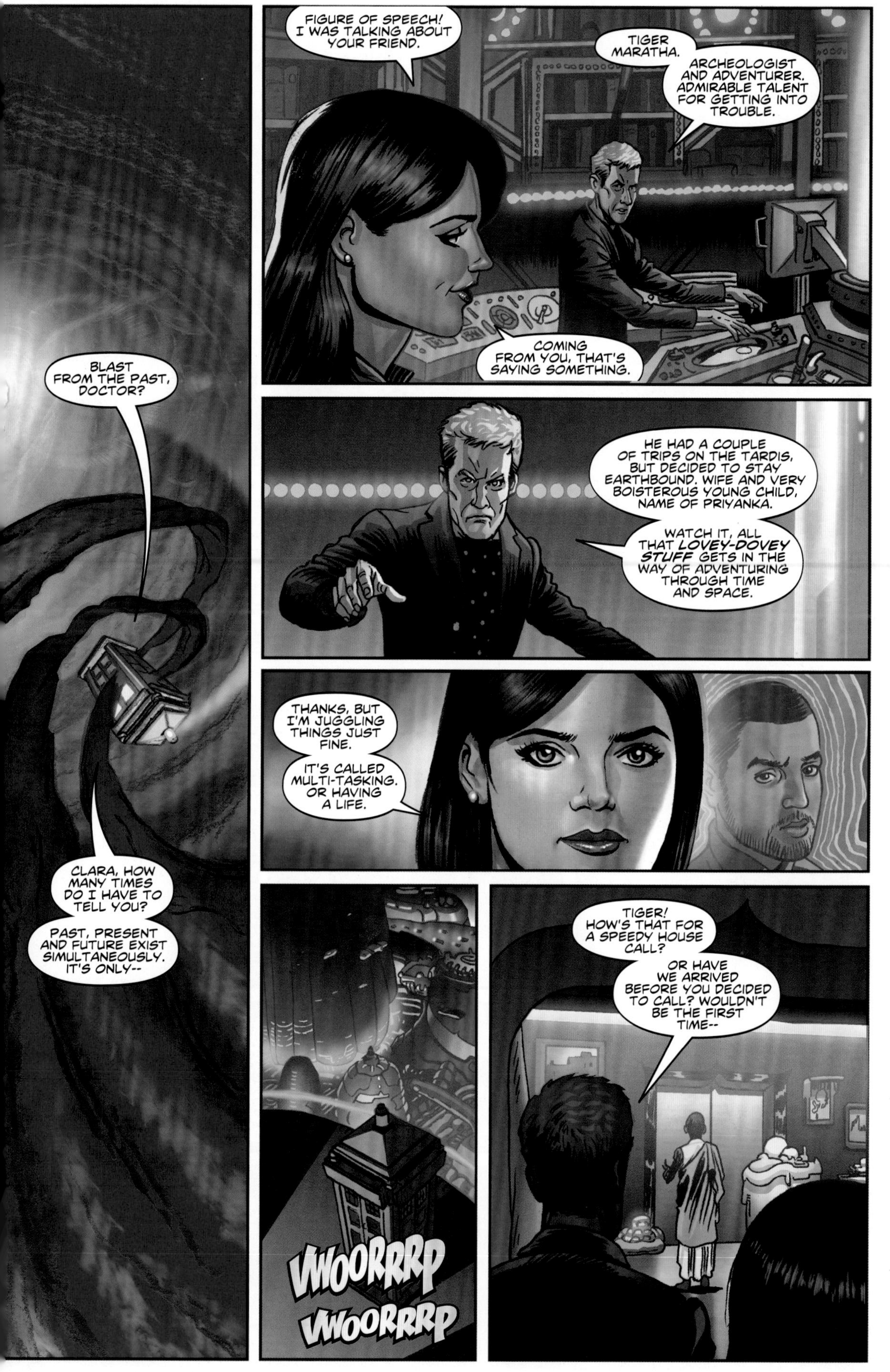
BLAST FROM THE PAST, DOCTOR?
CLARA, HOW MANY TIMES DO I HAVE TO TELL YOU?
PAST, PRESENT AND FUTURE EXIST SIMULTANEOUSLY. IT'S ONLY--
FIGURE OF SPEECH! I WAS TALKING ABOUT YOUR FRIEND.
TIGER MARATHA.
ARCHEOLOGIST AND ADVENTURER. ADMIRABLE TALENT FOR GETTING INTO TROUBLE.
COMING FROM YOU, THAT'S SAYING SOMETHING.
HE HAD A COUPLE OF TRIPS ON THE TARDIS, BUT DECIDED TO STAY EARTHBOUND. WIFE AND VERY BOISTEROUS YOUNG CHILD, NAME OF PRIYANKA.
WATCH IT, ALL THAT LOVEY-DOVEY STUFF GETS IN THE WAY OF ADVENTURING THROUGH TIME AND SPACE.
THANKS, BUT I'M JUGGLING THINGS JUST FINE.
IT'S CALLED MULTI-TASKING. OR HAVING A LIFE.
VWOORRRP
VWOORRRP
TIGER! HOW'S THAT FOR A SPEEDY HOUSE CALL?
OR HAVE WE ARRIVED BEFORE YOU DECIDED TO CALL? WOULDN'T BE THE FIRST TIME--

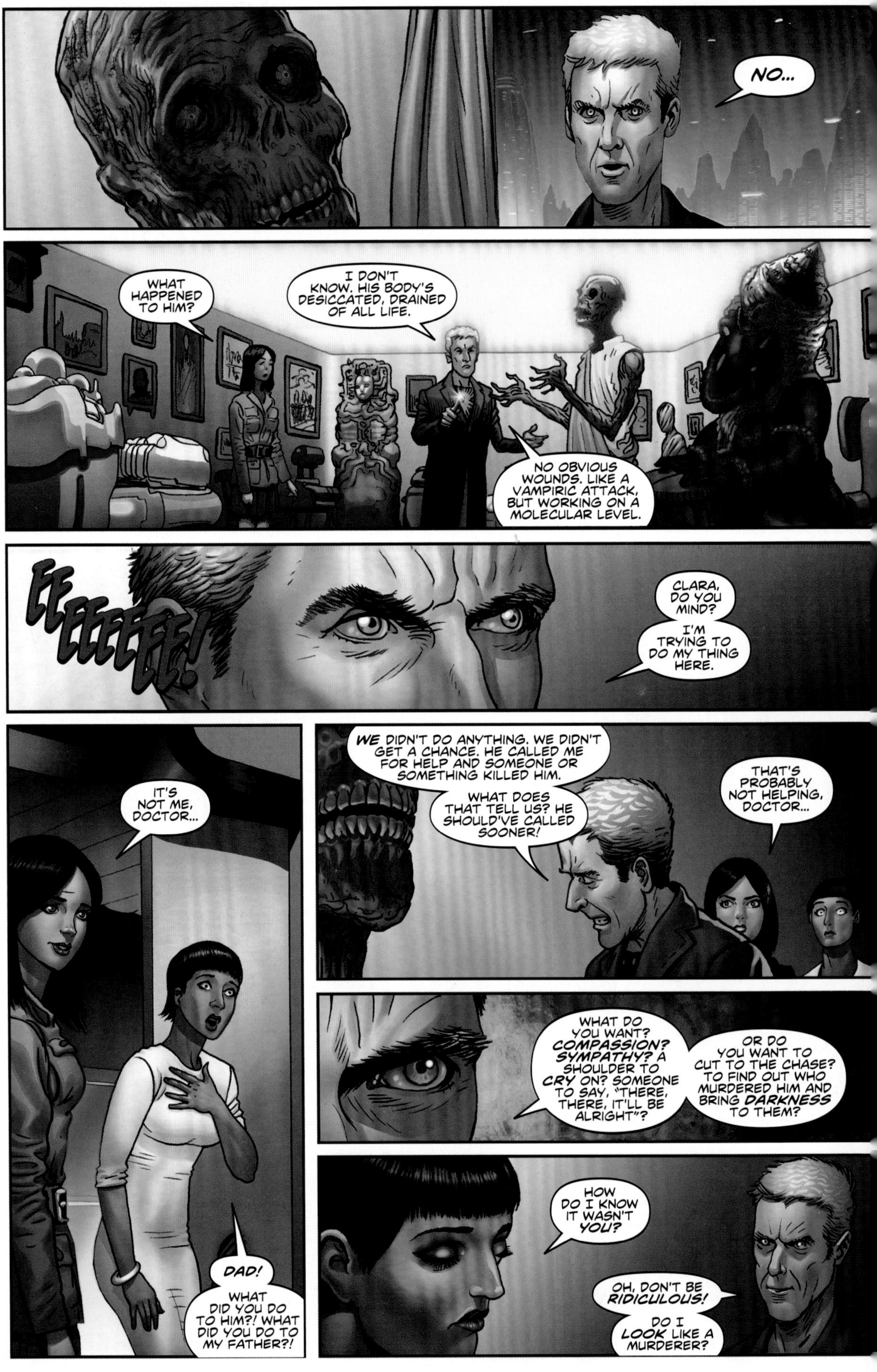
NO...
WHAT HAPPENED TO HIM?
I DON'T KNOW. HIS BODY'S DESICCATED, DRAINED OF ALL LIFE.
NO OBVIOUS WOUNDS. LIKE A VAMPIRIC ATTACK, BUT WORKING ON A MOLECULAR LEVEL.
EEEEEEEE!
CLARA, DO YOU MIND?
I'M TRYING TO DO MY THING HERE.
IT'S NOT ME, DOCTOR...
DAD!
WHAT DID YOU DO TO HIM?! WHAT DID YOU DO TO MY FATHER?!
WE DIDN'T DO ANYTHING. WE DIDN'T GET A CHANCE. HE CALLED ME FOR HELP AND SOMEONE OR SOMETHING KILLED HIM.
WHAT DOES THAT TELL US? HE SHOULD'VE CALLED SOONER!
THAT'S PROBABLY NOT HELPING, DOCTOR...
WHAT DO YOU WANT? COMPASSION? SYMPATHY? A SHOULDER TO CRY ON? SOMEONE TO SAY, "THERE, THERE, IT'LL BE ALRIGHT"?
OR DO YOU WANT TO CUT TO THE CHASE? TO FIND OUT WHO MURDERED HIM AND BRING DARKNESS TO THEM?
HOW DO I KNOW IT WASN'T YOU?
OH, DON'T BE RIDICULOUS!
DO I LOOK LIKE A MURDERER?

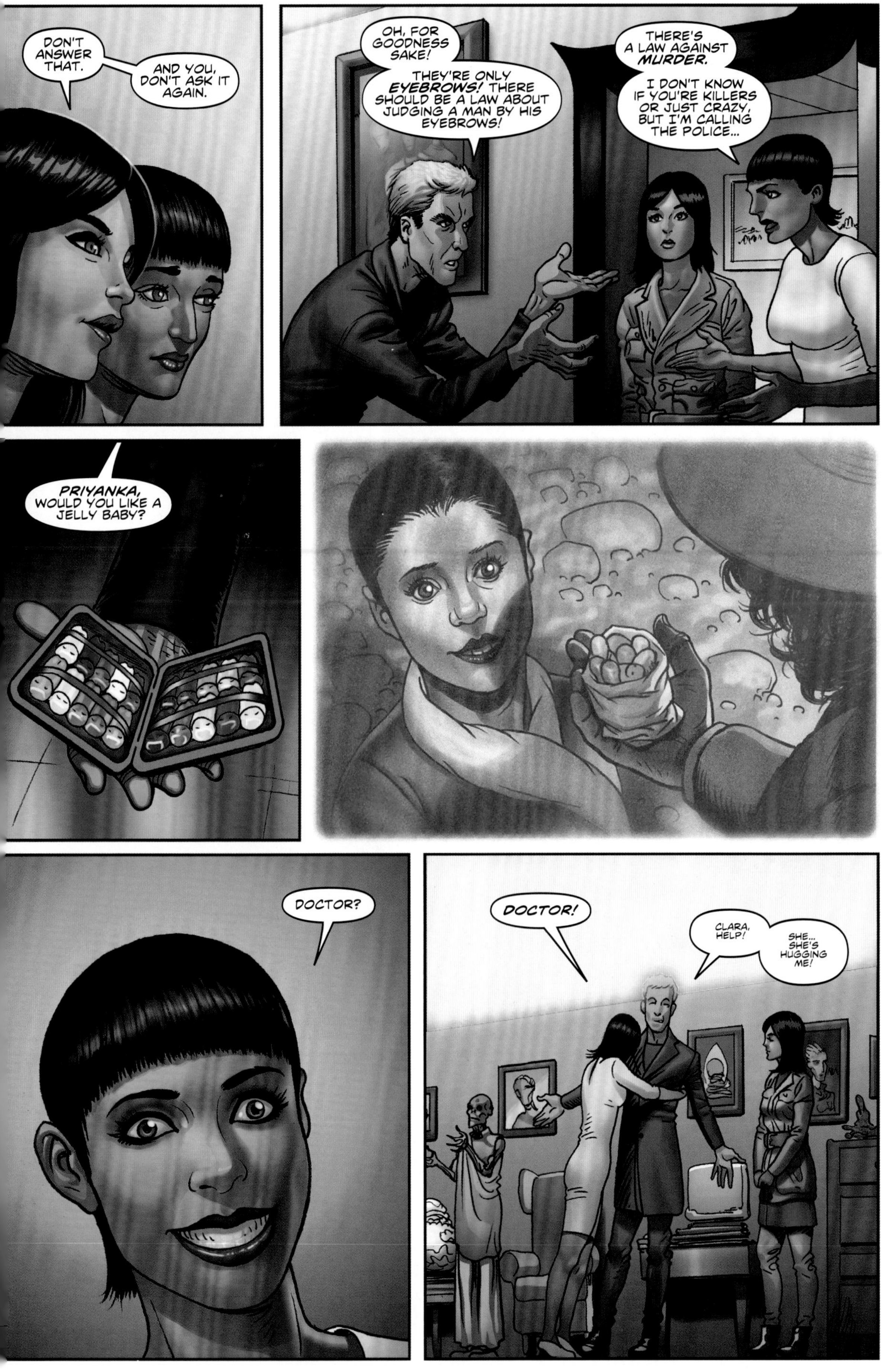

DON'T ANSWER THAT.
AND YOU, DON'T ASK IT AGAIN.
OH, FOR GOODNESS SAKE!
THEY'RE ONLY EYEBROWS! THERE SHOULD BE A LAW ABOUT JUDGING A MAN BY HIS EYEBROWS!
THERE'S A LAW AGAINST MURDER.
I DON'T KNOW IF YOU'RE KILLERS OR JUST CRAZY, BUT I'M CALLING THE POLICE...
PRIYANKA, WOULD YOU LIKE A JELLY BABY?
DOCTOR?
DOCTOR!
CLARA, HELP!
SHE... SHE'S HUGGING ME!

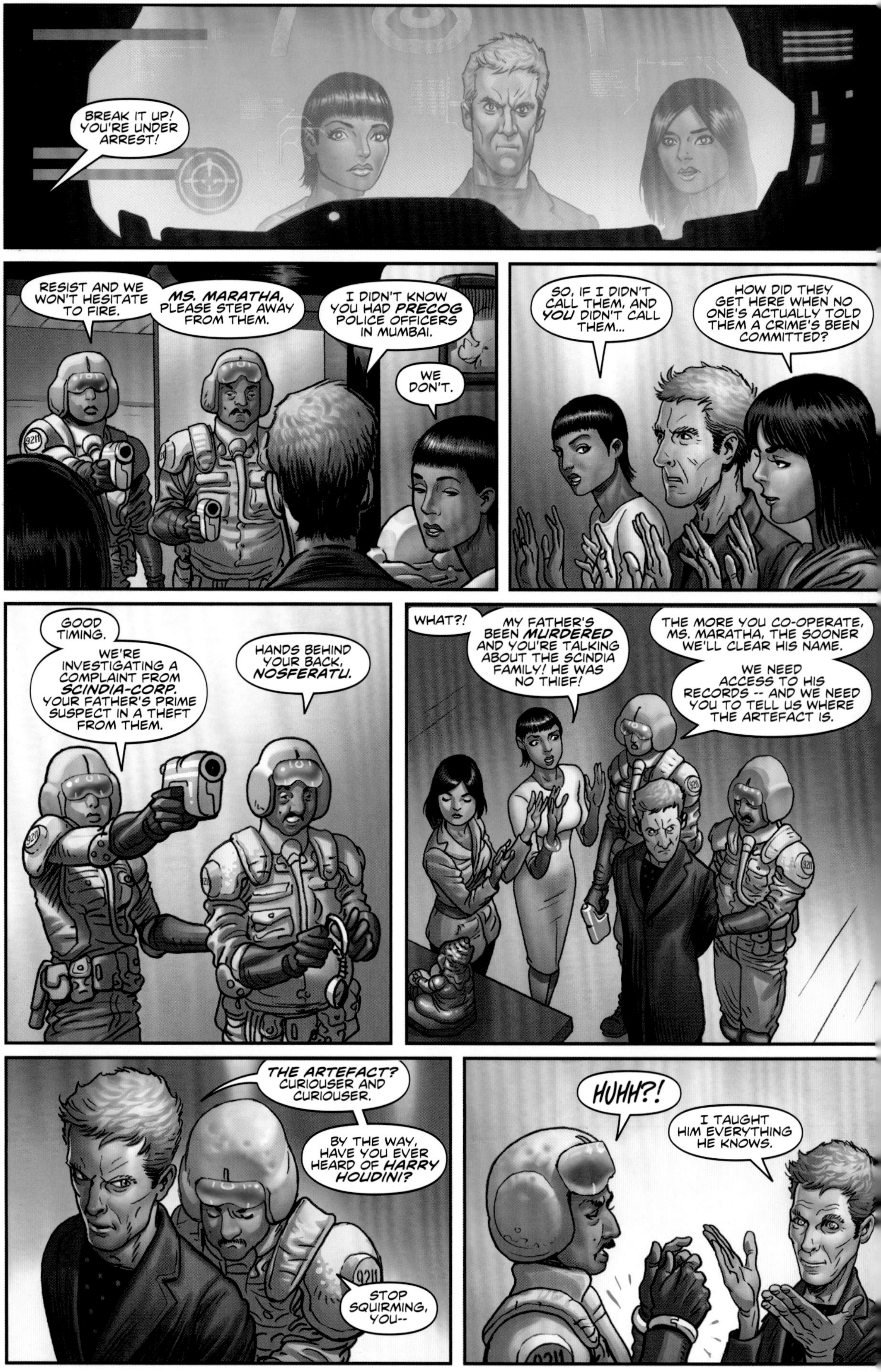

BREAK IT UP! YOU'RE UNDER ARREST!
RESIST AND WE WON'T HESITATE TO FIRE.
MS. MARATHA, PLEASE STEP AWAY FROM THEM.
I DIDN'T KNOW YOU HAD PRECOG POLICE OFFICERS IN MUMBAI.
WE DON'T.
SO, IF I DIDN'T CALL THEM, AND YOU DIDN'T CALL THEM...
HOW DID THEY GET HERE WHEN NO ONE'S ACTUALLY TOLD THEM A CRIME'S BEEN COMMITTED?
GOOD TIMING.
WE'RE INVESTIGATING A COMPLAINT FROM SCINDIA-CORP. YOUR FATHER'S PRIME SUSPECT IN A THEFT FROM THEM.
HANDS BEHIND YOUR BACK, NOSFERATU.
WHAT?!
MY FATHER'S BEEN MURDERED AND YOU'RE TALKING ABOUT THE SCINDIA FAMILY! HE WAS NO THIEF!
THE MORE YOU CO-OPERATE, MS. MARATHA, THE SOONER WE'LL CLEAR HIS NAME.
WE NEED ACCESS TO HIS RECORDS -- AND WE NEED YOU TO TELL US WHERE THE ARTEFACT IS.
THE ARTEFACT? CURIOUSER AND CURIOUSER.
BY THE WAY, HAVE YOU EVER HEARD OF HARRY HOUDINI?
STOP SQUIRMING, YOU--
HUHH?!
I TAUGHT HIM EVERYTHING HE KNOWS.

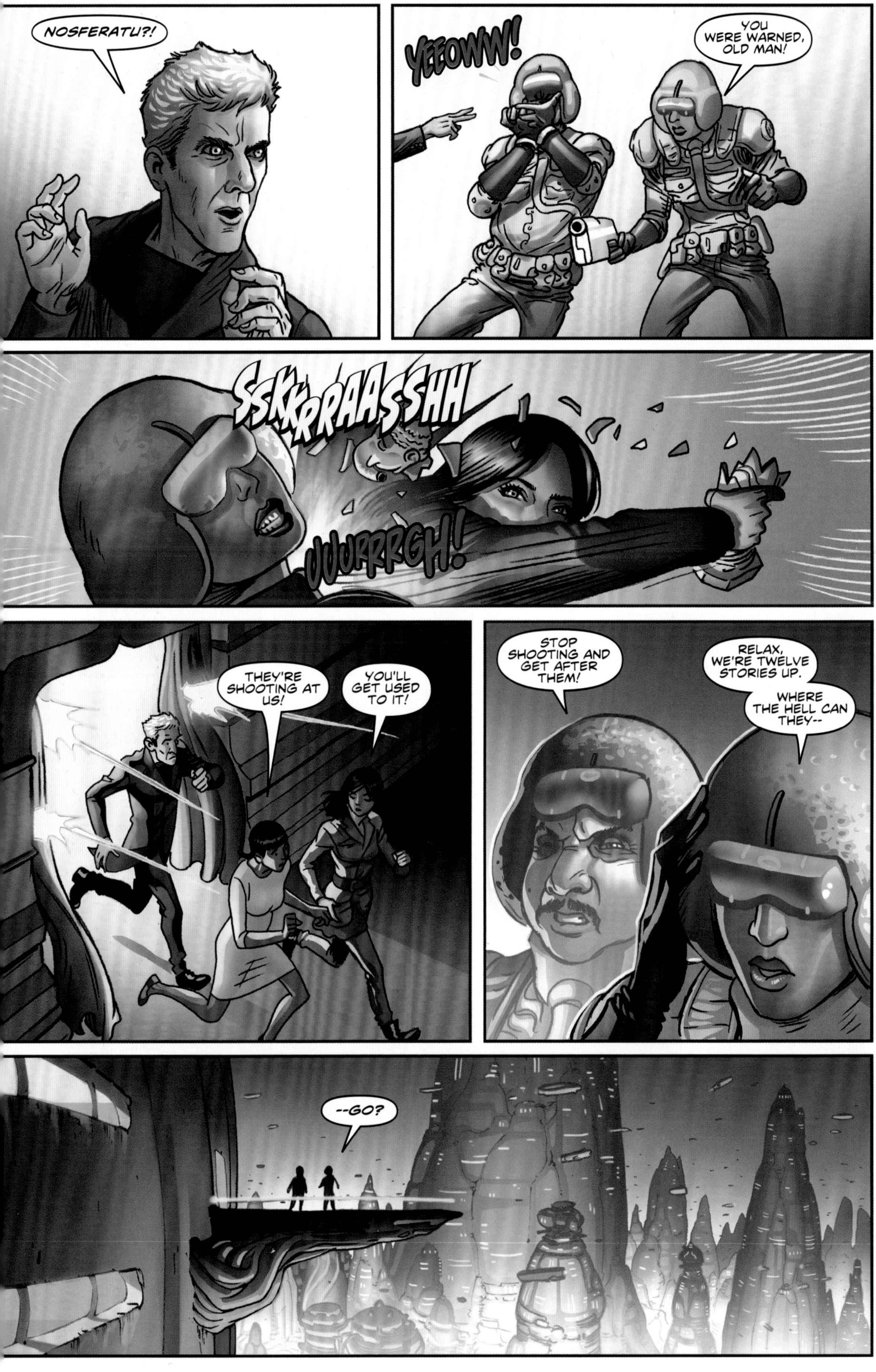
NOSFERATU?!
YEEOWW!
YOU WERE WARNED, OLD MAN!
SSKKRRAASSHH
UUURRRGH!
THEY'RE SHOOTING AT US!
YOU'LL GET USED TO IT!
STOP SHOOTING AND GET AFTER THEM!
RELAX, WE'RE TWELVE STORIES UP.
WHERE THE HELL CAN THEY--
--GO?

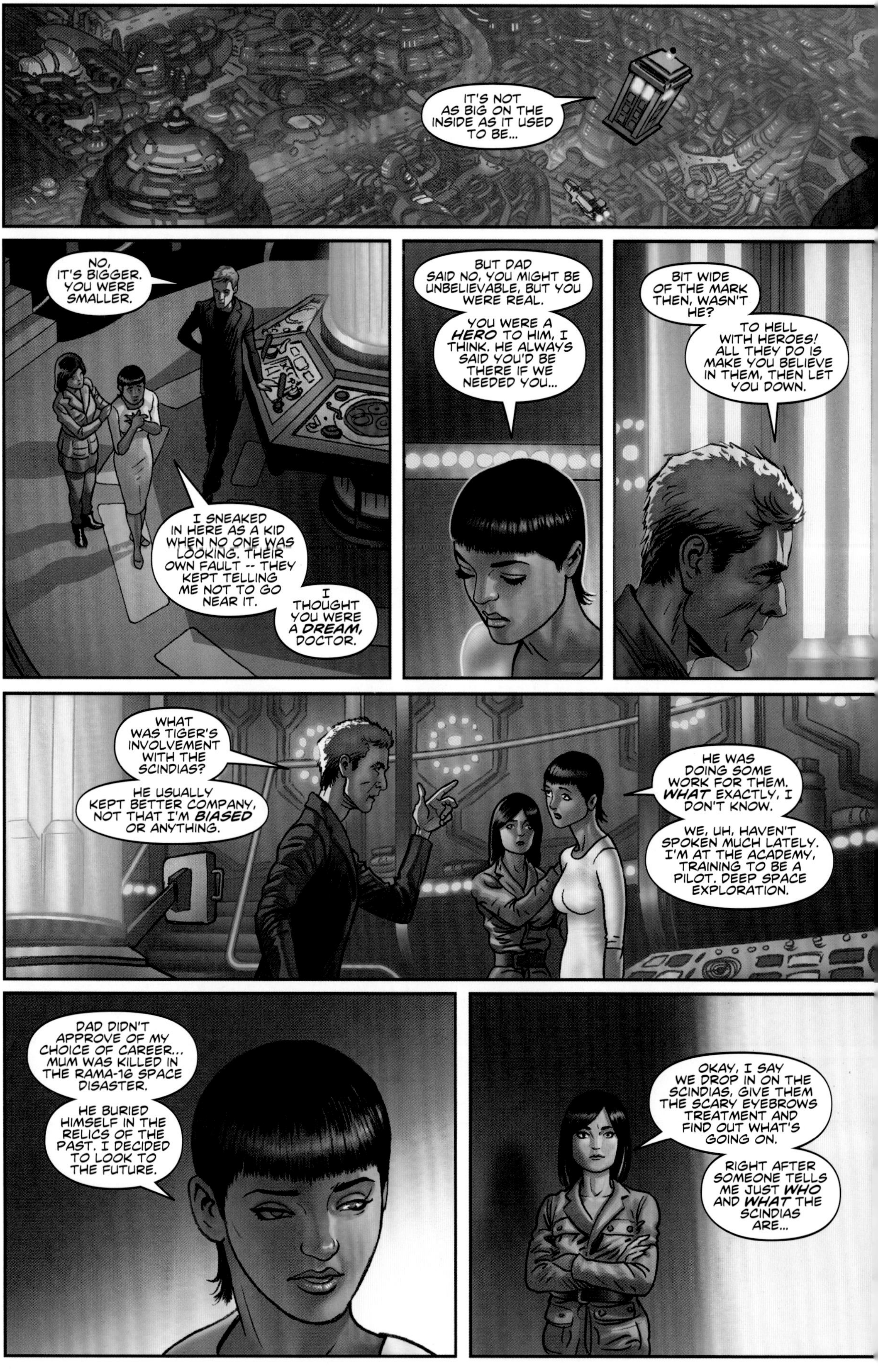
IT'S NOT AS BIG ON THE INSIDE AS IT USED TO BE...
NO, IT'S BIGGER. YOU WERE SMALLER.
I SNEAKED IN HERE AS A KID WHEN NO ONE WAS LOOKING. THEIR OWN FAULT -- THEY KEPT TELLING ME NOT TO GO NEAR IT.
I THOUGHT YOU WERE A *DREAM,* DOCTOR.
BUT DAD SAID NO, YOU MIGHT BE UNBELIEVABLE, BUT YOU WERE REAL.
YOU WERE A *HERO* TO HIM, I THINK. HE ALWAYS SAID YOU'D BE THERE IF WE NEEDED YOU...
BIT WIDE OF THE MARK THEN, WASN'T HE?
TO HELL WITH HEROES! ALL THEY DO IS MAKE YOU BELIEVE IN THEM, THEN LET YOU DOWN.
WHAT WAS TIGER'S INVOLVEMENT WITH THE SCINDIAS?
HE USUALLY KEPT BETTER COMPANY, NOT THAT I'M *BIASED* OR ANYTHING.
HE WAS DOING SOME WORK FOR THEM. *WHAT* EXACTLY, I DON'T KNOW.
WE, UH, HAVEN'T SPOKEN MUCH LATELY. I'M AT THE ACADEMY, TRAINING TO BE A PILOT. DEEP SPACE EXPLORATION.
DAD DIDN'T APPROVE OF MY CHOICE OF CAREER... MUM WAS KILLED IN THE RAMA-16 SPACE DISASTER.
HE BURIED HIMSELF IN THE RELICS OF THE PAST. I DECIDED TO LOOK TO THE FUTURE.
OKAY, I SAY WE DROP IN ON THE SCINDIAS, GIVE THEM THE SCARY EYEBROWS TREATMENT AND FIND OUT WHAT'S GOING ON.
RIGHT AFTER SOMEONE TELLS ME JUST *WHO* AND *WHAT* THE SCINDIAS ARE...

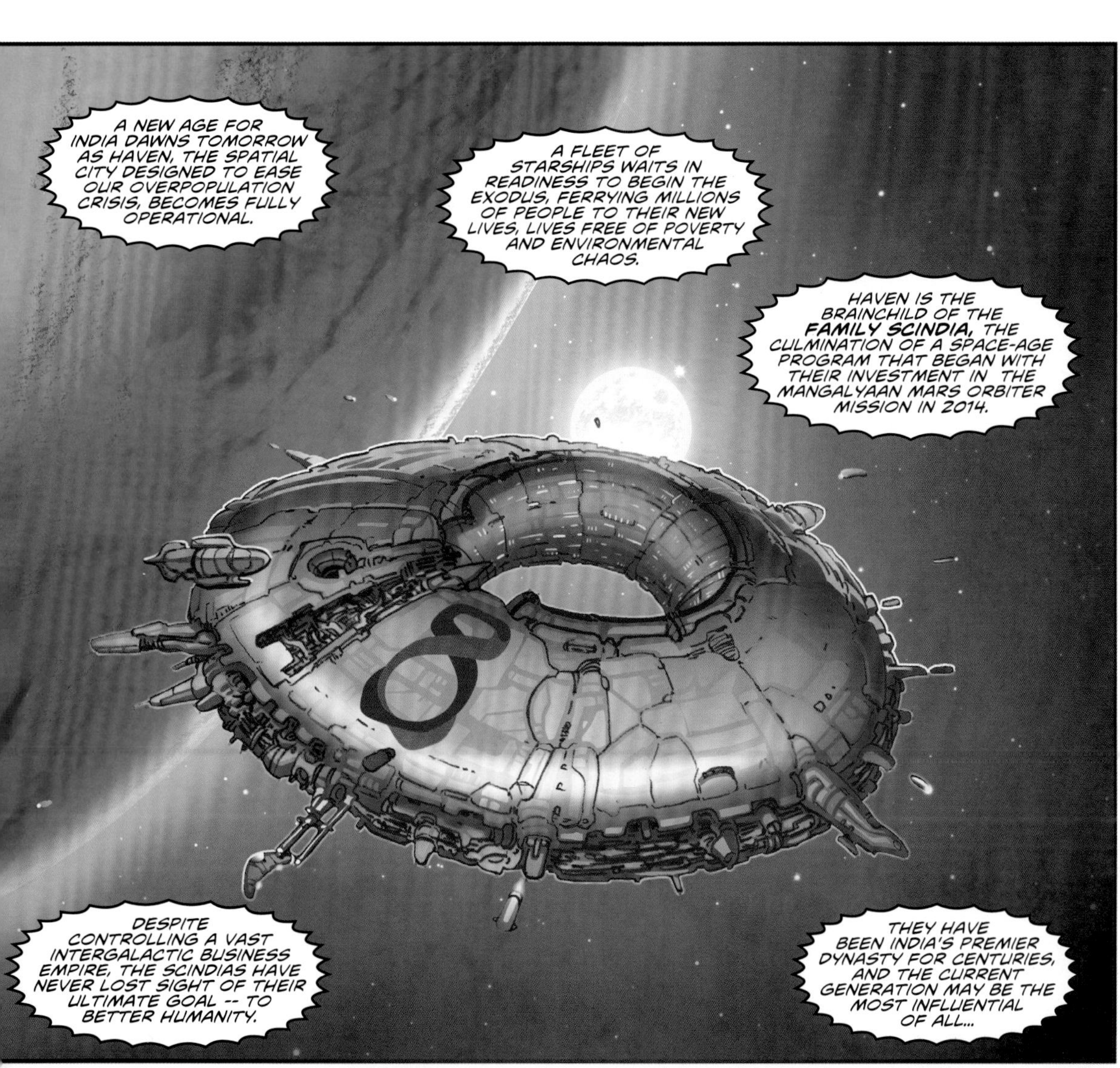
A NEW AGE FOR INDIA DAWNS TOMORROW AS HAVEN, THE SPATIAL CITY DESIGNED TO EASE OUR OVERPOPULATION CRISIS, BECOMES FULLY OPERATIONAL.
A FLEET OF STARSHIPS WAITS IN READINESS TO BEGIN THE EXODUS, FERRYING MILLIONS OF PEOPLE TO THEIR NEW LIVES, LIVES FREE OF POVERTY AND ENVIRONMENTAL CHAOS.
HAVEN IS THE BRAINCHILD OF THE FAMILY SCINDIA, THE CULMINATION OF A SPACE-AGE PROGRAM THAT BEGAN WITH THEIR INVESTMENT IN THE MANGALYAAN MARS ORBITER MISSION IN 2014.
DESPITE CONTROLLING A VAST INTERGALACTIC BUSINESS EMPIRE, THE SCINDIAS HAVE NEVER LOST SIGHT OF THEIR ULTIMATE GOAL -- TO BETTER HUMANITY.
THEY HAVE BEEN INDIA'S PREMIER DYNASTY FOR CENTURIES, AND THE CURRENT GENERATION MAY BE THE MOST INFLUENTIAL OF ALL...

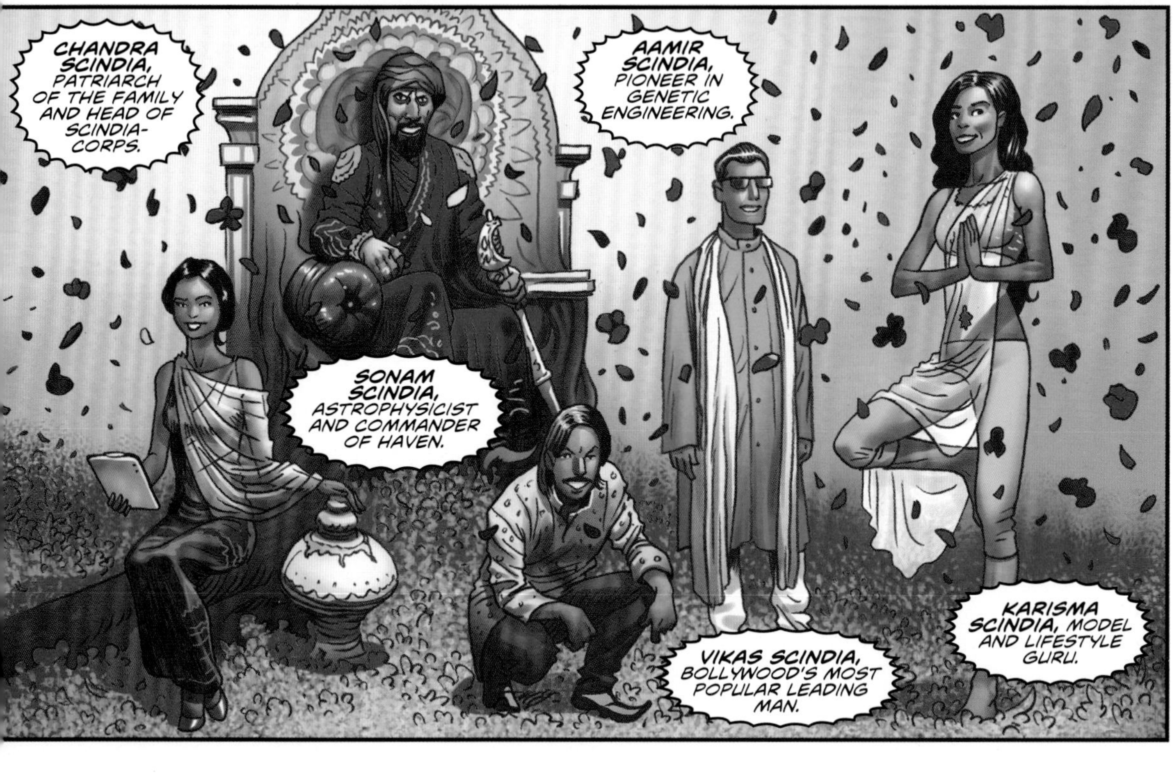
CHANDRA SCINDIA, PATRIARCH OF THE FAMILY AND HEAD OF SCINDIA-CORPS.
AAMIR SCINDIA, PIONEER IN GENETIC ENGINEERING.
SONAM SCINDIA, ASTROPHYSICIST AND COMMANDER OF HAVEN.
VIKAS SCINDIA, BOLLYWOOD'S MOST POPULAR LEADING MAN.
KARISMA SCINDIA, MODEL AND LIFESTYLE GURU.

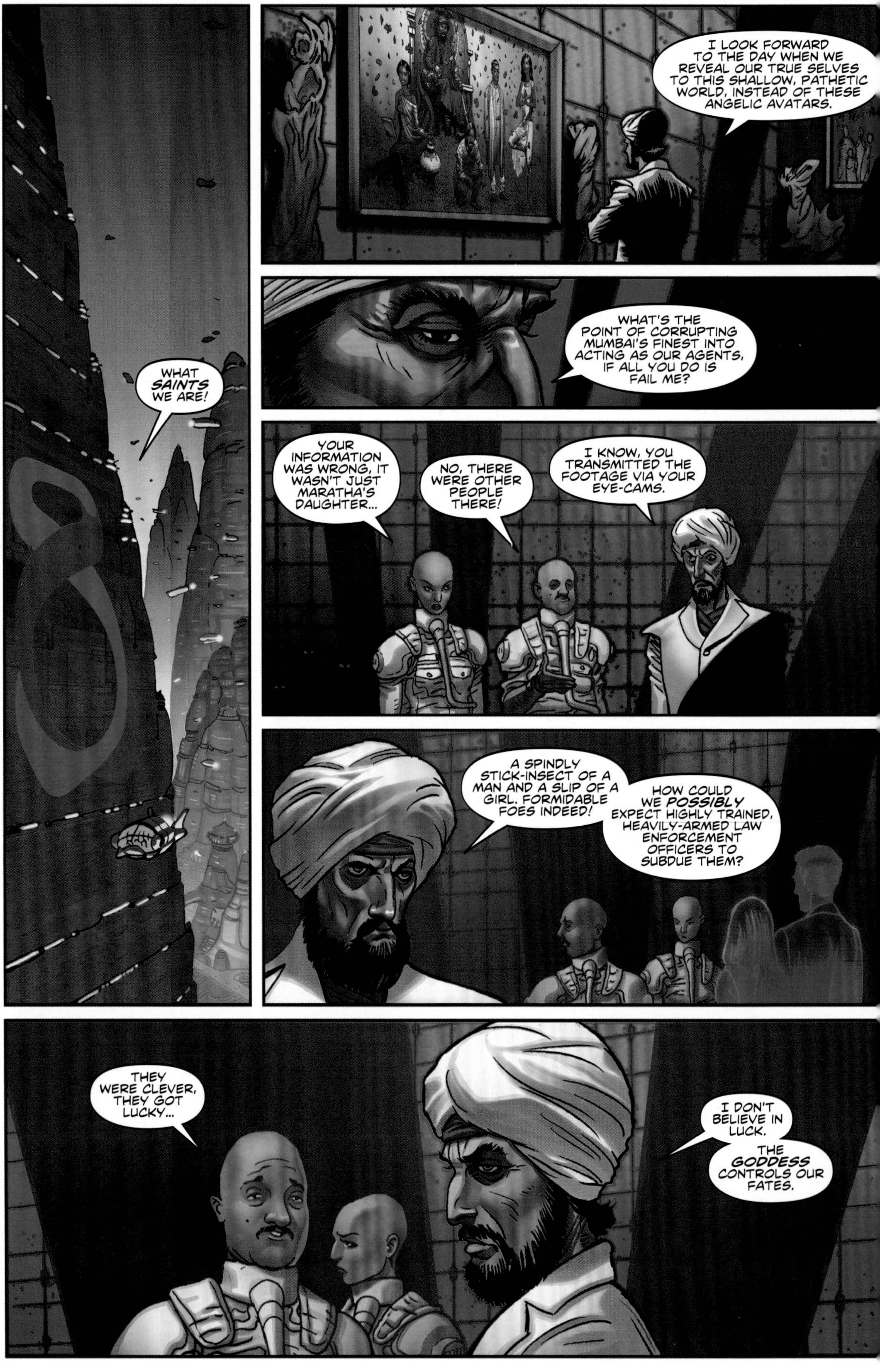
WHAT SAINTS WE ARE!
I LOOK FORWARD TO THE DAY WHEN WE REVEAL OUR TRUE SELVES TO THIS SHALLOW, PATHETIC WORLD, INSTEAD OF THESE ANGELIC AVATARS.
WHAT'S THE POINT OF CORRUPTING MUMBAI'S FINEST INTO ACTING AS OUR AGENTS, IF ALL YOU DO IS FAIL ME?
YOUR INFORMATION WAS WRONG, IT WASN'T JUST MARATHA'S DAUGHTER...
NO, THERE WERE OTHER PEOPLE THERE!
I KNOW, YOU TRANSMITTED THE FOOTAGE VIA YOUR EYE-CAMS.
A SPINDLY STICK-INSECT OF A MAN AND A SLIP OF A GIRL. FORMIDABLE FOES INDEED!
HOW COULD WE POSSIBLY EXPECT HIGHLY TRAINED, HEAVILY-ARMED LAW ENFORCEMENT OFFICERS TO SUBDUE THEM?
THEY WERE CLEVER, THEY GOT LUCKY...
I DON'T BELIEVE IN LUCK.
THE GODDESS CONTROLS OUR FATES.

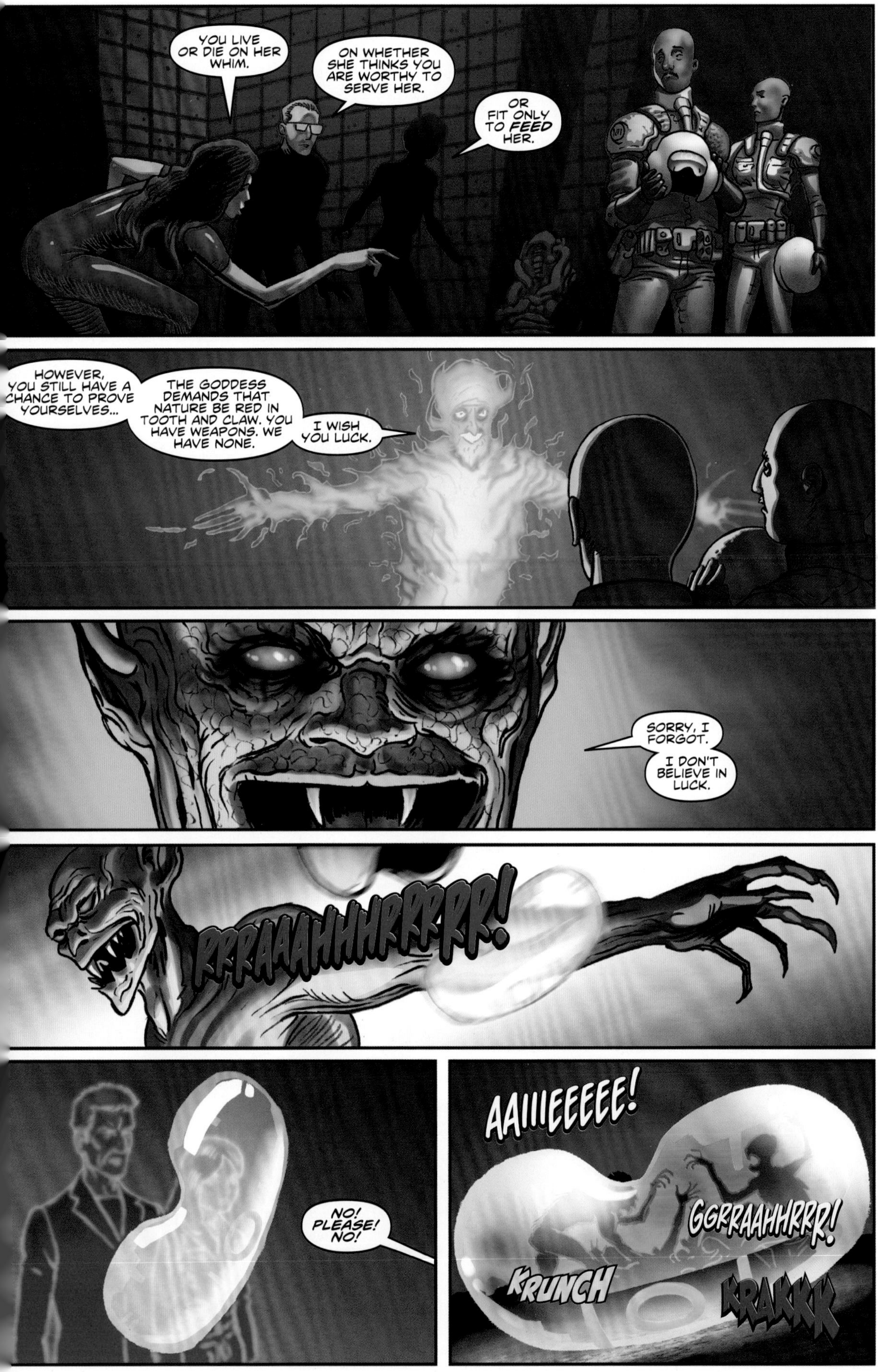
YOU LIVE OR DIE ON HER WHIM.
ON WHETHER SHE THINKS YOU ARE WORTHY TO SERVE HER.
OR FIT ONLY TO FEED HER.
HOWEVER, YOU STILL HAVE A CHANCE TO PROVE YOURSELVES...
THE GODDESS DEMANDS THAT NATURE BE RED IN TOOTH AND CLAW. YOU HAVE WEAPONS. WE HAVE NONE.
I WISH YOU LUCK.
SORRY, I FORGOT.
I DON'T BELIEVE IN LUCK.
RRRAAAHHHRRRRR!
NO! PLEASE! NO!
AAIIIEEEEE!
GGRRAAHHRRR!
KRUNCH
KRAKKK

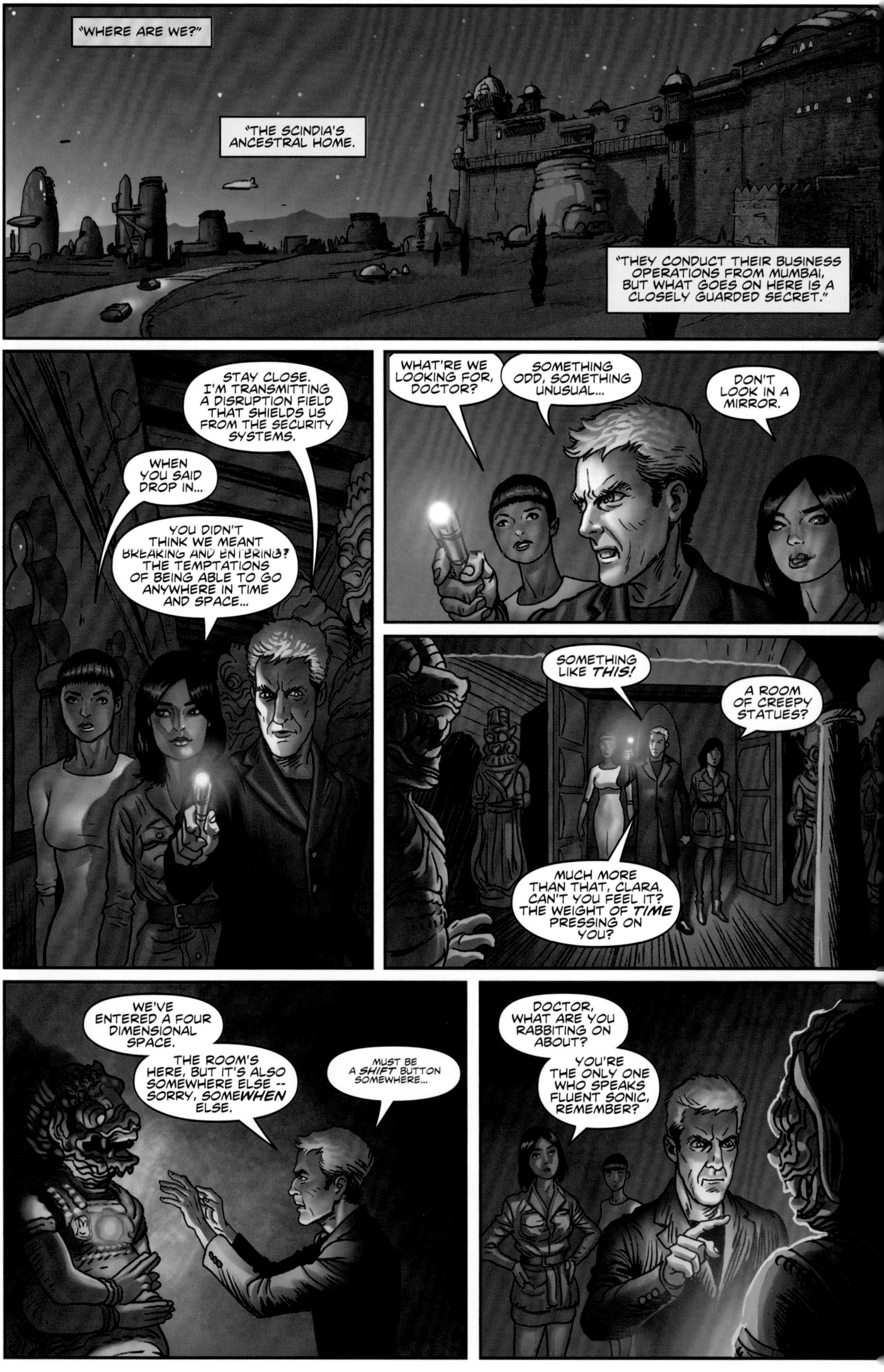
"WHERE ARE WE?"
"THE SCINDIA'S ANCESTRAL HOME.
"THEY CONDUCT THEIR BUSINESS OPERATIONS FROM MUMBAI, BUT WHAT GOES ON HERE IS A CLOSELY GUARDED SECRET."
STAY CLOSE. I'M TRANSMITTING A DISRUPTION FIELD THAT SHIELDS US FROM THE SECURITY SYSTEMS.
WHEN YOU SAID DROP IN...
YOU DIDN'T THINK WE MEANT BREAKING AND ENTERING? THE TEMPTATIONS OF BEING ABLE TO GO ANYWHERE IN TIME AND SPACE...
WHAT'RE WE LOOKING FOR, DOCTOR?
SOMETHING ODD, SOMETHING UNUSUAL...
DON'T LOOK IN A MIRROR.
SOMETHING LIKE THIS!
A ROOM OF CREEPY STATUES?
MUCH MORE THAN THAT, CLARA. CAN'T YOU FEEL IT? THE WEIGHT OF TIME PRESSING ON YOU?
WE'VE ENTERED A FOUR DIMENSIONAL SPACE.
THE ROOM'S HERE, BUT IT'S ALSO SOMEWHERE ELSE -- SORRY, SOMEWHEN ELSE.
MUST BE A SHIFT BUTTON SOMEWHERE...
DOCTOR, WHAT ARE YOU RABBITING ON ABOUT?
YOU'RE THE ONLY ONE WHO SPEAKS FLUENT SONIC, REMEMBER?

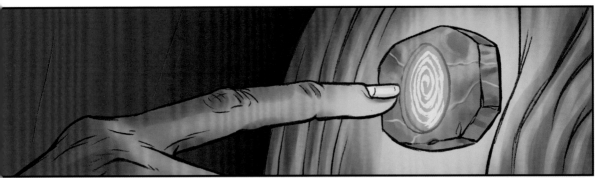

THIS ROOM, MAYBE THE ENTIRE FORTRESS, EXISTS FOUR-DIMENSIONALLY.

IT OCCUPIES THE SAME PHYSICAL LOCATION, BUT EXISTS SIMULTANEOUSLY IN OTHER TIME PERIODS.

A DOOR INTO THE PAST.

A DOOR YOU'LL WISH YOU'D *NEVER* OPENED.

I DO SO LOVE IT WHEN OUR PREY IS CONSIDERATE ENOUGH TO LOOK FOR US.

TONIGHT'S HUNT WILL BE SHORT BUT *SAVAGE.*

SHAME YOU'RE SUCH A POOR OFFERING, ALL SKIN AND BONE.

STILL, THE GODDESS CAN NEVER HAVE TOO MANY DEATHS.

MY, WHAT BIG *TEETH* YOU HAVE, GRANDMA.

AND AS FOR YOUR *BREATH...*

RRRAAAHHHRRRR!

PPTT-CHOW
PPTT-CHOW

AT LAST! THANK YOU!

WHAT WERE YOU TRYING TO DO, MAKE ME ASK *NICELY*?

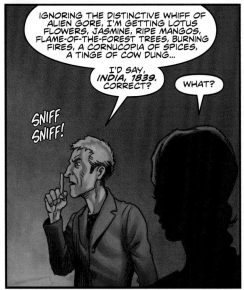

IGNORING THE DISTINCTIVE WHIFF OF ALIEN GORE, I'M GETTING LOTUS FLOWERS, JASMINE, RIPE MANGOS, FLAME-OF-THE-FOREST TREES, BURNING FIRES, A CORNUCOPIA OF SPICES, A TINGE OF COW DUNG...

I'D SAY, *INDIA, 1839.* CORRECT?

WHAT?

SNIFF SNIFF!

THE YEAR. WHAT YEAR IS IT?

ARE YOU SURE? I'M NOT USUALLY WRONG.

1825.

LOOK AT THIS NOSE.

IT CAN SNIFF OUT A TIME PERIOD WITHIN SIX MONTHS OF THE ACTUAL DATE.

ONLY A *FOOL* OR A *MADMAN* WOULDN'T KNOW THE YEAR IN WHICH HE IS LIVING.

I'M ACCUSED OF BEING BOTH. FREQUENTLY.

BY THE WAY, ARE YOUR BULLETS TIPPED WITH *ANTI-MATTER*, PACKED WITH *NANO-EXPLOSIVES*, OR DIPPED IN THE VENOM OF A *MYRAX-SIX VIPER-SKORPION*?

☠☠☠

WHY DOES NOTHING YOU SAY MAKE *SENSE*?!

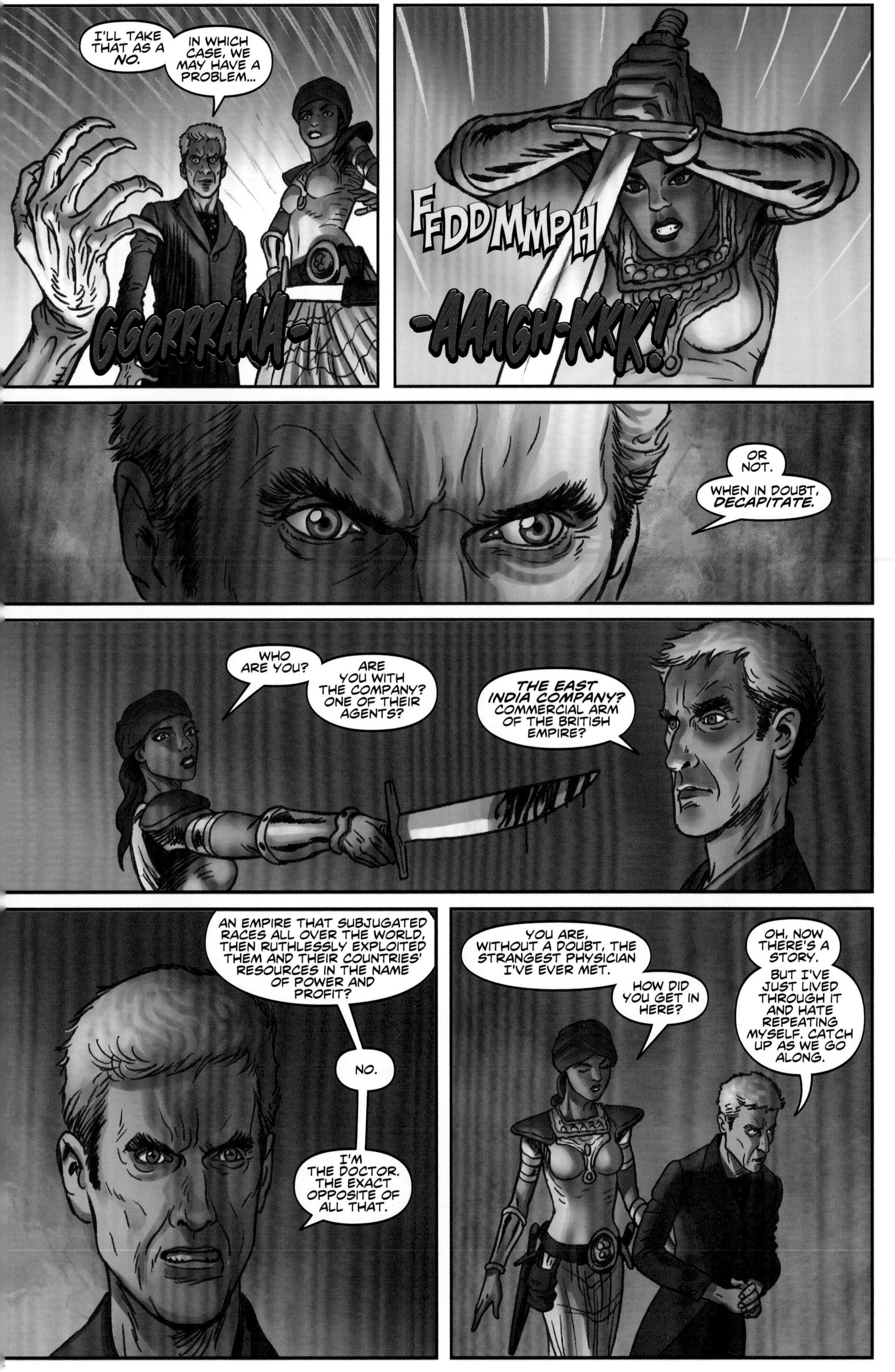
I'LL TAKE THAT AS A NO.
IN WHICH CASE, WE MAY HAVE A PROBLEM...
GGGRRRAAA-
FFDDMMPH
-AAAGH-KKK!
OR NOT.
WHEN IN DOUBT, DECAPITATE.
WHO ARE YOU?
ARE YOU WITH THE COMPANY? ONE OF THEIR AGENTS?
THE EAST INDIA COMPANY? COMMERCIAL ARM OF THE BRITISH EMPIRE?
AN EMPIRE THAT SUBJUGATED RACES ALL OVER THE WORLD, THEN RUTHLESSLY EXPLOITED THEM AND THEIR COUNTRIES' RESOURCES IN THE NAME OF POWER AND PROFIT?
NO.
I'M THE DOCTOR. THE EXACT OPPOSITE OF ALL THAT.
YOU ARE, WITHOUT A DOUBT, THE STRANGEST PHYSICIAN I'VE EVER MET.
HOW DID YOU GET IN HERE?
OH, NOW THERE'S A STORY.
BUT I'VE JUST LIVED THROUGH IT AND HATE REPEATING MYSELF. CATCH UP AS WE GO ALONG.

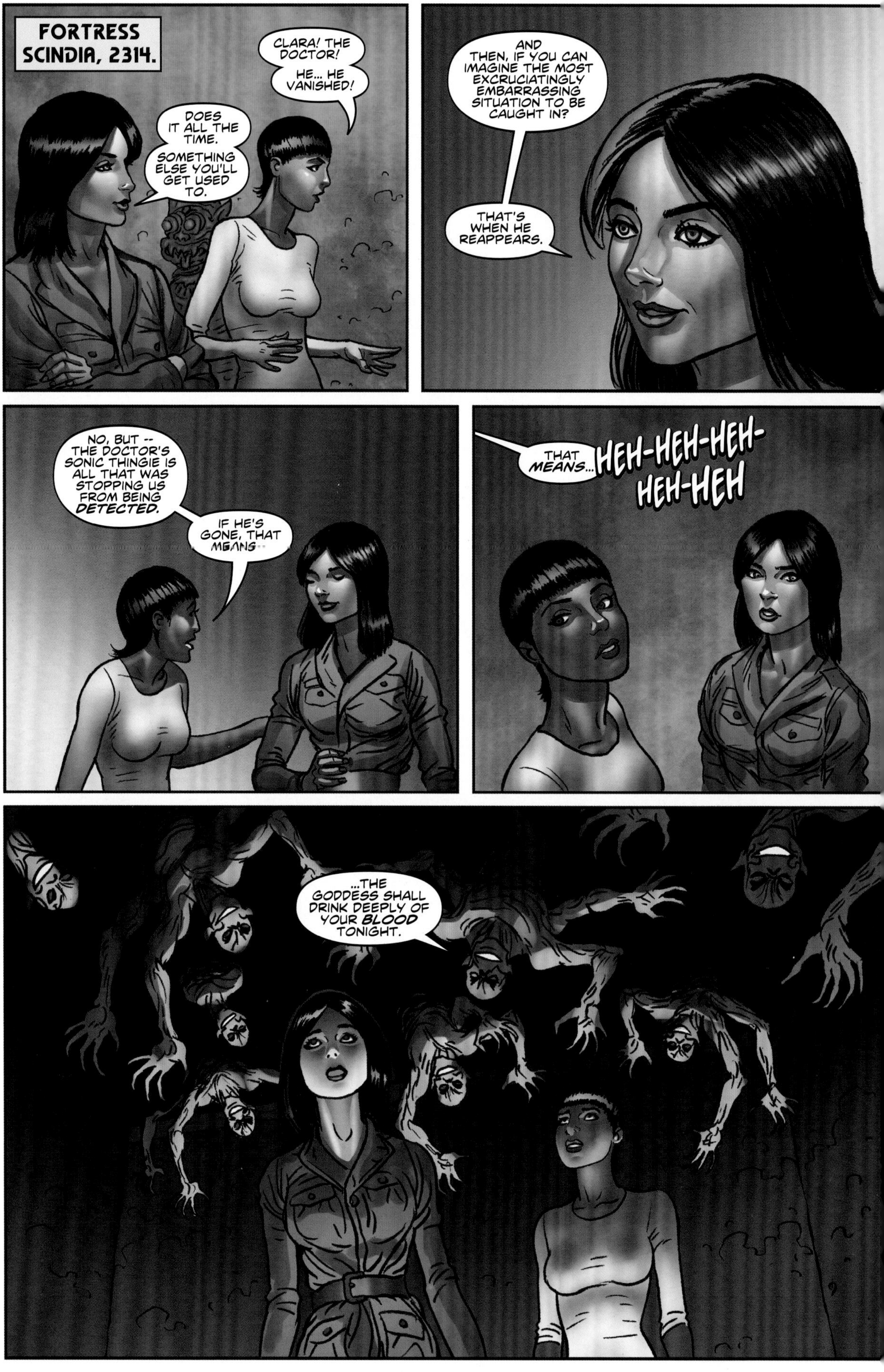
FORTRESS SCINDIA, 2314.
CLARA! THE DOCTOR!
HE... HE VANISHED!
DOES IT ALL THE TIME.
SOMETHING ELSE YOU'LL GET USED TO.
AND THEN, IF YOU CAN IMAGINE THE MOST EXCRUCIATINGLY EMBARRASSING SITUATION TO BE CAUGHT IN?
THAT'S WHEN HE REAPPEARS.
NO, BUT -- THE DOCTOR'S SONIC THINGIE IS ALL THAT WAS STOPPING US FROM BEING DETECTED.
IF HE'S GONE, THAT MEANS--
THAT MEANS...
HEH-HEH-HEH-HEH-HEH
...THE GODDESS SHALL DRINK DEEPLY OF YOUR BLOOD TONIGHT.

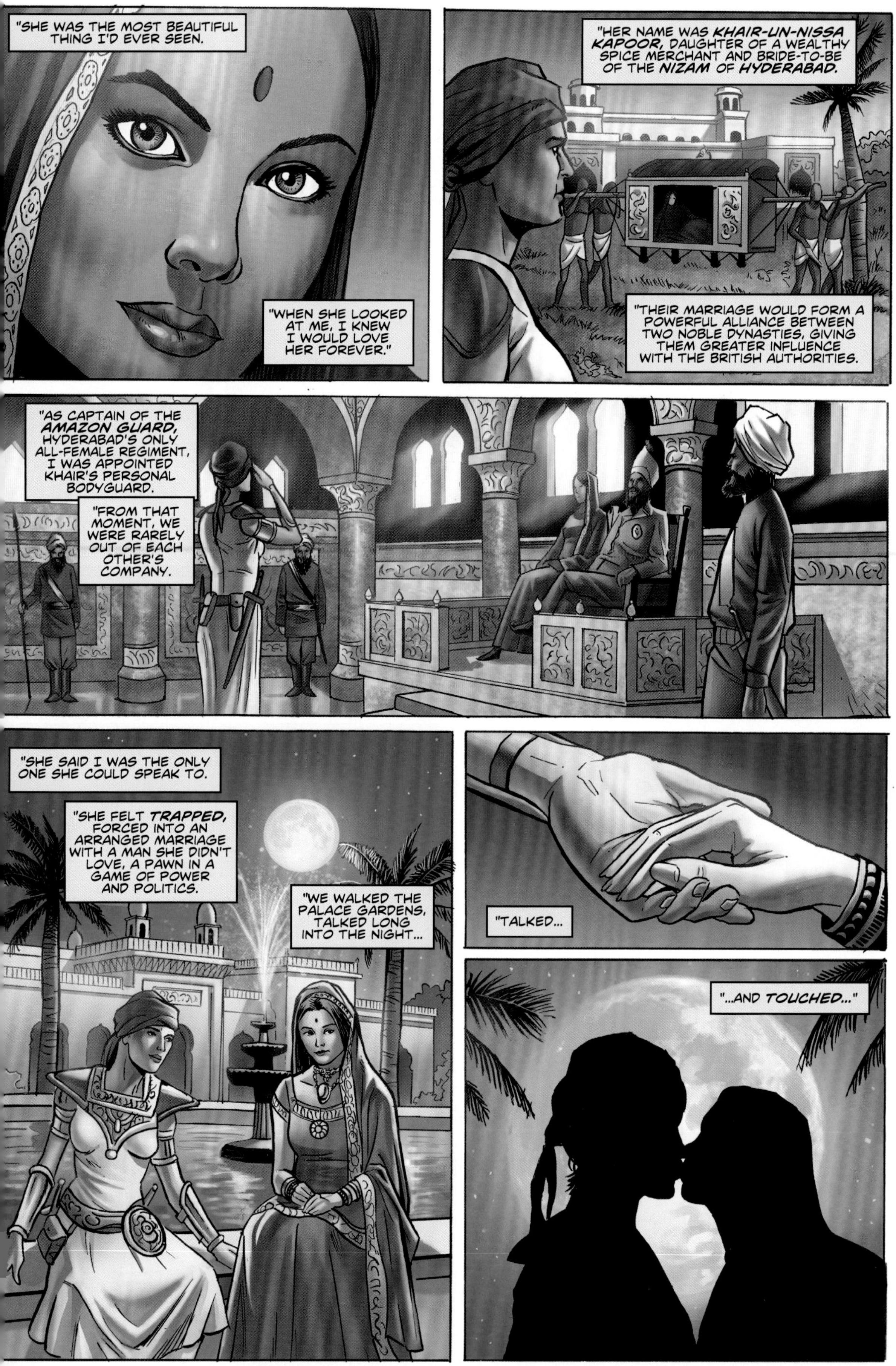
"SHE WAS THE MOST BEAUTIFUL THING I'D EVER SEEN.
"WHEN SHE LOOKED AT ME, I KNEW I WOULD LOVE HER FOREVER."
"HER NAME WAS KHAIR-UN-NISSA KAPOOR, DAUGHTER OF A WEALTHY SPICE MERCHANT AND BRIDE-TO-BE OF THE NIZAM OF HYDERABAD.
"THEIR MARRIAGE WOULD FORM A POWERFUL ALLIANCE BETWEEN TWO NOBLE DYNASTIES, GIVING THEM GREATER INFLUENCE WITH THE BRITISH AUTHORITIES.
"AS CAPTAIN OF THE AMAZON GUARD, HYDERABAD'S ONLY ALL-FEMALE REGIMENT, I WAS APPOINTED KHAIR'S PERSONAL BODYGUARD.
"FROM THAT MOMENT, WE WERE RARELY OUT OF EACH OTHER'S COMPANY.
"SHE SAID I WAS THE ONLY ONE SHE COULD SPEAK TO.
"SHE FELT TRAPPED, FORCED INTO AN ARRANGED MARRIAGE WITH A MAN SHE DIDN'T LOVE, A PAWN IN A GAME OF POWER AND POLITICS.
"WE WALKED THE PALACE GARDENS, TALKED LONG INTO THE NIGHT...
"TALKED...
"...AND TOUCHED..."

I... I'VE NEVER SPOKEN OF THESE THINGS BEFORE, BUT YOU SEEM LIKE YOU --

DON'T CARE?

LIKE IT DOESN'T MATTER TO YOU.

MAN LOVES WOMAN. MAN LOVES MAN. WOMAN LOVES WOMAN. WHO CARES?

PEOPLE *HATING* EACH OTHER, THAT'S WHAT BOTHERS ME. THAT'S WHEN THE TROUBLE STARTS.

PERHAPS I SHOULD'VE BEEN STRONGER, PUSHED HER AWAY, BUT ALL MY LIFE I'VE FELT DIFFERENT.

SHE WANTED ME TO BE WHO I *AM*, LOVED ME FOR IT.

"MY PARENTS DESPAIRED OF ME WHEN I WAS YOUNG, ALWAYS FIGHTING AND GETTING INTO TROUBLE.

"MOTHER SAID THAT IF I KEPT BEATING UP ALL THE BOYS, I'D NEVER FIND A HUSBAND. *'GOOD!'* I TOLD HER.

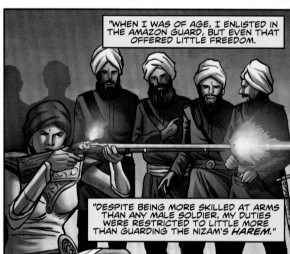

"WHEN I WAS OF AGE, I ENLISTED IN THE AMAZON GUARD, BUT EVEN THAT OFFERED LITTLE FREEDOM.

"DESPITE BEING MORE SKILLED AT ARMS THAN ANY MALE SOLDIER, MY DUTIES WERE RESTRICTED TO LITTLE MORE THAN GUARDING THE NIZAM'S *HAREM*."

"WE DECIDED TO RUN AWAY, BUILD A NEW LIFE TOGETHER IN A FARAWAY LAND.

"WE WOULD SLIP AWAY FROM THE PALACE SEPARATELY AND RENDEZVOUS AT *THE MALLELA THEERTHAM FALLS* IN *NALLAMALA FOREST*.

"I NEVER MADE IT OUT OF THE BARRACKS.

"OUR SECRET WAS NO LONGER SECRET."

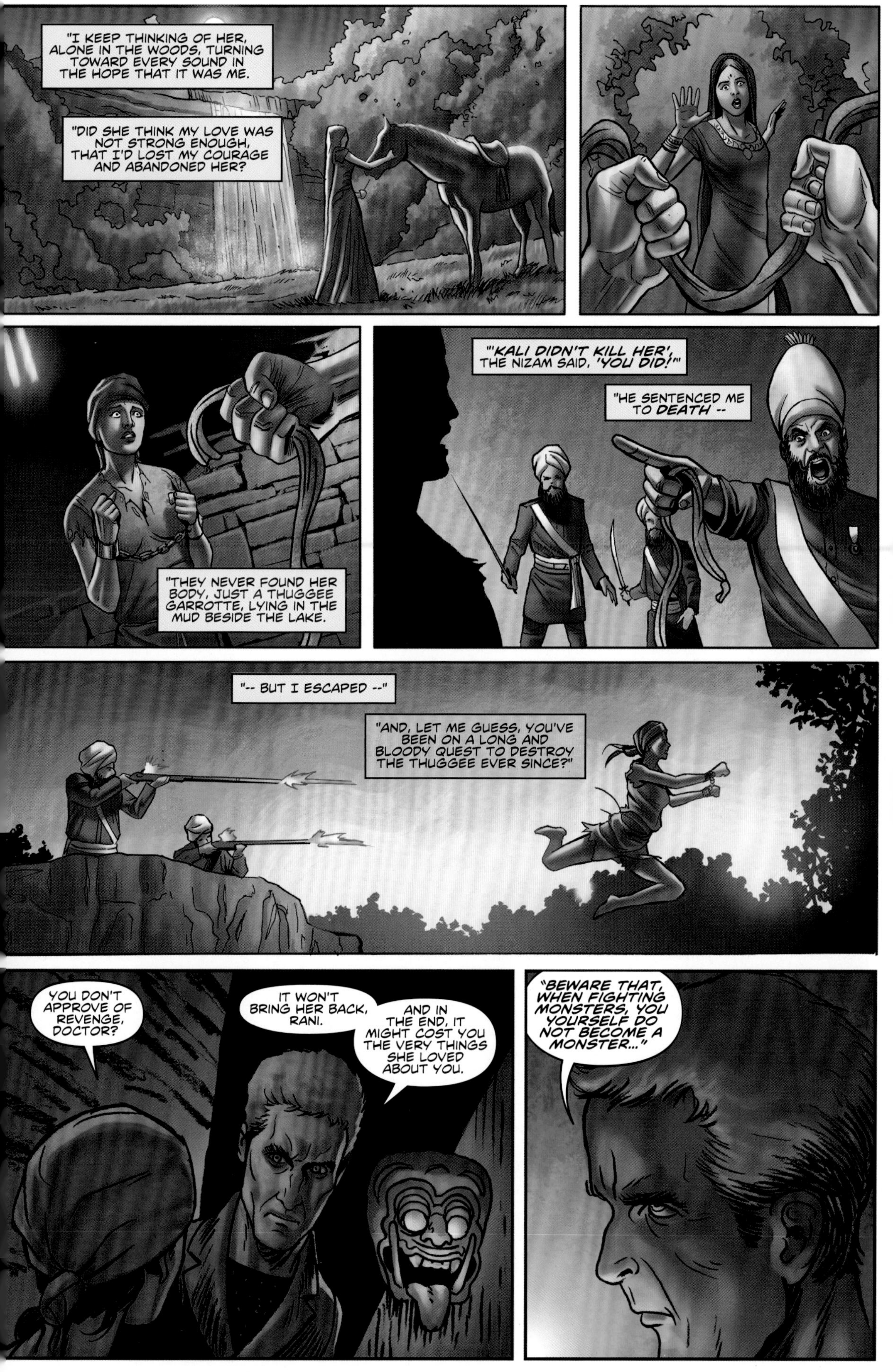
"I KEEP THINKING OF HER, ALONE IN THE WOODS, TURNING TOWARD EVERY SOUND IN THE HOPE THAT IT WAS ME.
"DID SHE THINK MY LOVE WAS NOT STRONG ENOUGH, THAT I'D LOST MY COURAGE AND ABANDONED HER?
"THEY NEVER FOUND HER BODY, JUST A THUGGEE GARROTTE, LYING IN THE MUD BESIDE THE LAKE.
"'KALI DIDN'T KILL HER', THE NIZAM SAID, 'YOU DID!'"
"HE SENTENCED ME TO DEATH --
"-- BUT I ESCAPED --"
"AND, LET ME GUESS, YOU'VE BEEN ON A LONG AND BLOODY QUEST TO DESTROY THE THUGGEE EVER SINCE?"
YOU DON'T APPROVE OF REVENGE, DOCTOR?
IT WON'T BRING HER BACK, RANI.
AND IN THE END, IT MIGHT COST YOU THE VERY THINGS SHE LOVED ABOUT YOU.
"BEWARE THAT, WHEN FIGHTING MONSTERS, YOU YOURSELF DO NOT BECOME A MONSTER..."

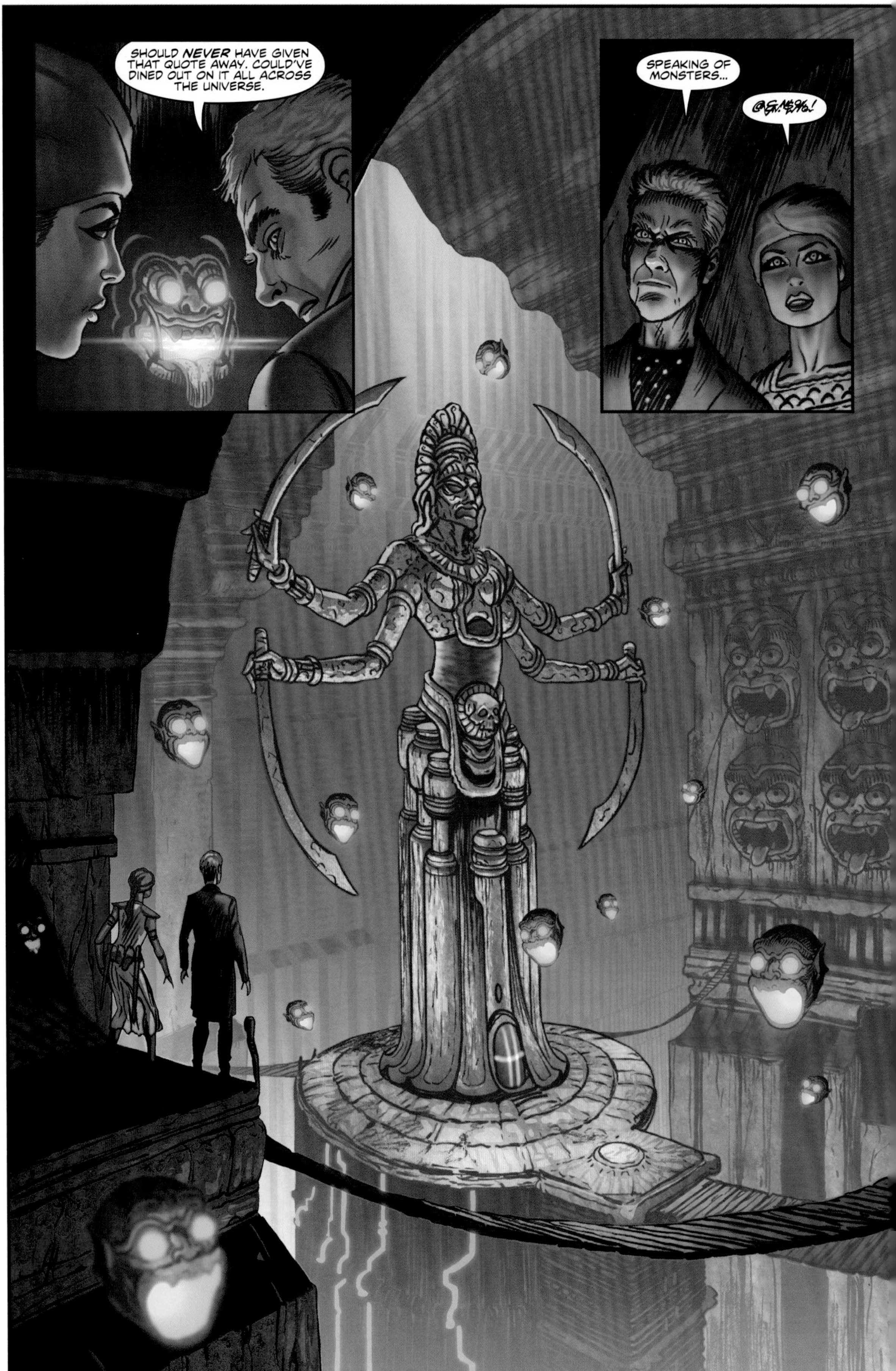
SHOULD NEVER HAVE GIVEN THAT QUOTE AWAY. COULD'VE DINED OUT ON IT ALL ACROSS THE UNIVERSE.
SPEAKING OF MONSTERS...

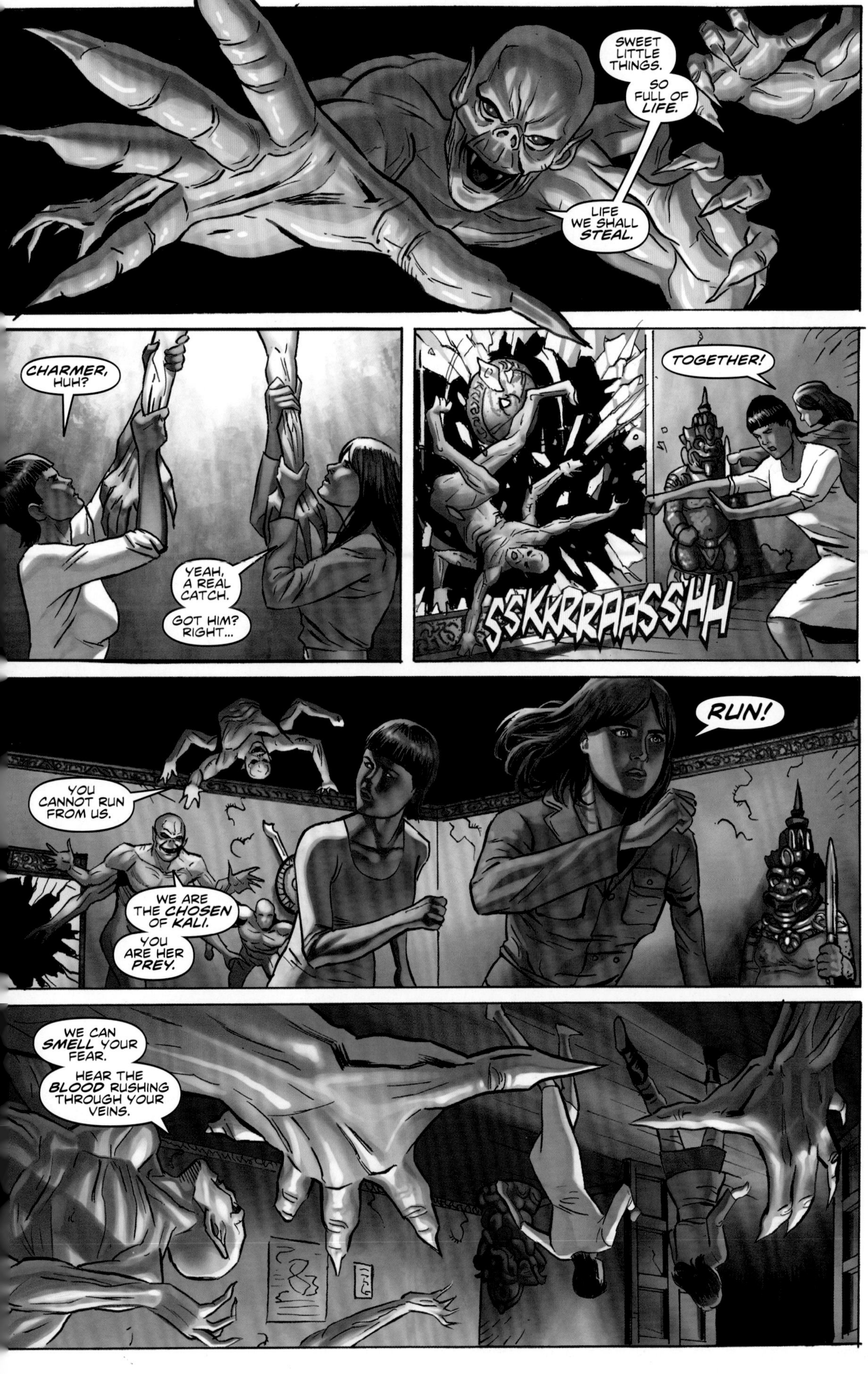

SWEET LITTLE THINGS.
SO FULL OF LIFE.
LIFE WE SHALL STEAL.
CHARMER, HUH?
YEAH, A REAL CATCH.
GOT HIM? RIGHT...
TOGETHER!
SSKKRRAASSHH
RUN!
YOU CANNOT RUN FROM US.
WE ARE THE CHOSEN OF KALI.
YOU ARE HER PREY.
WE CAN SMELL YOUR FEAR.
HEAR THE BLOOD RUSHING THROUGH YOUR VEINS.

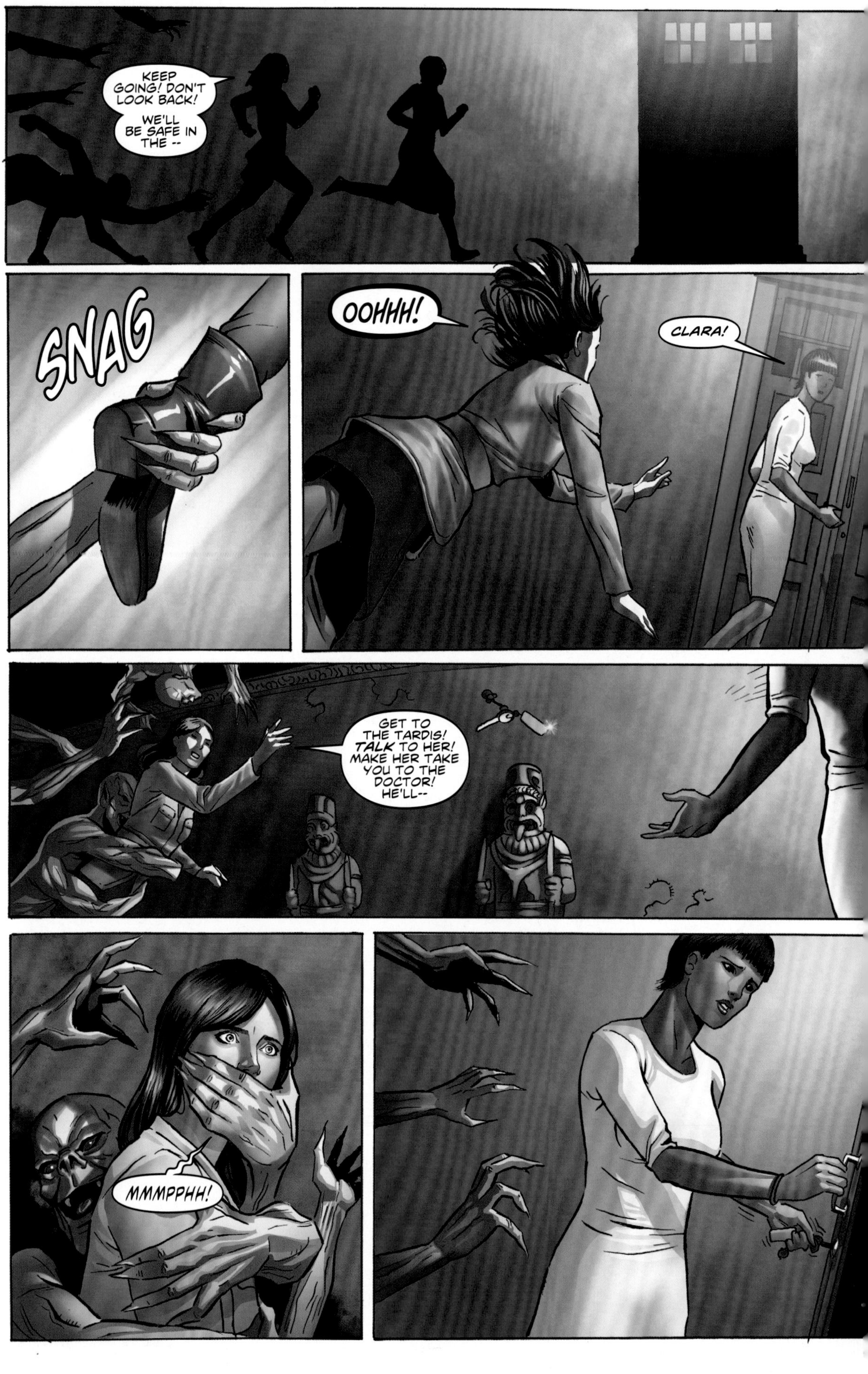
KEEP GOING! DON'T LOOK BACK!
WE'LL BE SAFE IN THE --
SNAG
OOHHH!
CLARA!
GET TO THE TARDIS! TALK TO HER! MAKE HER TAKE YOU TO THE DOCTOR! HE'LL--
MMMPPHH!

DEMONS!

WILL YOU STOP TRYING TO SHOOT EVERYTHING?

IT'S JUST A GLORIFIED OIL-LAMP, ALBEIT WITH A GRUESOME DESIGN SENSE AND SOME ANTI-GRAV TECHNOLOGY.

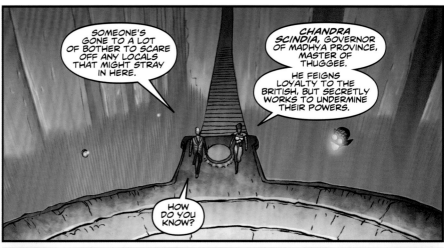

SOMEONE'S GONE TO A LOT OF BOTHER TO SCARE OFF ANY LOCALS THAT MIGHT STRAY IN HERE.

CHANDRA SCINDIA, GOVERNOR OF MADHYA PROVINCE, MASTER OF THUGGEE.

HE FEIGNS LOYALTY TO THE BRITISH, BUT SECRETLY WORKS TO UNDERMINE THEIR POWERS.

HOW DO YOU KNOW?

I DANGLED ONE OF HIS DACOITS OVER A *TIGER* PIT IN CALCUTTA.

HE CONFESSED EVERYTHING.

VERY QUICKLY.

SUCH *DARKNESS.* WHAT IS IT, DOCTOR?

A *NECRO-CLOUD.*

MANY CULTURES IN THE UNIVERSE BELIEVE THAT ALL LIFE IS JUST ENERGY, DEATH MERELY THE *TRANSMUTATION* OF ONE FORM OF ENERGY INTO ANOTHER.

SOME UNSCRUPULOUS RACES HARVEST SENTIENT LIFE-FORCES FOR *SUSTENANCE,* OR TO USE AS A POWER SOURCE, CONTAINING THEM WITHIN A NECRO-CLOUD.

THE *SPIRITS* OF THE DEAD.

IF YOU WANT TO GET *PHILOSOPHICAL* ABOUT IT.

PLEASE, DON'T.

KHAIR-UN-NISSA'S IN THERE, DOCTOR. I CAN *FEEL* HER.

BUT SHE'S *LOST* TO ME, ISN'T SHE?

LOST FOREVER...

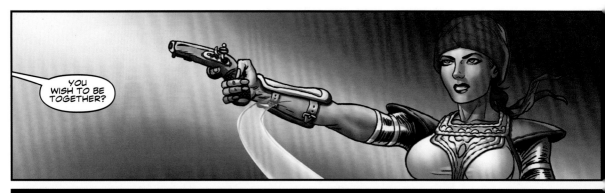

YOU WISH TO BE TOGETHER?

WE WILL *SEND* YOU TO HER.

WITH *PLEASURE.*

ALL YOU NEED DO IS GIVE YOUR LIFE TO THE GODDESS.

THE GODDESS.

THE GODDESS.

THE GODDESS.

THE GODDESS. THE GODDESS. THE GODDESS. THE GODDESS. THE GODDESS. THE GODDESS. THE GODDESS. THE GODDESS. THE GODDESS.

I WONDERED WHY WHAT'S OBVIOUSLY AN IMPORTANT LOCATION APPEARED TO BE UNGUARDED.

THESE SPIDERY-MEN MUST HAVE *STEALTH* CAPABILITIES CODED INTO THEIR DNA.

THE MORE YOU SAY, THE *LESS* I UNDERSTAND.

FOR KALI!

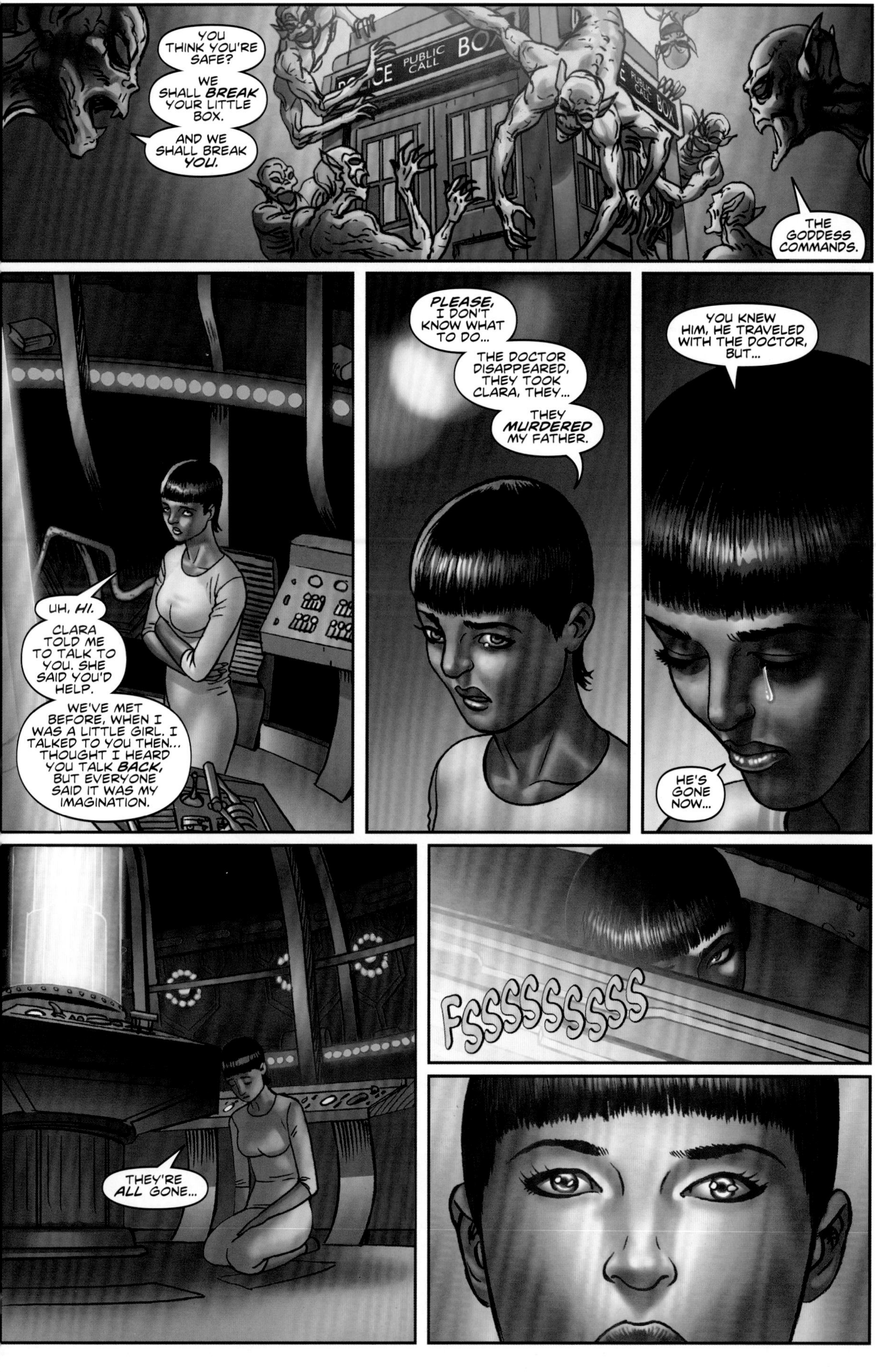
YOU THINK YOU'RE SAFE?
WE SHALL **BREAK** YOUR LITTLE BOX.
AND WE SHALL BREAK **YOU.**
POLICE PUBLIC CALL BOX
THE GODDESS COMMANDS.
UH, **HI.**
CLARA TOLD ME TO TALK TO YOU. SHE SAID YOU'D HELP.
WE'VE MET BEFORE, WHEN I WAS A LITTLE GIRL. I TALKED TO YOU THEN... THOUGHT I HEARD YOU TALK **BACK,** BUT EVERYONE SAID IT WAS MY IMAGINATION.
PLEASE, I DON'T KNOW WHAT TO DO...
THE DOCTOR DISAPPEARED, THEY TOOK CLARA, THEY...
THEY **MURDERED** MY FATHER.
YOU KNEW HIM, HE TRAVELED WITH THE DOCTOR, BUT...
HE'S GONE NOW...
THEY'RE **ALL** GONE...
FSSSSSSSSS

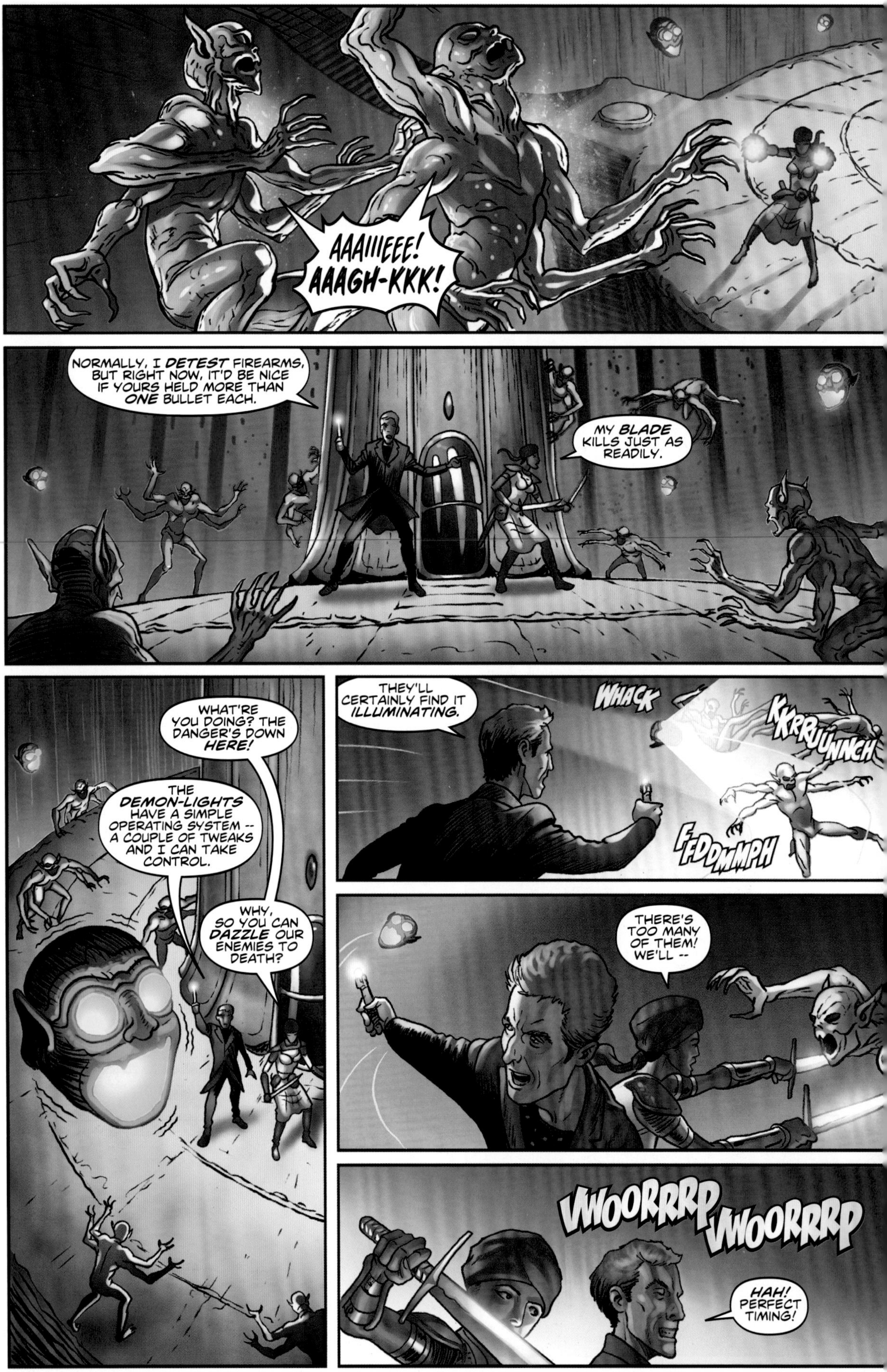
AAAIIIEEE! AAAGH-KKK!
NORMALLY, I DETEST FIREARMS, BUT RIGHT NOW, IT'D BE NICE IF YOURS HELD MORE THAN ONE BULLET EACH.
MY BLADE KILLS JUST AS READILY.
WHAT'RE YOU DOING? THE DANGER'S DOWN HERE!
THE DEMON-LIGHTS HAVE A SIMPLE OPERATING SYSTEM -- A COUPLE OF TWEAKS AND I CAN TAKE CONTROL.
WHY, SO YOU CAN DAZZLE OUR ENEMIES TO DEATH?
THEY'LL CERTAINLY FIND IT ILLUMINATING.
WHACK
KKRRUUNNCH
FFDDMMPH
THERE'S TOO MANY OF THEM! WE'LL --
VWOORRRP VWOORRRP
HAH! PERFECT TIMING!

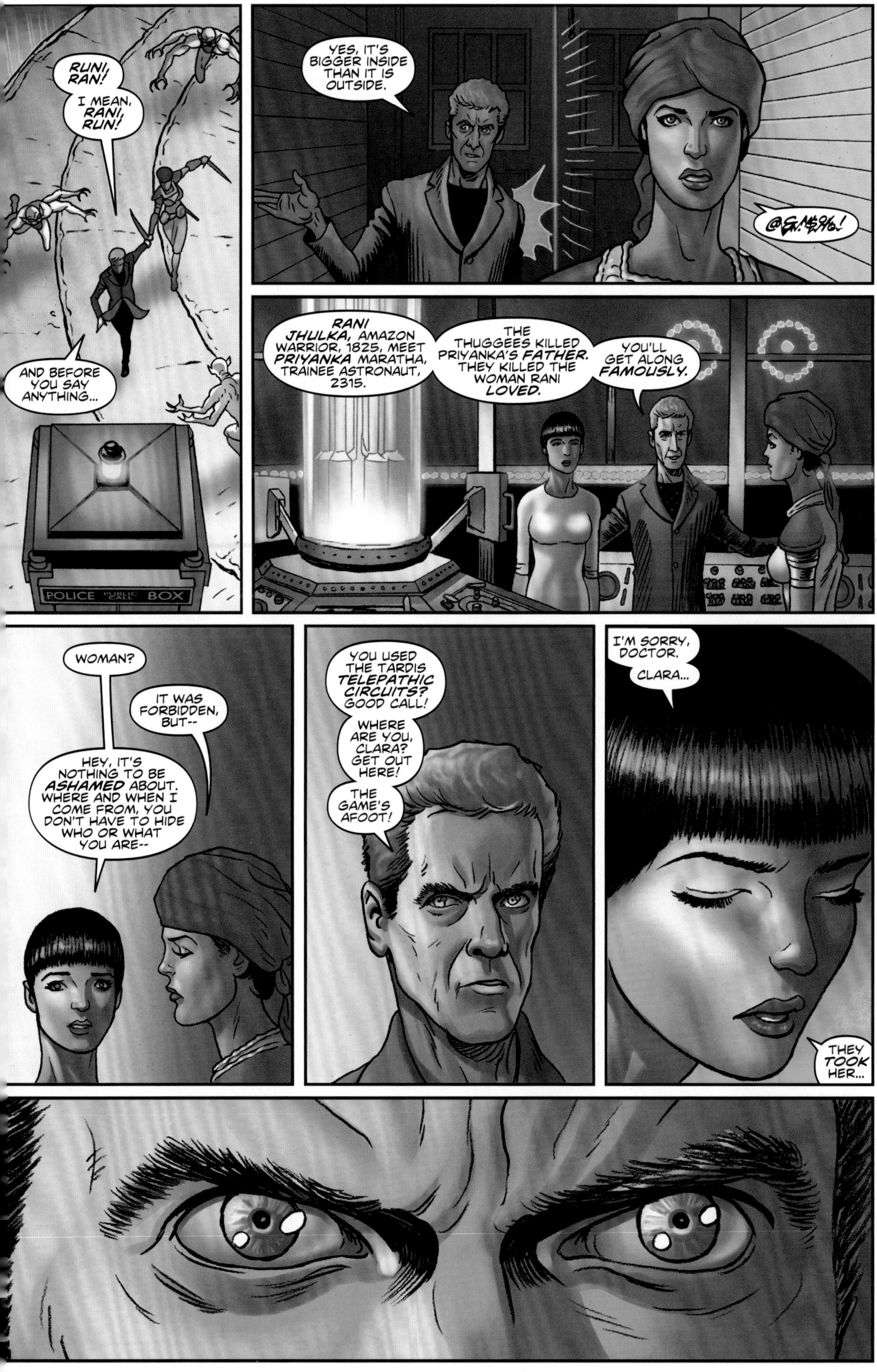
RUN! RAN!
I MEAN, RANI, RUN!
AND BEFORE YOU SAY ANYTHING...
POLICE PUBLIC CALL BOX
YES, IT'S BIGGER INSIDE THAN IT IS OUTSIDE.
@£%!
RANI JHULKA, AMAZON WARRIOR, 1825, MEET PRIYANKA MARATHA, TRAINEE ASTRONAUT, 2315.
THE THUGGEES KILLED PRIYANKA'S FATHER. THEY KILLED THE WOMAN RANI LOVED.
YOU'LL GET ALONG FAMOUSLY.
WOMAN?
IT WAS FORBIDDEN, BUT--
HEY, IT'S NOTHING TO BE ASHAMED ABOUT. WHERE AND WHEN I COME FROM, YOU DON'T HAVE TO HIDE WHO OR WHAT YOU ARE--
YOU USED THE TARDIS TELEPATHIC CIRCUITS? GOOD CALL!
WHERE ARE YOU, CLARA? GET OUT HERE!
THE GAME'S AFOOT!
I'M SORRY, DOCTOR.
CLARA...
THEY TOOK HER...

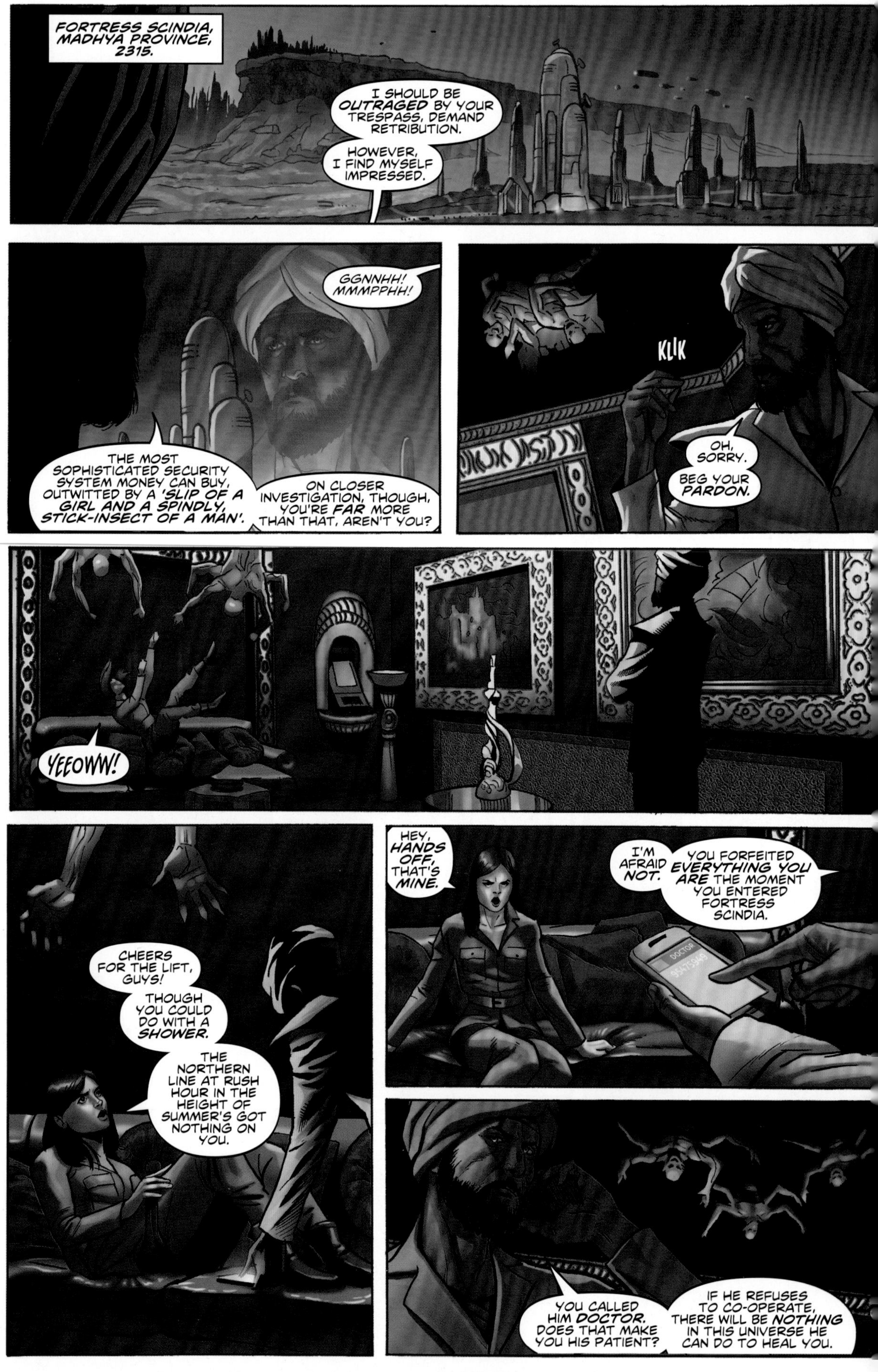
FORTRESS SCINDIA, MADHYA PROVINCE, 2315.
I SHOULD BE OUTRAGED BY YOUR TRESPASS, DEMAND RETRIBUTION.
HOWEVER, I FIND MYSELF IMPRESSED.
GGNNHH! MMMPPHH!
THE MOST SOPHISTICATED SECURITY SYSTEM MONEY CAN BUY, OUTWITTED BY A 'SLIP OF A GIRL AND A SPINDLY, STICK-INSECT OF A MAN'.
ON CLOSER INVESTIGATION, THOUGH, YOU'RE FAR MORE THAN THAT, AREN'T YOU?
KLIK
OH, SORRY.
BEG YOUR PARDON.
YEEOWW!
CHEERS FOR THE LIFT, GUYS!
THOUGH YOU COULD DO WITH A SHOWER.
THE NORTHERN LINE AT RUSH HOUR IN THE HEIGHT OF SUMMER'S GOT NOTHING ON YOU.
HEY, HANDS OFF, THAT'S MINE.
I'M AFRAID NOT.
YOU FORFEITED EVERYTHING YOU ARE THE MOMENT YOU ENTERED FORTRESS SCINDIA.
DOCTOR
YOU CALLED HIM DOCTOR. DOES THAT MAKE YOU HIS PATIENT?
IF HE REFUSES TO CO-OPERATE, THERE WILL BE NOTHING IN THIS UNIVERSE HE CAN DO TO HEAL YOU.

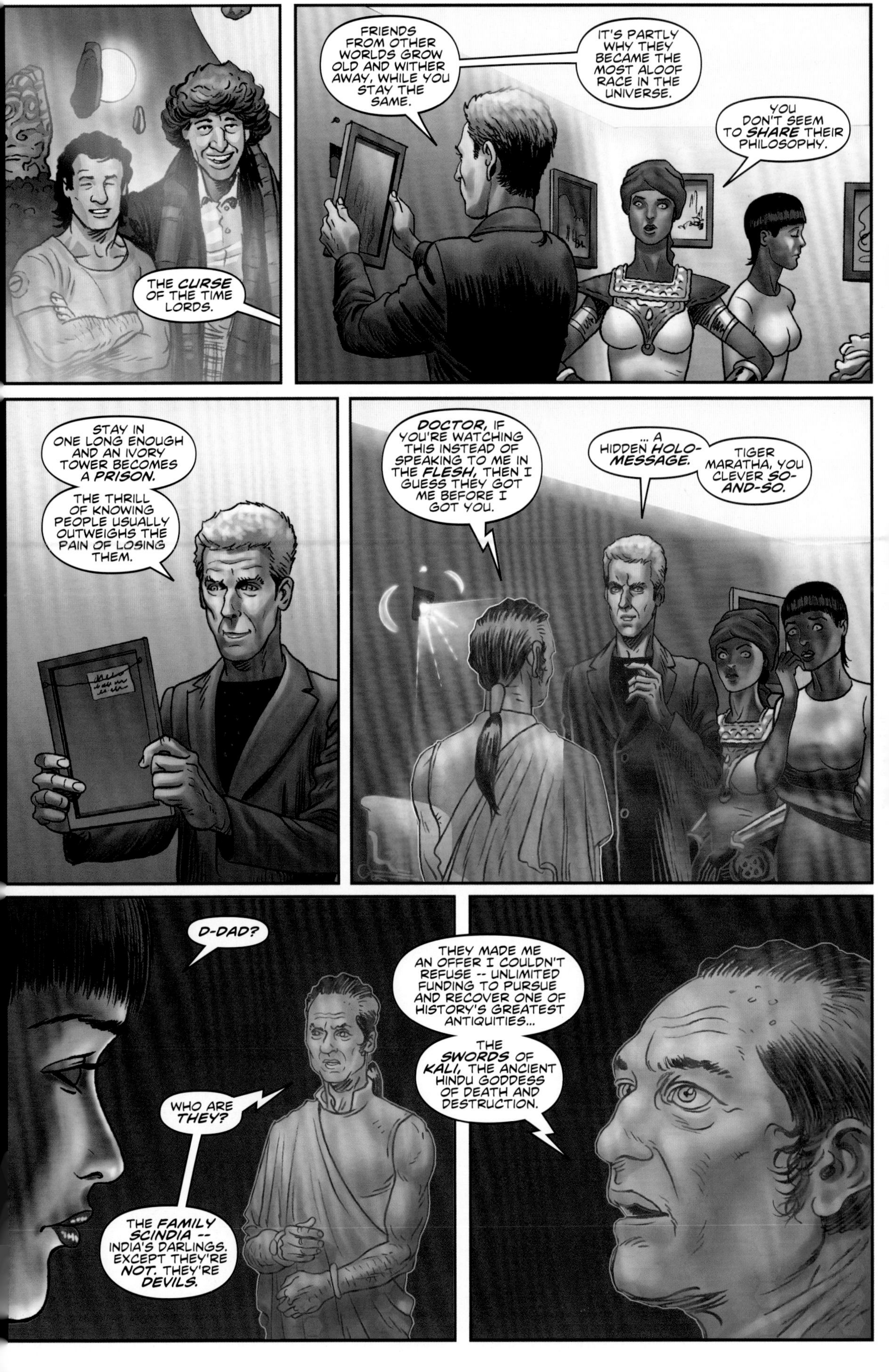
THE CURSE OF THE TIME LORDS.
FRIENDS FROM OTHER WORLDS GROW OLD AND WITHER AWAY, WHILE YOU STAY THE SAME.
IT'S PARTLY WHY THEY BECAME THE MOST ALOOF RACE IN THE UNIVERSE.
YOU DON'T SEEM TO SHARE THEIR PHILOSOPHY.
STAY IN ONE LONG ENOUGH AND AN IVORY TOWER BECOMES A PRISON.
THE THRILL OF KNOWING PEOPLE USUALLY OUTWEIGHS THE PAIN OF LOSING THEM.
DOCTOR, IF YOU'RE WATCHING THIS INSTEAD OF SPEAKING TO ME IN THE FLESH, THEN I GUESS THEY GOT ME BEFORE I GOT YOU.
... A HIDDEN HOLO-MESSAGE.
TIGER MARATHA, YOU CLEVER SO-AND-SO.
D-DAD?
WHO ARE THEY?
THE FAMILY SCINDIA -- INDIA'S DARLINGS. EXCEPT THEY'RE NOT. THEY'RE DEVILS.
THEY MADE ME AN OFFER I COULDN'T REFUSE -- UNLIMITED FUNDING TO PURSUE AND RECOVER ONE OF HISTORY'S GREATEST ANTIQUITIES...
THE SWORDS OF KALI, THE ANCIENT HINDU GODDESS OF DEATH AND DESTRUCTION.

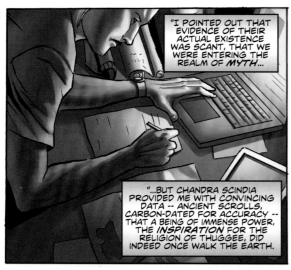

"I POINTED OUT THAT EVIDENCE OF THEIR ACTUAL EXISTENCE WAS SCANT, THAT WE WERE ENTERING THE REALM OF *MYTH*...

"...BUT CHANDRA SCINDIA PROVIDED ME WITH CONVINCING DATA -- ANCIENT SCROLLS, CARBON-DATED FOR ACCURACY -- THAT A BEING OF IMMENSE POWER, THE *INSPIRATION* FOR THE RELIGION OF THUGGEE, DID INDEED ONCE WALK THE EARTH.

"THE SCROLLS TOLD OF AN EPIC WAR BETWEEN KALI AND OTHER BEINGS, BATTLES THAT *LAID WASTE* TO THE WORLD.

"THE GODDESS WAS DESTROYED, HER BODY *INCINERATED* AND HER SWORDS, POSSESSED OF A POWER TOO DANGEROUS FOR MANKIND TO WIELD, SECRETED AWAY IN HIDDEN TEMPLES.

"IT WAS LIKE THE *OLD DAYS* AGAIN, DOCTOR.

"I TRAVELLED THE GLOBE, PIECING TOGETHER CLUES AND FIGHTING OFF RIVALS UNTIL I PINPOINTED THE LOCATION OF THE *FOUR TEMPLES* -- CO-ORDINATES INCLUDED IN THIS MESSAGE -- AND SET ABOUT RECOVERING THE ARTEFACTS.

"BREAKING INTO THE TEMPLES, I EXPECTED THE USUAL *'DEATH-TRAPS OF THE ANCIENTS'*, BUT IT WAS FAR MORE HAIR-RAISING THAN THAT.

"EXTRA-TERRESTRIAL TECHNOLOGY AND KILLER ANDROIDS.

"IF I HADN'T BEEN FAMILIAR WITH SUCH THINGS FROM MY TIME ABOARD THE TARDIS, I'D *NEVER* HAVE SURVIVED.

"I GOT THE SWORDS, THOUGH, THE FIRST *THREE* AT LEAST.

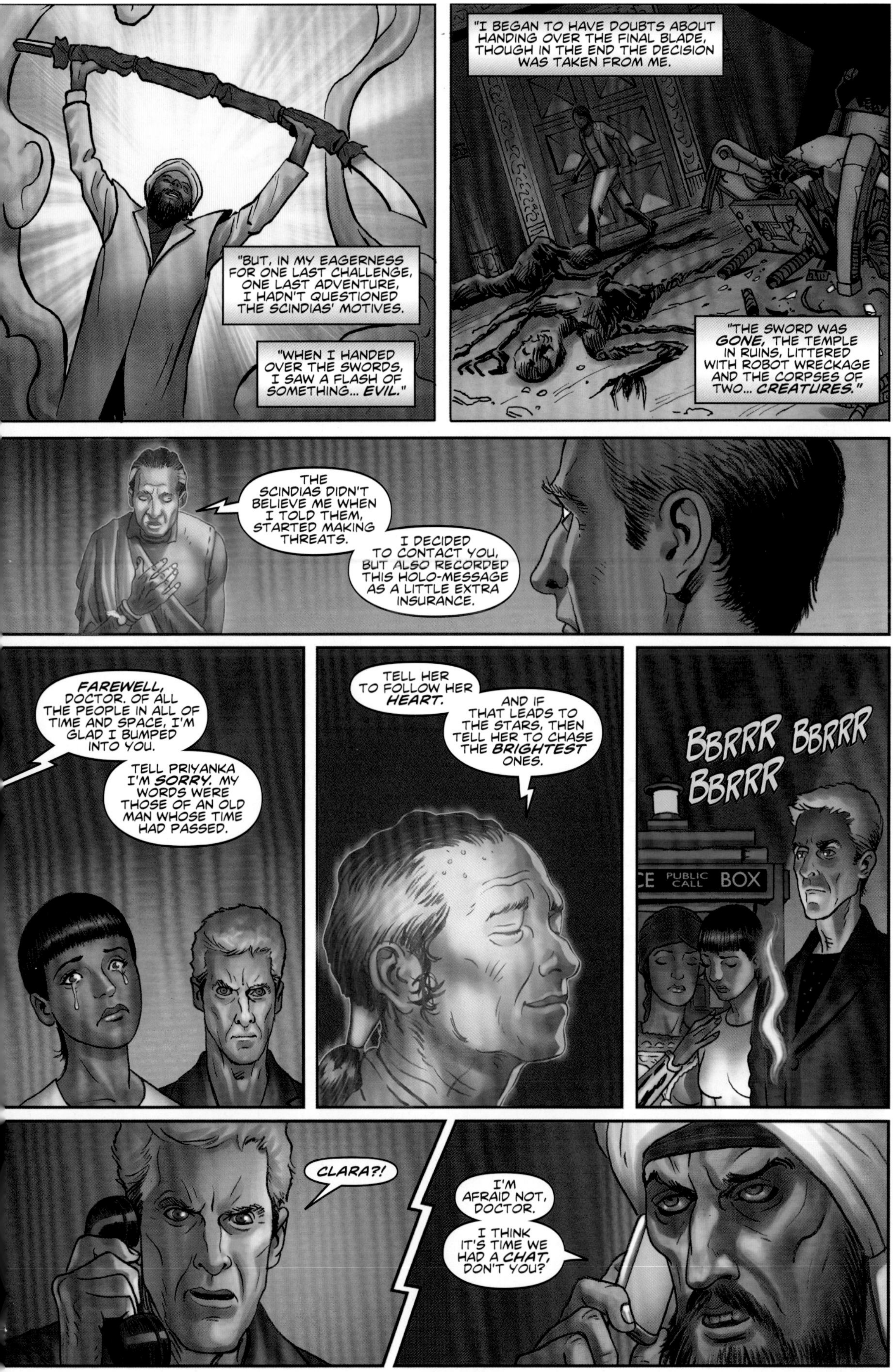
"BUT, IN MY EAGERNESS FOR ONE LAST CHALLENGE, ONE LAST ADVENTURE, I HADN'T QUESTIONED THE SCINDIAS' MOTIVES.
"WHEN I HANDED OVER THE SWORDS, I SAW A FLASH OF SOMETHING... EVIL."
"I BEGAN TO HAVE DOUBTS ABOUT HANDING OVER THE FINAL BLADE, THOUGH IN THE END THE DECISION WAS TAKEN FROM ME.
"THE SWORD WAS GONE, THE TEMPLE IN RUINS, LITTERED WITH ROBOT WRECKAGE AND THE CORPSES OF TWO... CREATURES."
THE SCINDIAS DIDN'T BELIEVE ME WHEN I TOLD THEM, STARTED MAKING THREATS.
I DECIDED TO CONTACT YOU, BUT ALSO RECORDED THIS HOLO-MESSAGE AS A LITTLE EXTRA INSURANCE.
FAREWELL, DOCTOR. OF ALL THE PEOPLE IN ALL OF TIME AND SPACE, I'M GLAD I BUMPED INTO YOU.
TELL PRIYANKA I'M SORRY. MY WORDS WERE THOSE OF AN OLD MAN WHOSE TIME HAD PASSED.
TELL HER TO FOLLOW HER HEART.
AND IF THAT LEADS TO THE STARS, THEN TELL HER TO CHASE THE BRIGHTEST ONES.
BBRRR BBRRR BBRRR
CE PUBLIC CALL BOX
CLARA?!
I'M AFRAID NOT, DOCTOR.
I THINK IT'S TIME WE HAD A CHAT, DON'T YOU?

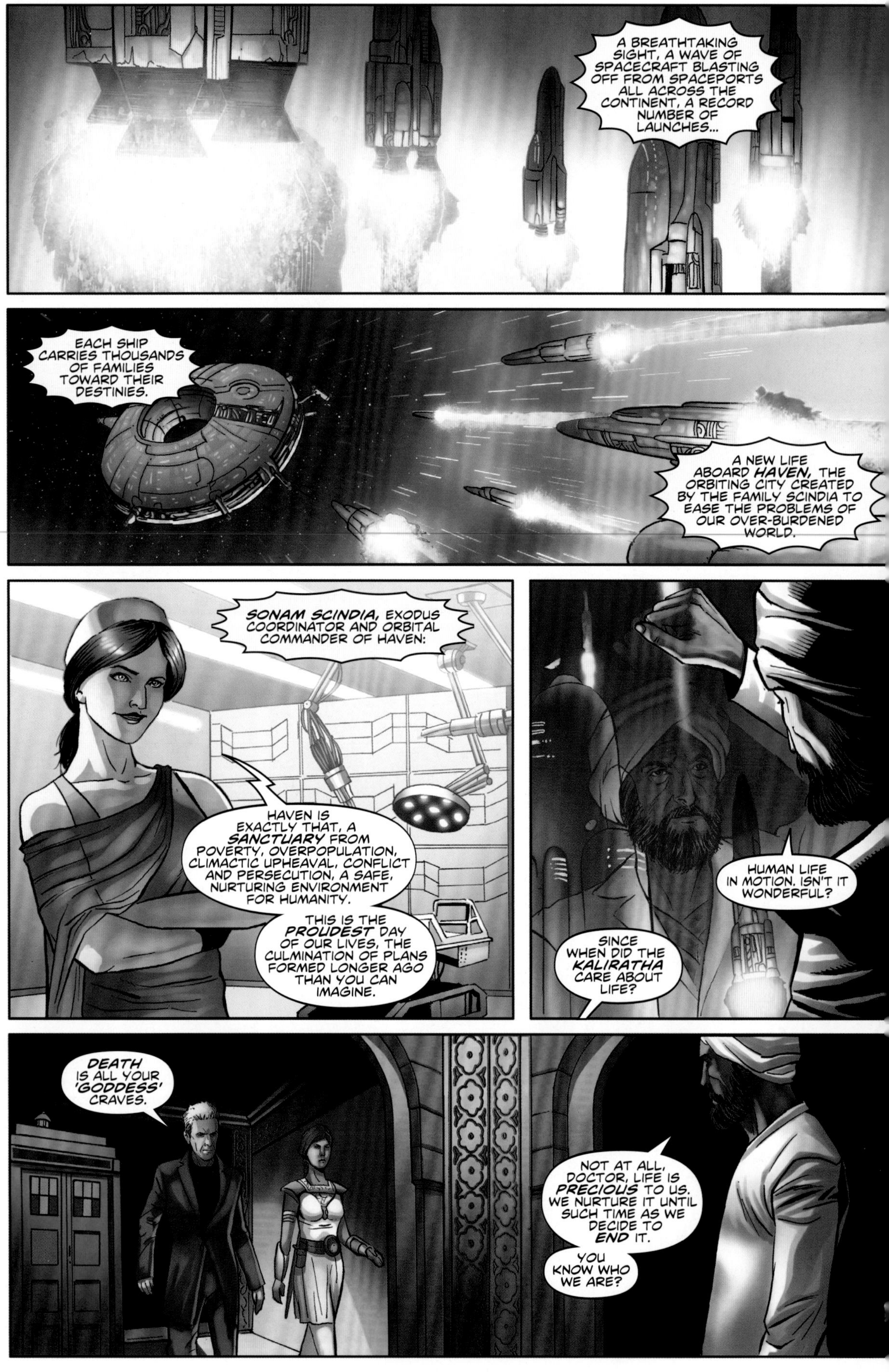
A BREATHTAKING SIGHT, A WAVE OF SPACECRAFT BLASTING OFF FROM SPACEPORTS ALL ACROSS THE CONTINENT, A RECORD NUMBER OF LAUNCHES...
EACH SHIP CARRIES THOUSANDS OF FAMILIES TOWARD THEIR DESTINIES.
A NEW LIFE ABOARD HAVEN, THE ORBITING CITY CREATED BY THE FAMILY SCINDIA TO EASE THE PROBLEMS OF OUR OVER-BURDENED WORLD.
SONAM SCINDIA, EXODUS COORDINATOR AND ORBITAL COMMANDER OF HAVEN:
HAVEN IS EXACTLY THAT, A SANCTUARY FROM POVERTY, OVERPOPULATION, CLIMACTIC UPHEAVAL, CONFLICT AND PERSECUTION, A SAFE, NURTURING ENVIRONMENT FOR HUMANITY.
THIS IS THE PROUDEST DAY OF OUR LIVES, THE CULMINATION OF PLANS FORMED LONGER AGO THAN YOU CAN IMAGINE.
HUMAN LIFE IN MOTION. ISN'T IT WONDERFUL?
SINCE WHEN DID THE KALIRATHA CARE ABOUT LIFE?
DEATH IS ALL YOUR 'GODDESS' CRAVES.
NOT AT ALL, DOCTOR, LIFE IS PRECIOUS TO US. WE NURTURE IT UNTIL SUCH TIME AS WE DECIDE TO END IT.
YOU KNOW WHO WE ARE?

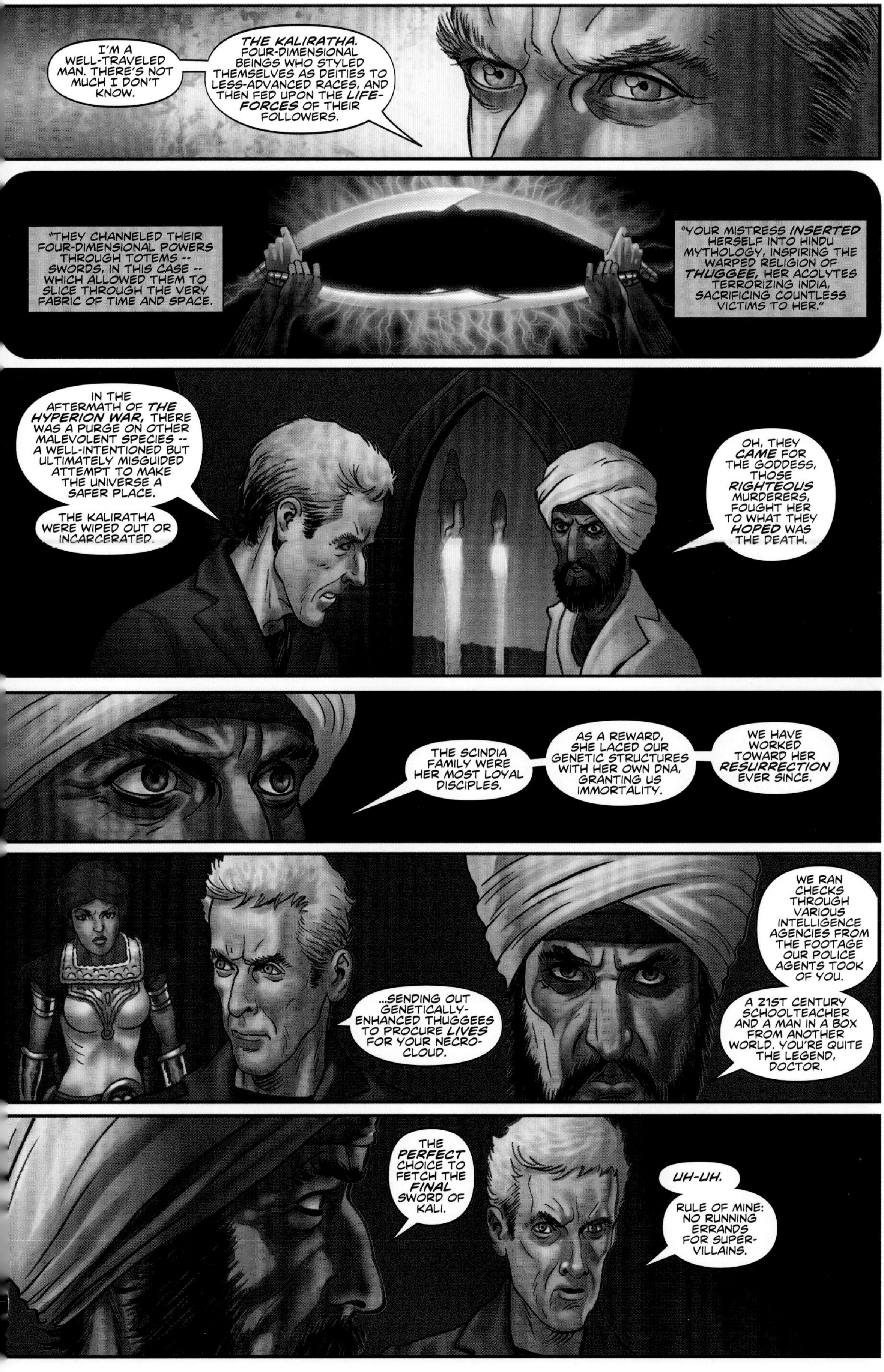
I'M A WELL-TRAVELED MAN. THERE'S NOT MUCH I DON'T KNOW.
THE KALIRATHA. FOUR-DIMENSIONAL BEINGS WHO STYLED THEMSELVES AS DEITIES TO LESS-ADVANCED RACES, AND THEN FED UPON THE LIFE-FORCES OF THEIR FOLLOWERS.
"THEY CHANNELED THEIR FOUR-DIMENSIONAL POWERS THROUGH TOTEMS -- SWORDS, IN THIS CASE -- WHICH ALLOWED THEM TO SLICE THROUGH THE VERY FABRIC OF TIME AND SPACE.
"YOUR MISTRESS INSERTED HERSELF INTO HINDU MYTHOLOGY, INSPIRING THE WARPED RELIGION OF THUGGEE, HER ACOLYTES TERRORIZING INDIA, SACRIFICING COUNTLESS VICTIMS TO HER."
IN THE AFTERMATH OF THE HYPERION WAR, THERE WAS A PURGE ON OTHER MALEVOLENT SPECIES -- A WELL-INTENTIONED BUT ULTIMATELY MISGUIDED ATTEMPT TO MAKE THE UNIVERSE A SAFER PLACE.
THE KALIRATHA WERE WIPED OUT OR INCARCERATED.
OH, THEY CAME FOR THE GODDESS, THOSE RIGHTEOUS MURDERERS, FOUGHT HER TO WHAT THEY HOPED WAS THE DEATH.
THE SCINDIA FAMILY WERE HER MOST LOYAL DISCIPLES.
AS A REWARD, SHE LACED OUR GENETIC STRUCTURES WITH HER OWN DNA, GRANTING US IMMORTALITY.
WE HAVE WORKED TOWARD HER RESURRECTION EVER SINCE.
...SENDING OUT GENETICALLY-ENHANCED THUGGEES TO PROCURE LIVES FOR YOUR NECRO-CLOUD.
WE RAN CHECKS THROUGH VARIOUS INTELLIGENCE AGENCIES FROM THE FOOTAGE OUR POLICE AGENTS TOOK OF YOU.
A 21ST CENTURY SCHOOLTEACHER AND A MAN IN A BOX FROM ANOTHER WORLD. YOU'RE QUITE THE LEGEND, DOCTOR.
THE PERFECT CHOICE TO FETCH THE FINAL SWORD OF KALI.
UH-UH.
RULE OF MINE: NO RUNNING ERRANDS FOR SUPER-VILLAINS.

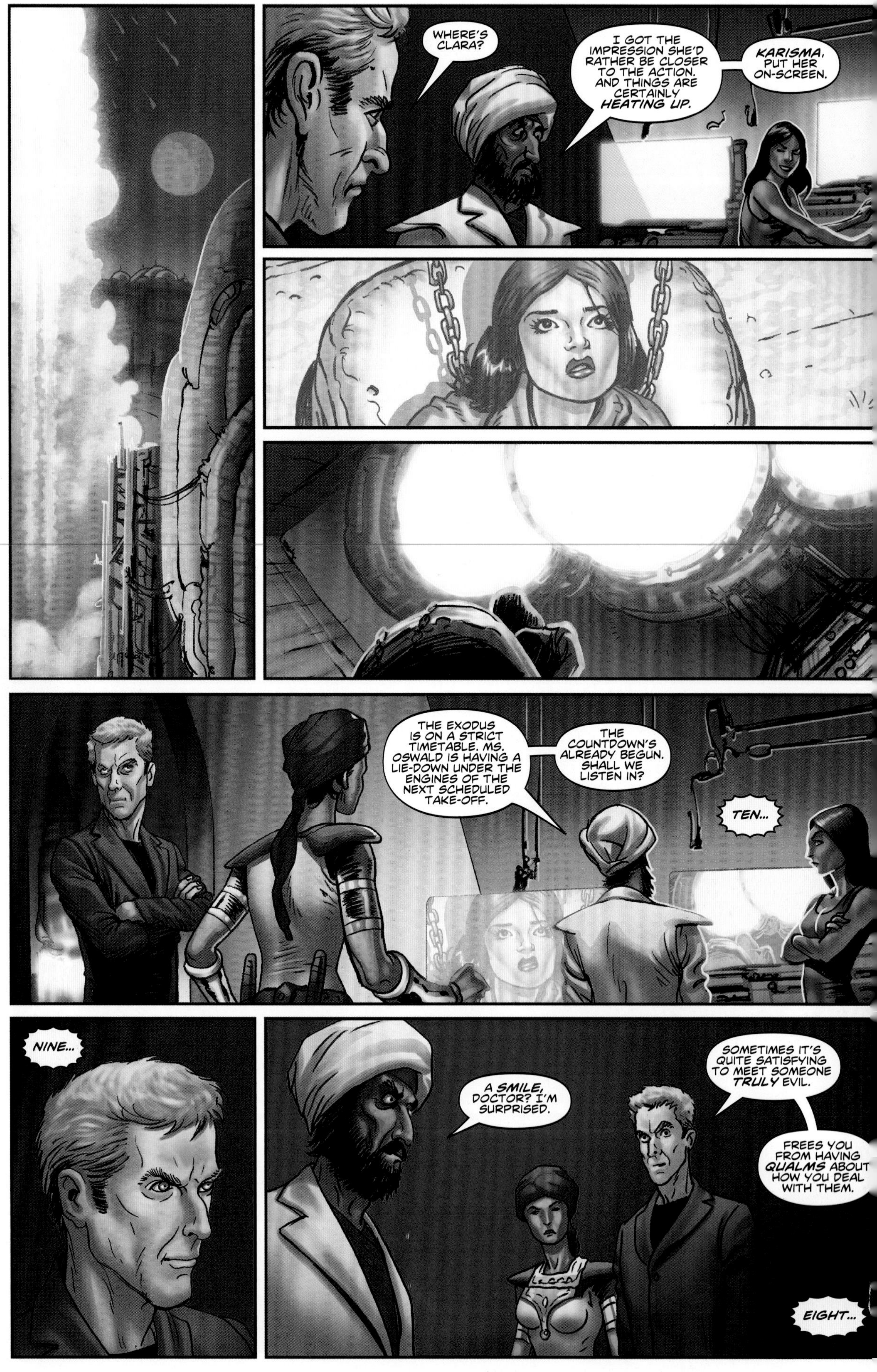
WHERE'S CLARA?
I GOT THE IMPRESSION SHE'D RATHER BE CLOSER TO THE ACTION. AND THINGS ARE CERTAINLY HEATING UP.
KARISMA, PUT HER ON-SCREEN.
THE EXODUS IS ON A STRICT TIMETABLE. MS. OSWALD IS HAVING A LIE-DOWN UNDER THE ENGINES OF THE NEXT SCHEDULED TAKE-OFF.
THE COUNTDOWN'S ALREADY BEGUN. SHALL WE LISTEN IN?
TEN...
NINE...
A SMILE, DOCTOR? I'M SURPRISED.
SOMETIMES IT'S QUITE SATISFYING TO MEET SOMEONE TRULY EVIL.
FREES YOU FROM HAVING QUALMS ABOUT HOW YOU DEAL WITH THEM.
EIGHT...

THERE'S ONLY ONE DEAL OPEN TO YOU, DOCTOR.

THE FOURTH SWORD OF KALI IN EXCHANGE FOR THE LIFE OF YOUR LITTLE HUMAN *PET.*

SEVEN...

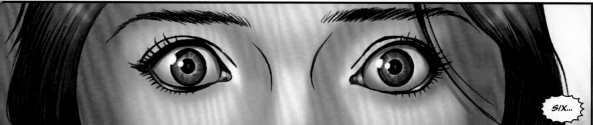

SIX...

FIVE...

TICK-*TOCK.* TICK-*TOCK.*

I CAN ALMOST SMELL HER *ROASTING* FROM HERE.

FOUR...

ENOUGH. I'LL FIND YOUR SWORD.

I SAID I'LL FIND IT!

BUT DOCTOR--

THREE...

DELAY THE LAUNCH.

BEST YOU LEAVE IMMEDIATELY, DOCTOR. *AAMIR* AND *KARISMA* WILL ACT AS CHAPERONES, TO DETER ANY TROUBLESOME IDEAS OR NOTIONS YOU MAY HAVE.

YOU KNOW THEY MEAN TO KILL US WHATEVER HAPPENS, DOCTOR.

OF COURSE.

WE'LL JUST HAVE TO SHOW THEM HOW *HARD* WE ARE TO KILL.

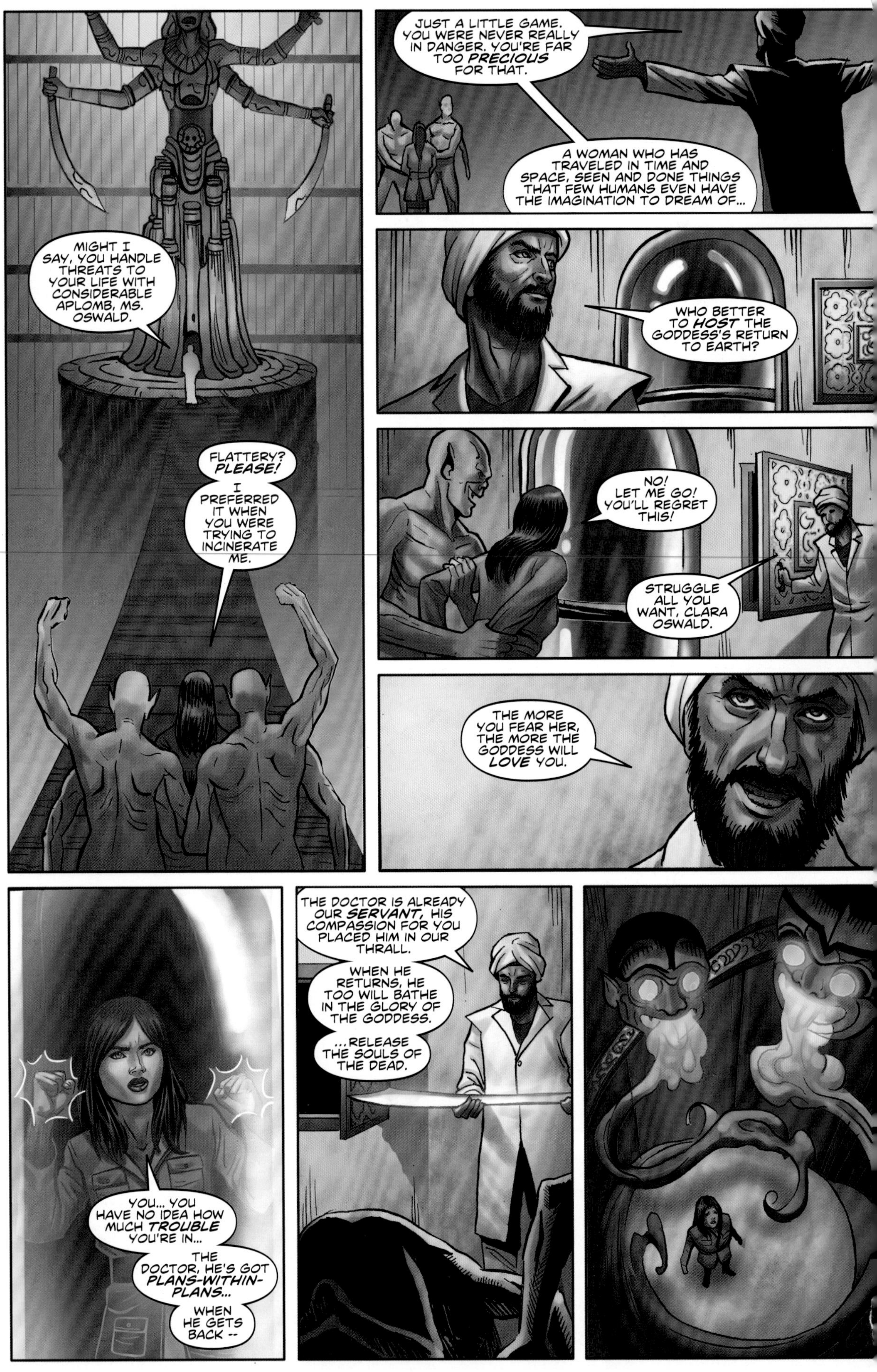
MIGHT I SAY, YOU HANDLE THREATS TO YOUR LIFE WITH CONSIDERABLE APLOMB, MS. OSWALD.
FLATTERY? PLEASE!
I PREFERRED IT WHEN YOU WERE TRYING TO INCINERATE ME.
JUST A LITTLE GAME. YOU WERE NEVER REALLY IN DANGER. YOU'RE FAR TOO PRECIOUS FOR THAT.
A WOMAN WHO HAS TRAVELED IN TIME AND SPACE, SEEN AND DONE THINGS THAT FEW HUMANS EVEN HAVE THE IMAGINATION TO DREAM OF...
WHO BETTER TO HOST THE GODDESS'S RETURN TO EARTH?
NO! LET ME GO! YOU'LL REGRET THIS!
STRUGGLE ALL YOU WANT, CLARA OSWALD.
THE MORE YOU FEAR HER, THE MORE THE GODDESS WILL LOVE YOU.
YOU... YOU HAVE NO IDEA HOW MUCH TROUBLE YOU'RE IN...
THE DOCTOR, HE'S GOT PLANS-WITHIN-PLANS...
WHEN HE GETS BACK --
THE DOCTOR IS ALREADY OUR SERVANT, HIS COMPASSION FOR YOU PLACED HIM IN OUR THRALL.
WHEN HE RETURNS, HE TOO WILL BATHE IN THE GLORY OF THE GODDESS.
...RELEASE THE SOULS OF THE DEAD.

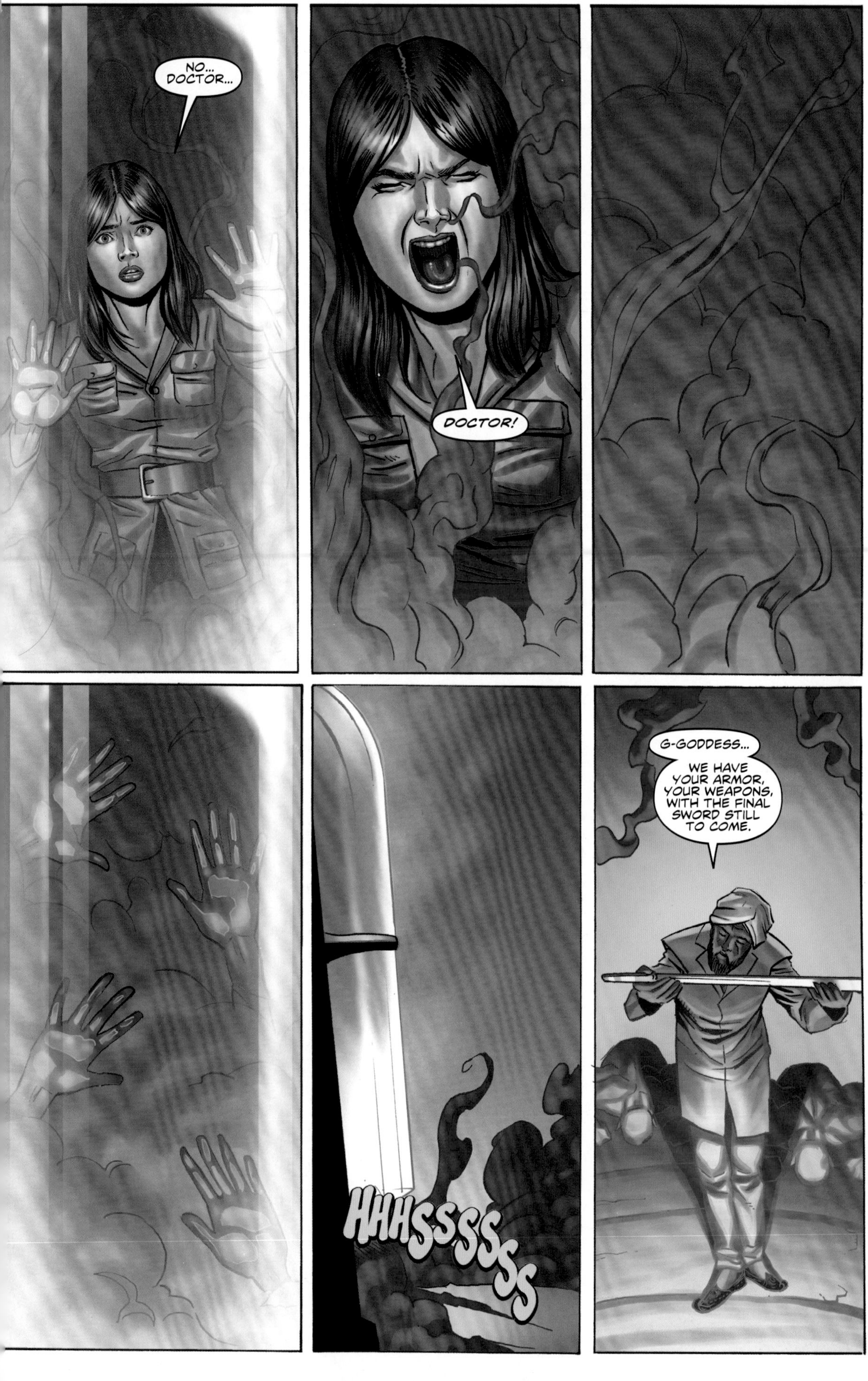
NO... DOCTOR...
DOCTOR!
HHHSSSSSS
G-GODDESS...
WE HAVE YOUR ARMOR, YOUR WEAPONS, WITH THE FINAL SWORD STILL TO COME.

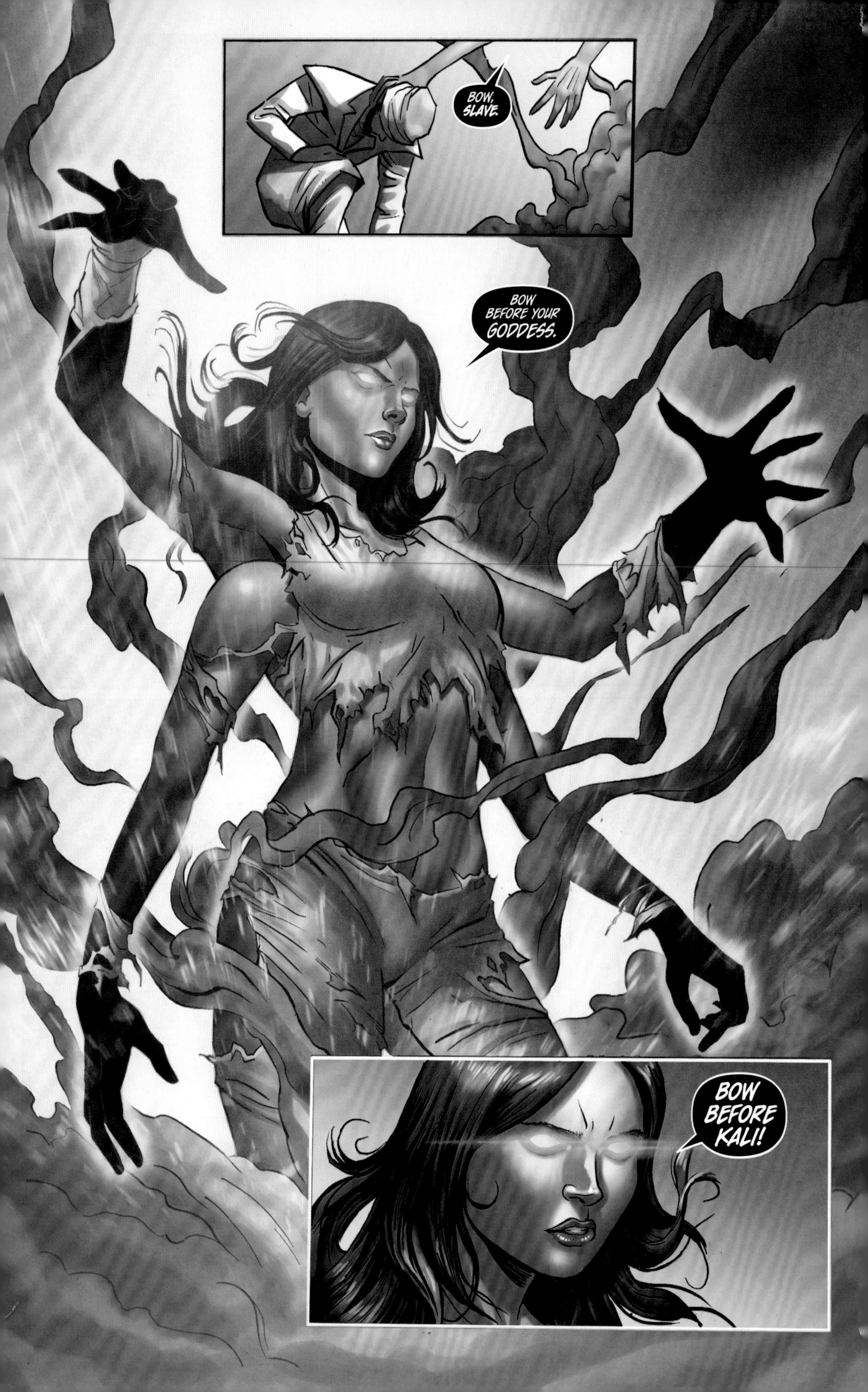
BOW, SLAVE.
BOW BEFORE YOUR GODDESS.
BOW BEFORE KALI!

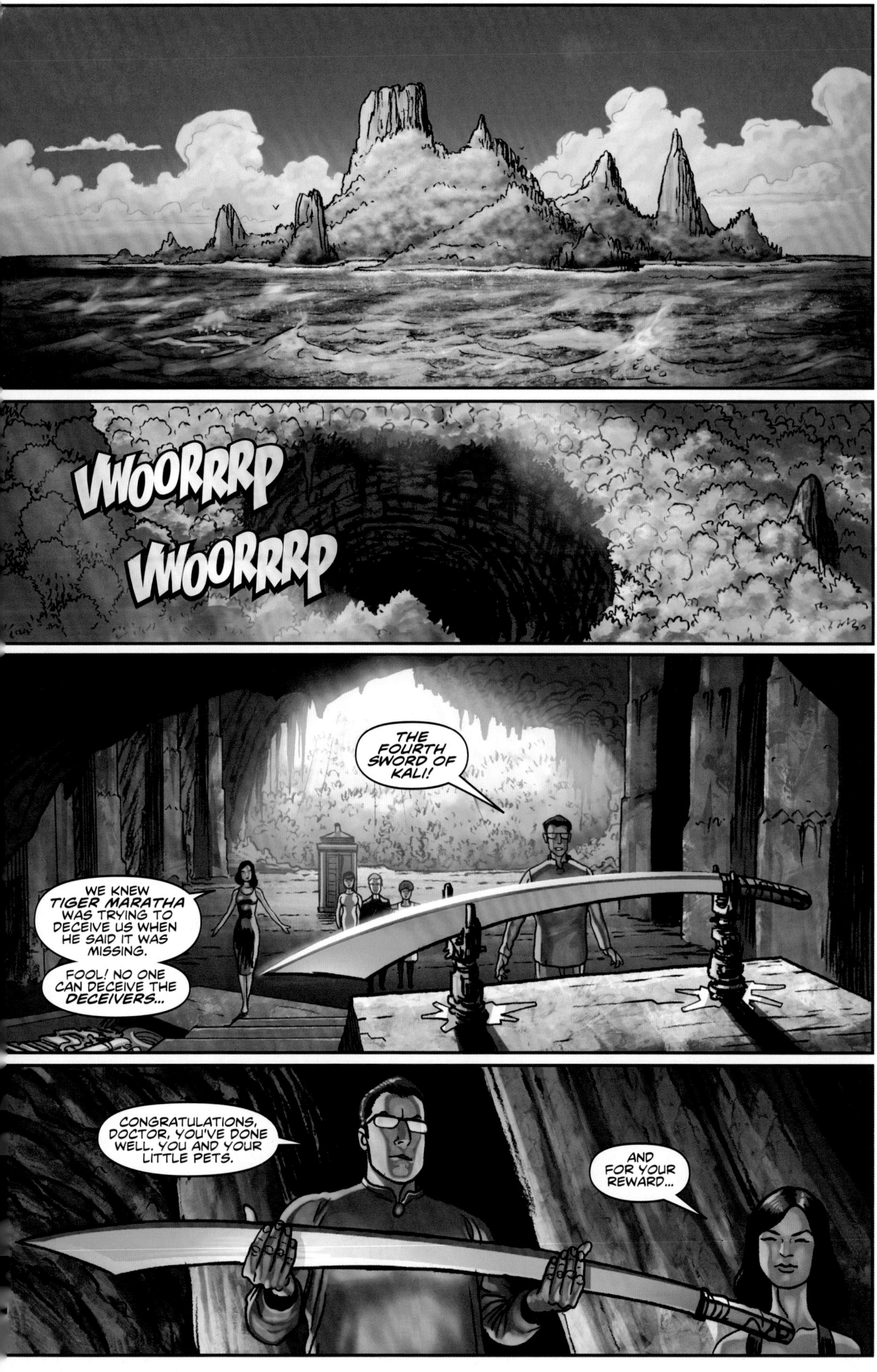
VWOORRRP
VWOORRRP
THE FOURTH SWORD OF KALI!
WE KNEW TIGER MARATHA WAS TRYING TO DECEIVE US WHEN HE SAID IT WAS MISSING.
FOOL! NO ONE CAN DECEIVE THE DECEIVERS...
CONGRATULATIONS, DOCTOR, YOU'VE DONE WELL. YOU AND YOUR LITTLE PETS.
AND FOR YOUR REWARD...

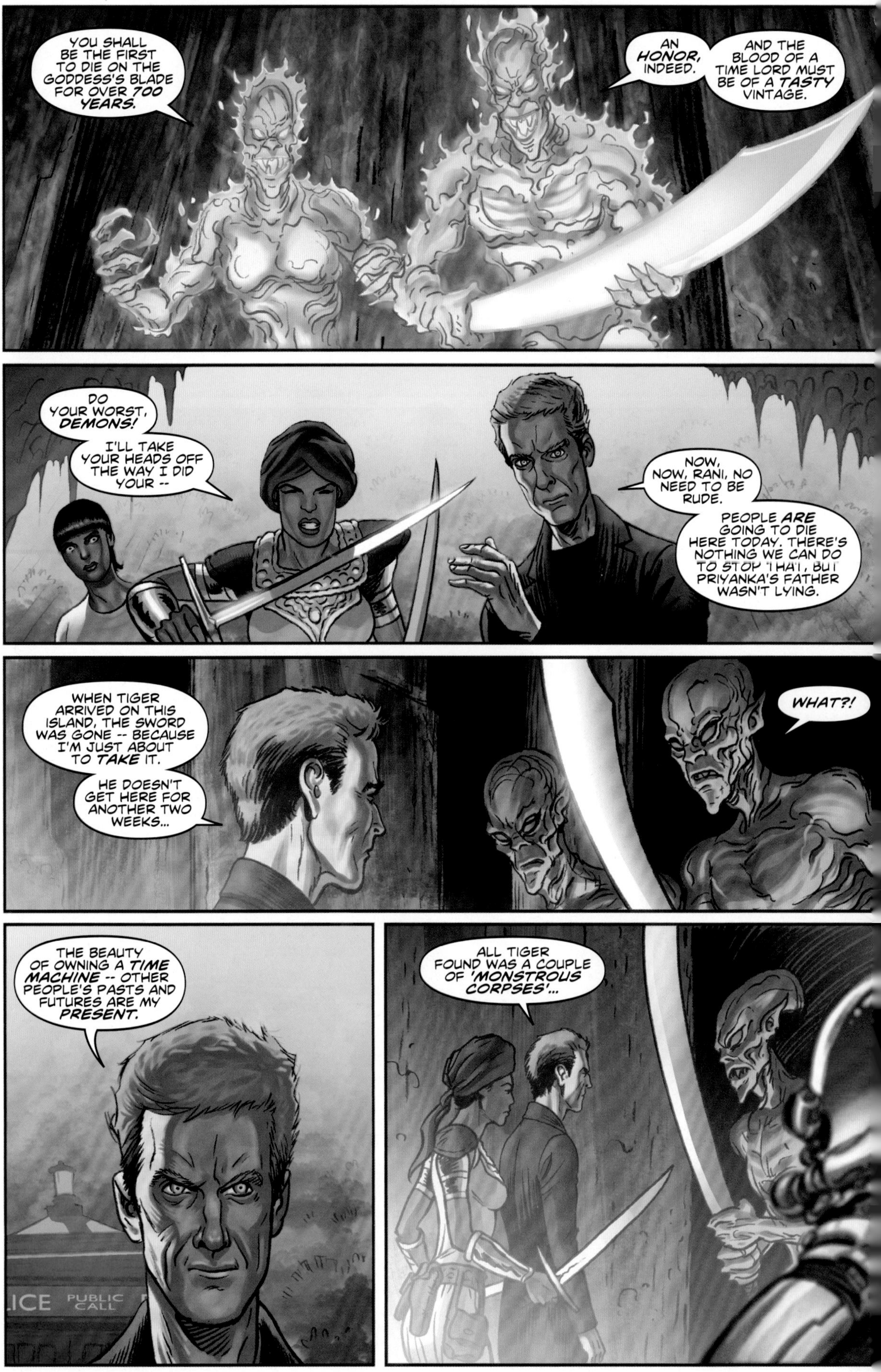
YOU SHALL BE THE FIRST TO DIE ON THE GODDESS'S BLADE FOR OVER 700 YEARS.
AN HONOR, INDEED.
AND THE BLOOD OF A TIME LORD MUST BE OF A TASTY VINTAGE.
DO YOUR WORST, DEMONS!
I'LL TAKE YOUR HEADS OFF THE WAY I DID YOUR --
NOW, NOW, RANI, NO NEED TO BE RUDE.
PEOPLE ARE GOING TO DIE HERE TODAY. THERE'S NOTHING WE CAN DO TO STOP THAT, BUT PRIYANKA'S FATHER WASN'T LYING.
WHEN TIGER ARRIVED ON THIS ISLAND, THE SWORD WAS GONE -- BECAUSE I'M JUST ABOUT TO TAKE IT.
HE DOESN'T GET HERE FOR ANOTHER TWO WEEKS...
WHAT?!
THE BEAUTY OF OWNING A TIME MACHINE -- OTHER PEOPLE'S PASTS AND FUTURES ARE MY PRESENT.
LICE PUBLIC CALL
ALL TIGER FOUND WAS A COUPLE OF 'MONSTROUS CORPSES'...

NOW, NO ONE THIS SIDE OF THE *JAGAROTH* COULD APPLY THAT DESCRIPTION TO MY TRAVELING COMPANIONS.

AND WHILE, I'M NO OIL PAINTING, *'MONSTROUS'* IS A BIT STRONG, SO I WONDER...

WHO COULD THOSE BODIES *POSSIBLY* BELONG TO?

FFFFFAAARRRGH!!

SECURITY BREACH!

KALIRATHA DNA DETECTED! ERADICATE IMMEDIATELY!

ERADICATE!

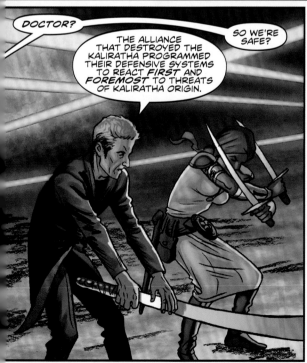

DOCTOR?

THE ALLIANCE THAT DESTROYED THE KALIRATHA PROGRAMMED THEIR DEFENSIVE SYSTEMS TO REACT *FIRST* AND *FOREMOST* TO THREATS OF KALIRATHA ORIGIN.

SO WE'RE SAFE?

'COURSE NOT, BUT A HEAD START'S BETTER THAN NOTHING.

RUN!

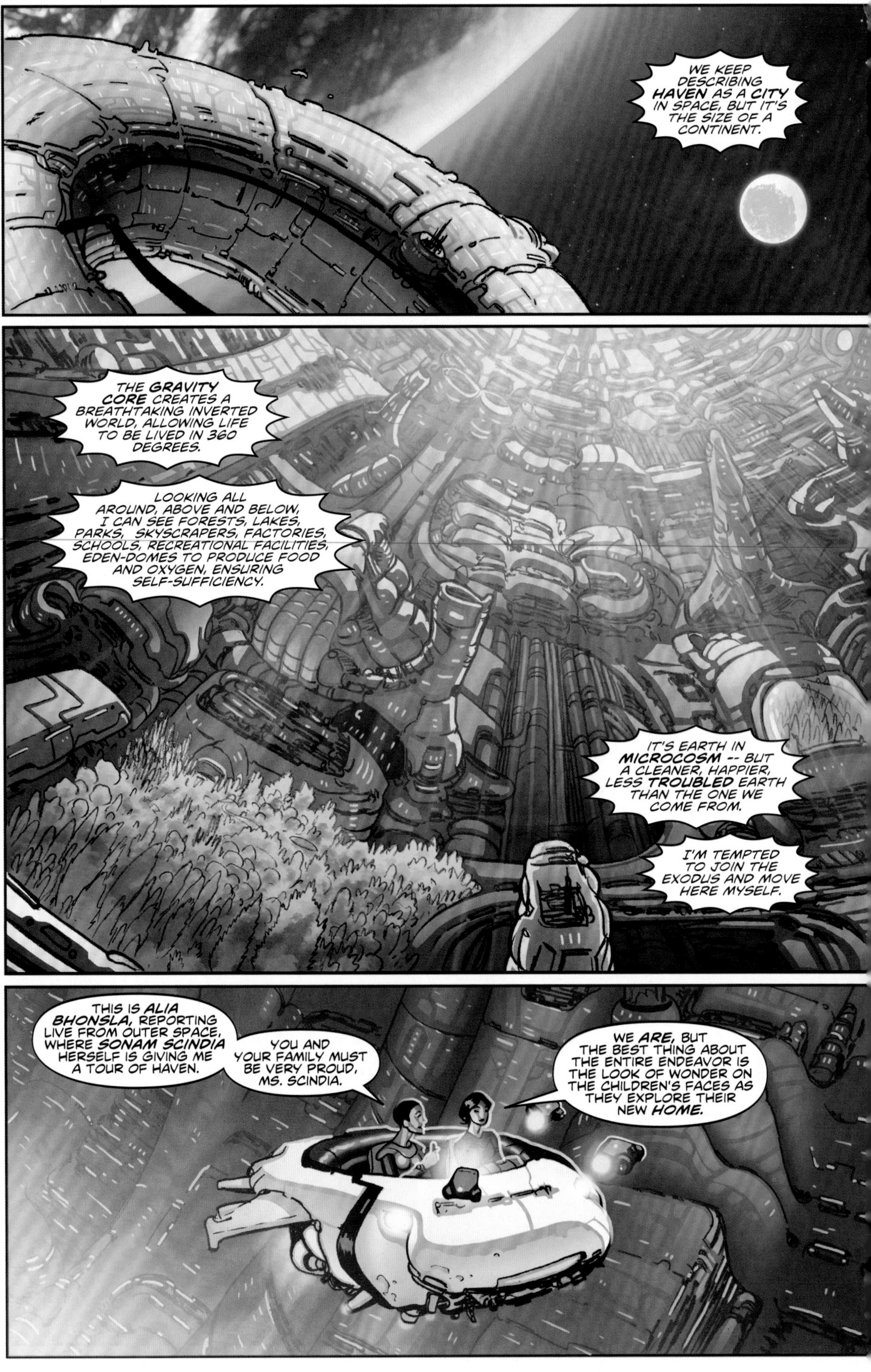
WE KEEP DESCRIBING HAVEN AS A CITY IN SPACE, BUT IT'S THE SIZE OF A CONTINENT.
THE GRAVITY CORE CREATES A BREATHTAKING INVERTED WORLD, ALLOWING LIFE TO BE LIVED IN 360 DEGREES.
LOOKING ALL AROUND, ABOVE AND BELOW, I CAN SEE FORESTS, LAKES, PARKS, SKYSCRAPERS, FACTORIES, SCHOOLS, RECREATIONAL FACILITIES, EDEN-DOMES TO PRODUCE FOOD AND OXYGEN, ENSURING SELF-SUFFICIENCY.
IT'S EARTH IN MICROCOSM -- BUT A CLEANER, HAPPIER, LESS TROUBLED EARTH THAN THE ONE WE COME FROM.
I'M TEMPTED TO JOIN THE EXODUS AND MOVE HERE MYSELF.
THIS IS ALIA BHONSLA, REPORTING LIVE FROM OUTER SPACE, WHERE SONAM SCINDIA HERSELF IS GIVING ME A TOUR OF HAVEN.
YOU AND YOUR FAMILY MUST BE VERY PROUD, MS. SCINDIA.
WE ARE, BUT THE BEST THING ABOUT THE ENTIRE ENDEAVOR IS THE LOOK OF WONDER ON THE CHILDREN'S FACES AS THEY EXPLORE THEIR NEW HOME.

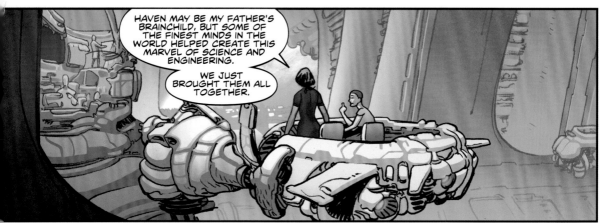

HAVEN MAY BE MY FATHER'S BRAINCHILD, BUT SOME OF THE FINEST MINDS IN THE WORLD HELPED CREATE THIS MARVEL OF SCIENCE AND ENGINEERING.

WE JUST BROUGHT THEM ALL TOGETHER.

AND WE MUSTN'T FORGET THE *CREW* OF HAVEN AND THEIR STERLING WORK.

TODAY'S OPENING COULDN'T HAVE GONE SMOOTHER, AND IT'S ALL THANKS TO THEM.

I'M SURE YOU ALL RECOGNIZE *ROSHAN 'ROCKETS' RANJEEV*, INDIA'S MOST FAMOUS ASTRONAUT AND NOW DEPUTY COMMANDER OF HAVEN.

WITHOUT 'ROCKETS', WE WOULDN'T BE ABLE TO STAY IN ORBIT...

PLEASE, YOU'RE TOO KIND. I'M JUST--

THAT'S WHY --

-- WE HAVE TO *KILL HIM* FIRST.

AAAAA- -AAAAAGH- KKKKK!

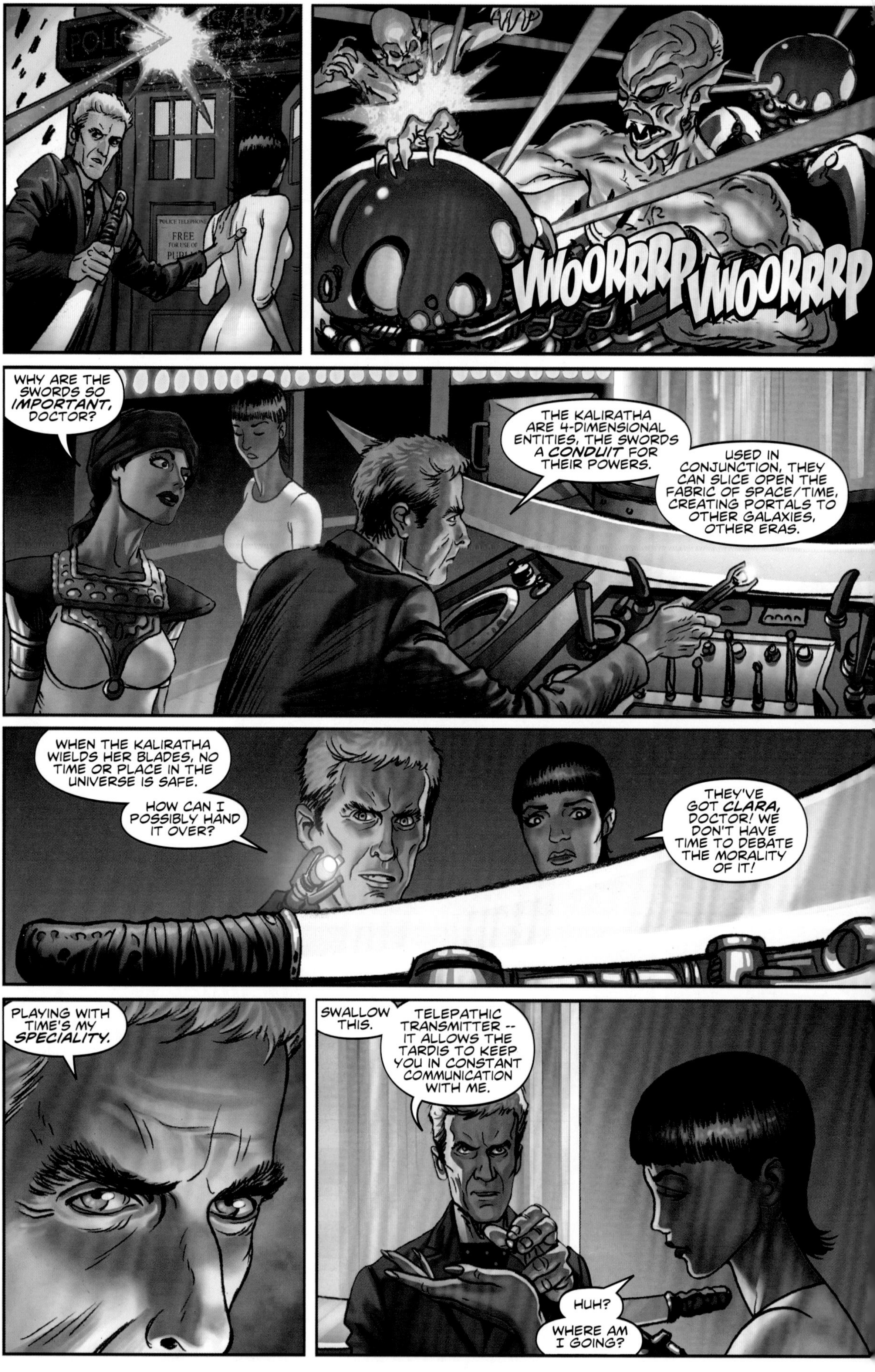
POLICE TELEPHONE
FREE
FOR USE OF
VWOORRRP VWOORRRP
WHY ARE THE SWORDS SO *IMPORTANT*, DOCTOR?
THE KALIRATHA ARE 4-DIMENSIONAL ENTITIES, THE SWORDS A *CONDUIT* FOR THEIR POWERS.
USED IN CONJUNCTION, THEY CAN SLICE OPEN THE FABRIC OF SPACE/TIME, CREATING PORTALS TO OTHER GALAXIES, OTHER ERAS.
WHEN THE KALIRATHA WIELDS HER BLADES, NO TIME OR PLACE IN THE UNIVERSE IS SAFE.
HOW CAN I POSSIBLY HAND IT OVER?
THEY'VE GOT *CLARA*, DOCTOR! WE DON'T HAVE TIME TO DEBATE THE MORALITY OF IT!
PLAYING WITH TIME'S MY *SPECIALITY*.
SWALLOW THIS.
TELEPATHIC TRANSMITTER -- IT ALLOWS THE TARDIS TO KEEP YOU IN CONSTANT COMMUNICATION WITH ME.
HUH?
WHERE AM I GOING?

CALL ME A *DOUR* GALLIFREYAN, BUT I'VE A SNEAKING SUSPICION THAT HAVEN, THE SCINDIAS' CITY IN SPACE, IS ABOUT TO COME DOWN TO EARTH WITH A VERY BIG *BANG*.

WARNING: EMERGENCY SYSTEMS SHUT DOWN.

WARNING: GRAVITY CORE DEACTIVATED.

WARNING: CATASTROPHIC RE-ENTRY COURSE INITIATED.

WARNING: TWELVE MINUTES TO EARTH IMPACT.

ATTENTION, THIS IS YOUR COMMANDER SPEAKING.

APOLOGIES FOR ANY *TURBULENCE* YOU MAY BE EXPERIENCING.

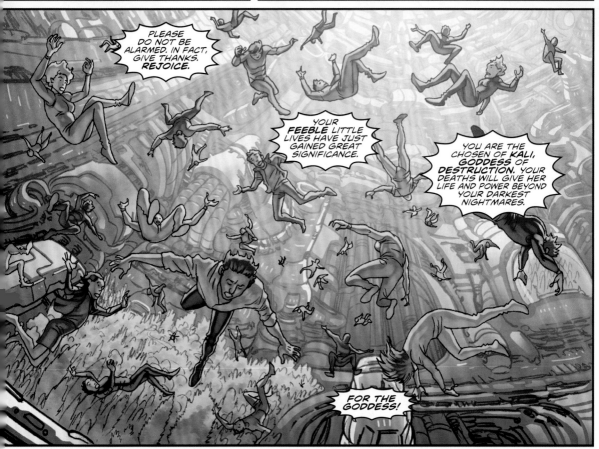

PLEASE DO NOT BE ALARMED. IN FACT, GIVE THANKS. *REJOICE.*

YOUR *FEEBLE* LITTLE LIVES HAVE JUST GAINED GREAT SIGNIFICANCE.

YOU ARE THE CHOSEN OF *KALI, GODDESS OF DESTRUCTION.* YOUR DEATHS WILL GIVE HER LIFE AND POWER BEYOND YOUR DARKEST NIGHTMARES.

FOR THE GODDESS!

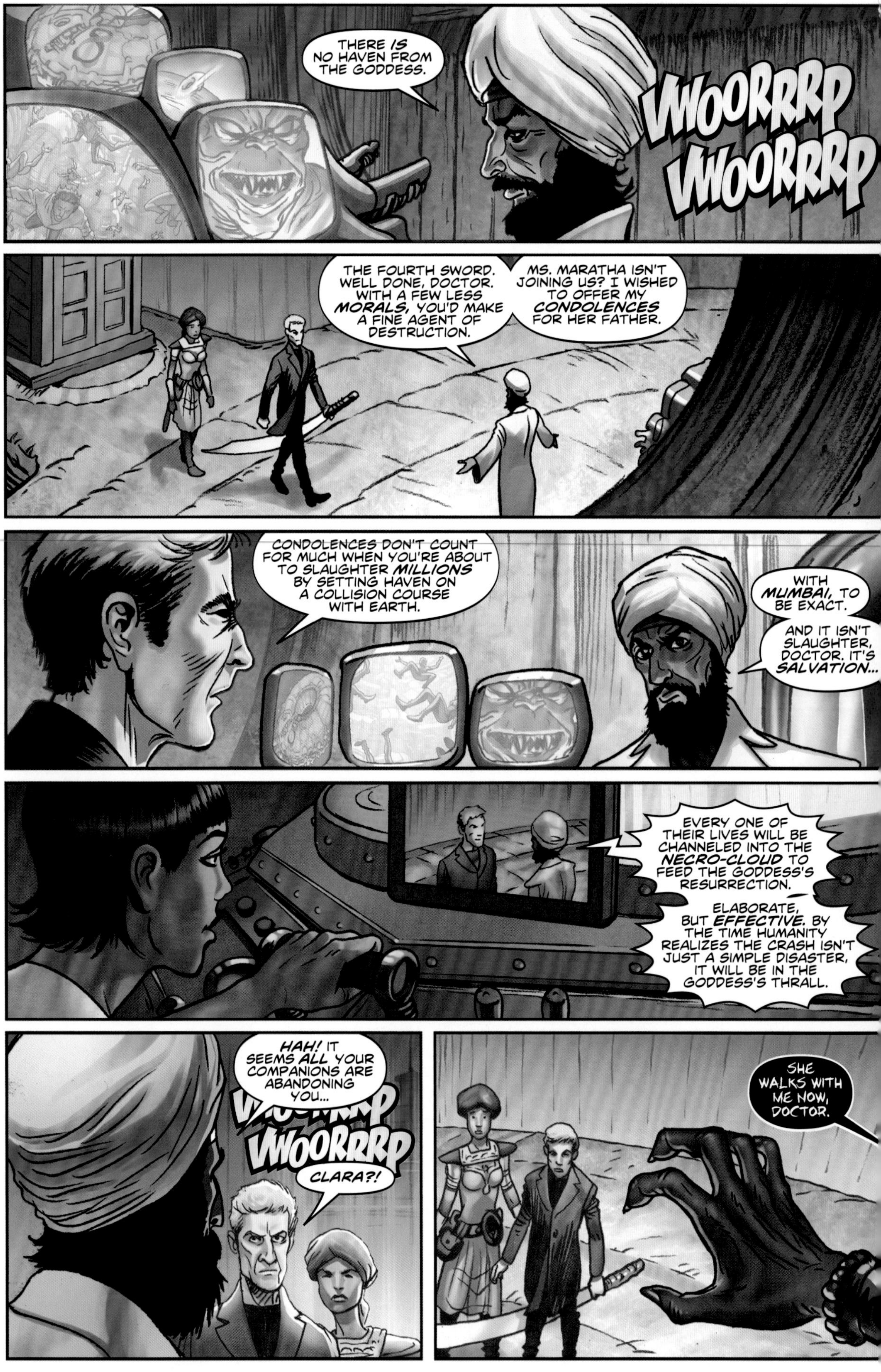
THERE IS NO HAVEN FROM THE GODDESS.
VWOORRRP VWOORRRP
THE FOURTH SWORD. WELL DONE, DOCTOR. WITH A FEW LESS MORALS, YOU'D MAKE A FINE AGENT OF DESTRUCTION.
MS. MARATHA ISN'T JOINING US? I WISHED TO OFFER MY CONDOLENCES FOR HER FATHER.
CONDOLENCES DON'T COUNT FOR MUCH WHEN YOU'RE ABOUT TO SLAUGHTER MILLIONS BY SETTING HAVEN ON A COLLISION COURSE WITH EARTH.
WITH MUMBAI, TO BE EXACT.
AND IT ISN'T SLAUGHTER, DOCTOR. IT'S SALVATION...
EVERY ONE OF THEIR LIVES WILL BE CHANNELED INTO THE NECRO-CLOUD TO FEED THE GODDESS'S RESURRECTION.
ELABORATE, BUT EFFECTIVE. BY THE TIME HUMANITY REALIZES THE CRASH ISN'T JUST A SIMPLE DISASTER, IT WILL BE IN THE GODDESS'S THRALL.
HAH! IT SEEMS ALL YOUR COMPANIONS ARE ABANDONING YOU...
VWOORRRP
CLARA?!
SHE WALKS WITH ME NOW, DOCTOR.

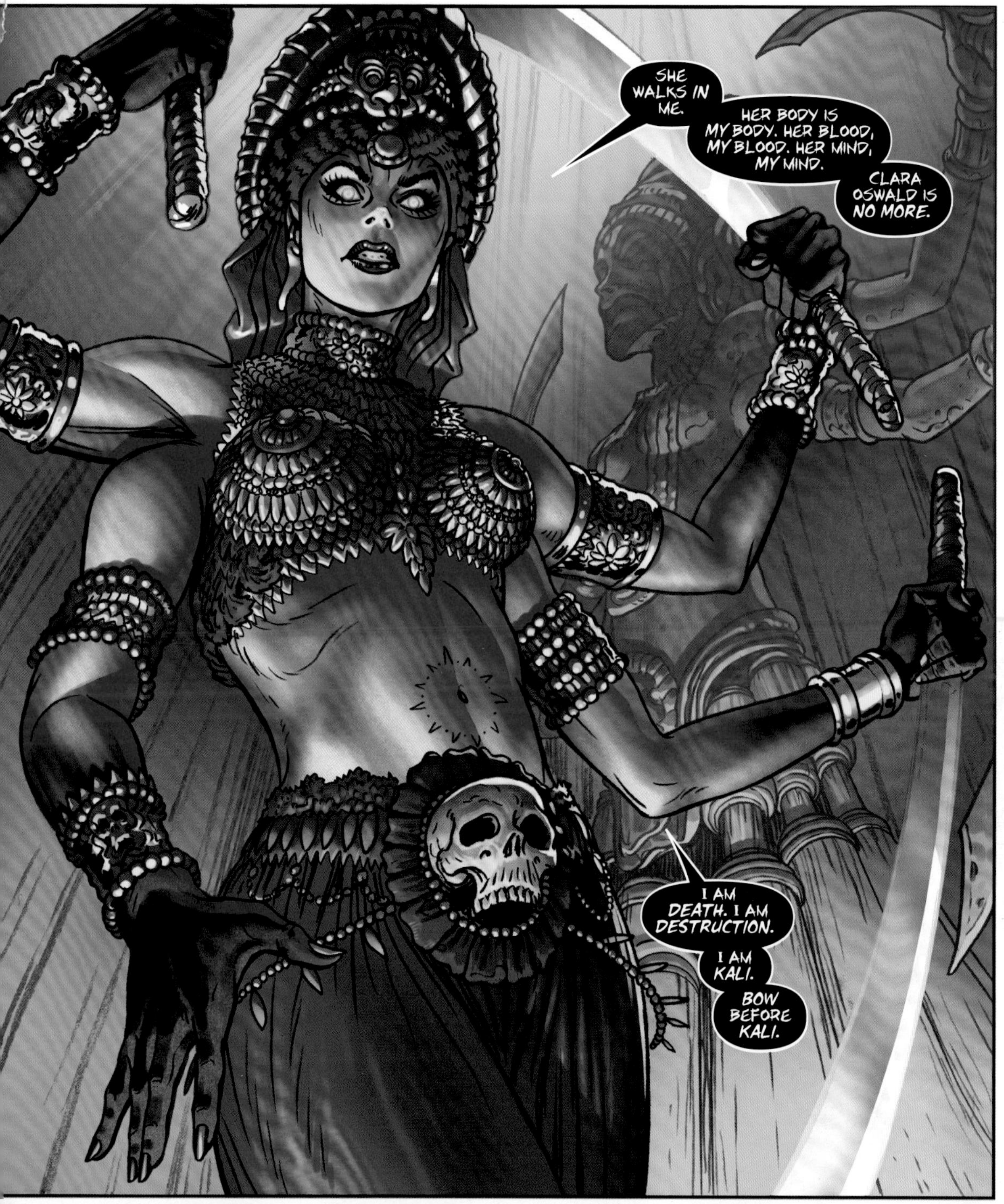
SHE WALKS IN ME.
HER BODY IS MY BODY. HER BLOOD, MY BLOOD. HER MIND, MY MIND.
CLARA OSWALD IS NO MORE.
I AM DEATH. I AM DESTRUCTION.
I AM KALI.
BOW BEFORE KALI.

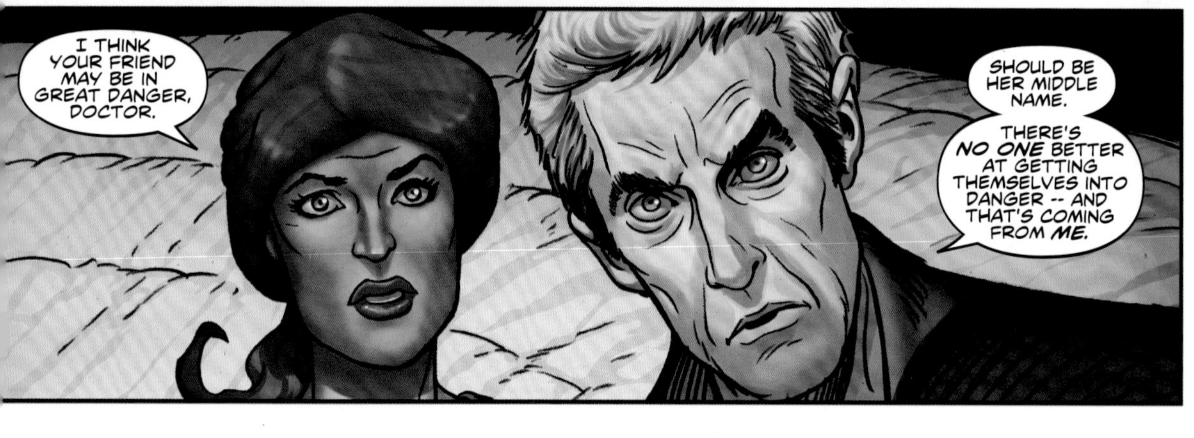
I THINK YOUR FRIEND MAY BE IN GREAT DANGER, DOCTOR.
SHOULD BE HER MIDDLE NAME.
THERE'S NO ONE BETTER AT GETTING THEMSELVES INTO DANGER -- AND THAT'S COMING FROM ME.

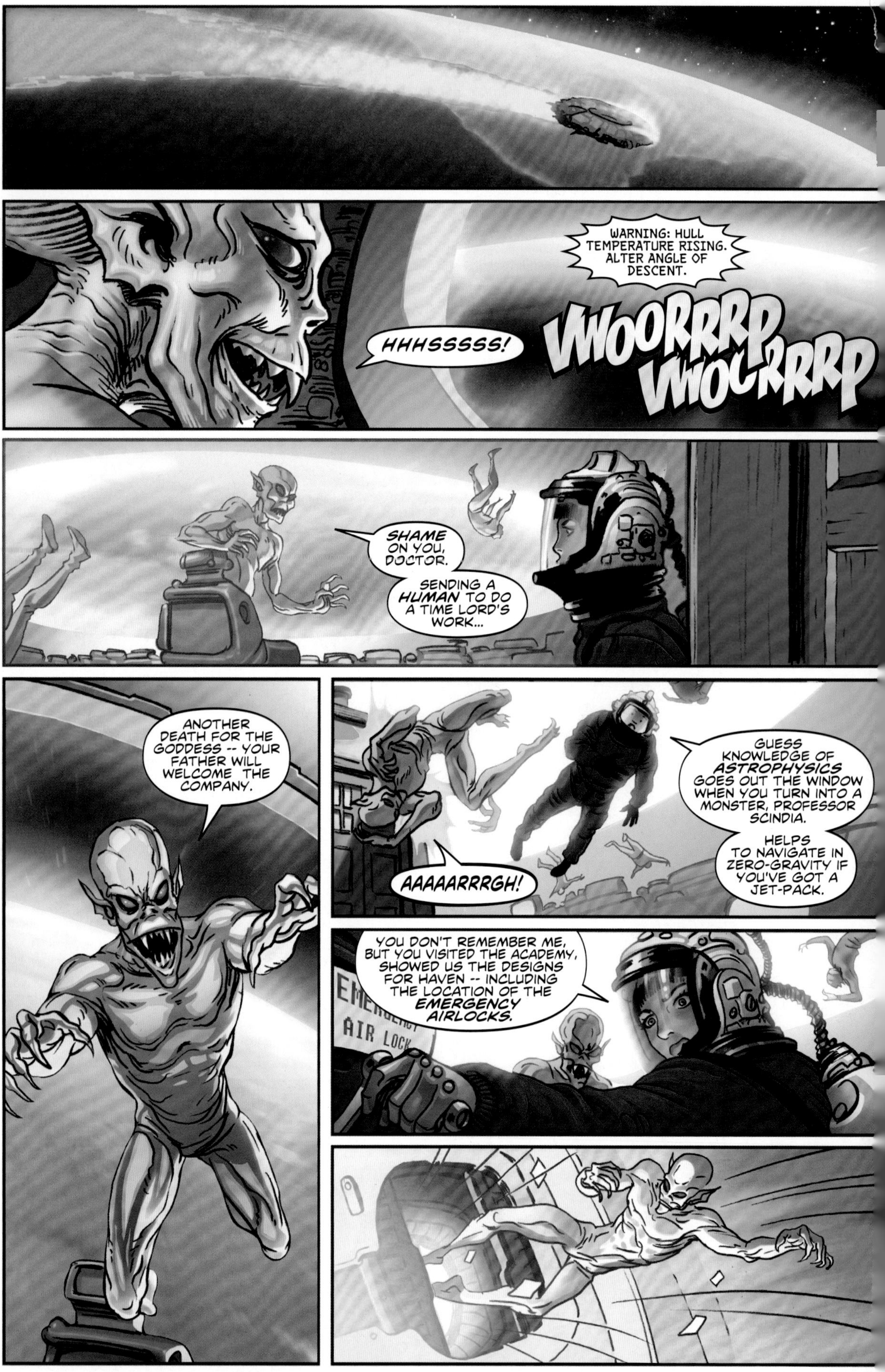
WARNING: HULL TEMPERATURE RISING. ALTER ANGLE OF DESCENT.
HHHSSSSS!
VWOORRRP VWOORRRP
SHAME ON YOU, DOCTOR.
SENDING A HUMAN TO DO A TIME LORD'S WORK...
ANOTHER DEATH FOR THE GODDESS -- YOUR FATHER WILL WELCOME THE COMPANY.
AAAAARRRGH!
GUESS KNOWLEDGE OF ASTROPHYSICS GOES OUT THE WINDOW WHEN YOU TURN INTO A MONSTER, PROFESSOR SCINDIA.
HELPS TO NAVIGATE IN ZERO-GRAVITY IF YOU'VE GOT A JET-PACK.
YOU DON'T REMEMBER ME, BUT YOU VISITED THE ACADEMY, SHOWED US THE DESIGNS FOR HAVEN -- INCLUDING THE LOCATION OF THE EMERGENCY AIRLOCKS.
EMERGENCY AIR LOCK

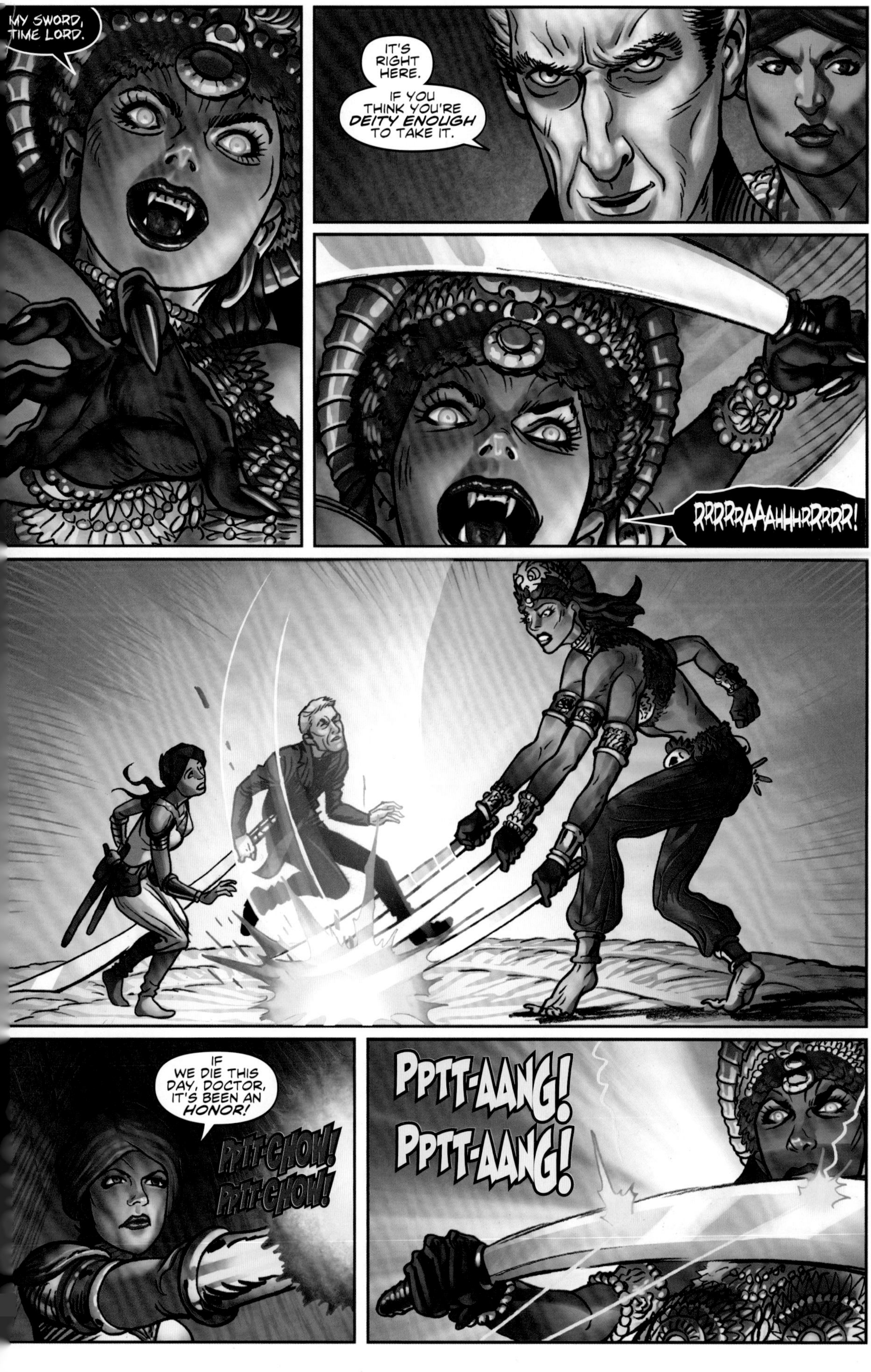
MY SWORD, TIME LORD.
IT'S RIGHT HERE.
IF YOU THINK YOU'RE *DEITY ENOUGH* TO TAKE IT.
DRDRDRAAAHHHRDRDRR!
IF WE DIE THIS DAY, DOCTOR, IT'S BEEN AN *HONOR!*
PPTT-CHOW! PPTT-CHOW!
PPTT-AANG! PPTT-AANG!

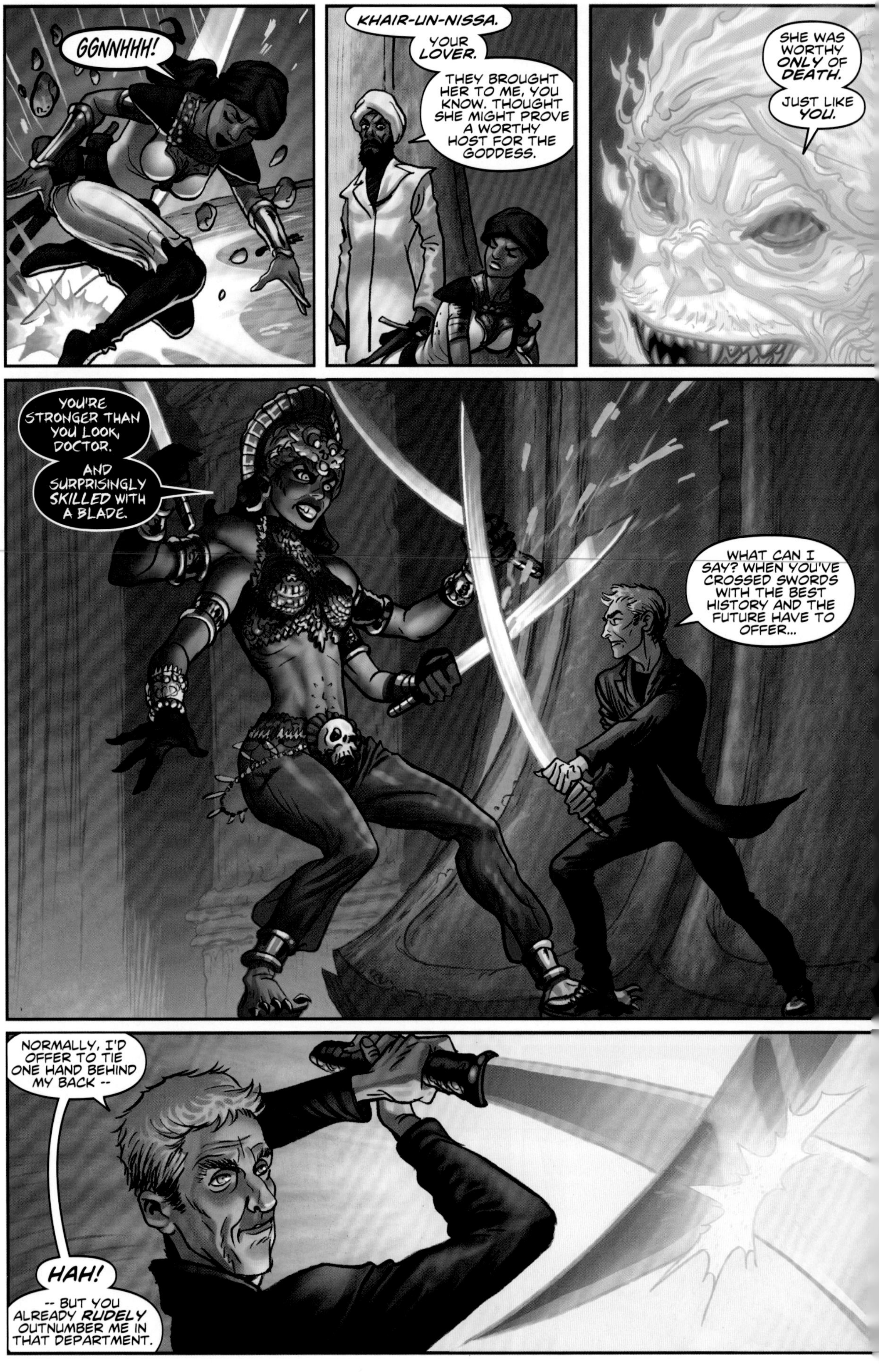

GGNNHHH!
KHAIR-UN-NISSA.
YOUR LOVER.
THEY BROUGHT HER TO ME, YOU KNOW. THOUGHT SHE MIGHT PROVE A WORTHY HOST FOR THE GODDESS.
SHE WAS WORTHY ONLY OF DEATH.
JUST LIKE YOU.
YOU'RE STRONGER THAN YOU LOOK, DOCTOR.
AND SURPRISINGLY SKILLED WITH A BLADE.
WHAT CAN I SAY? WHEN YOU'VE CROSSED SWORDS WITH THE BEST HISTORY AND THE FUTURE HAVE TO OFFER...
NORMALLY, I'D OFFER TO TIE ONE HAND BEHIND MY BACK --
HAH!
-- BUT YOU ALREADY RUDELY OUTNUMBER ME IN THAT DEPARTMENT.

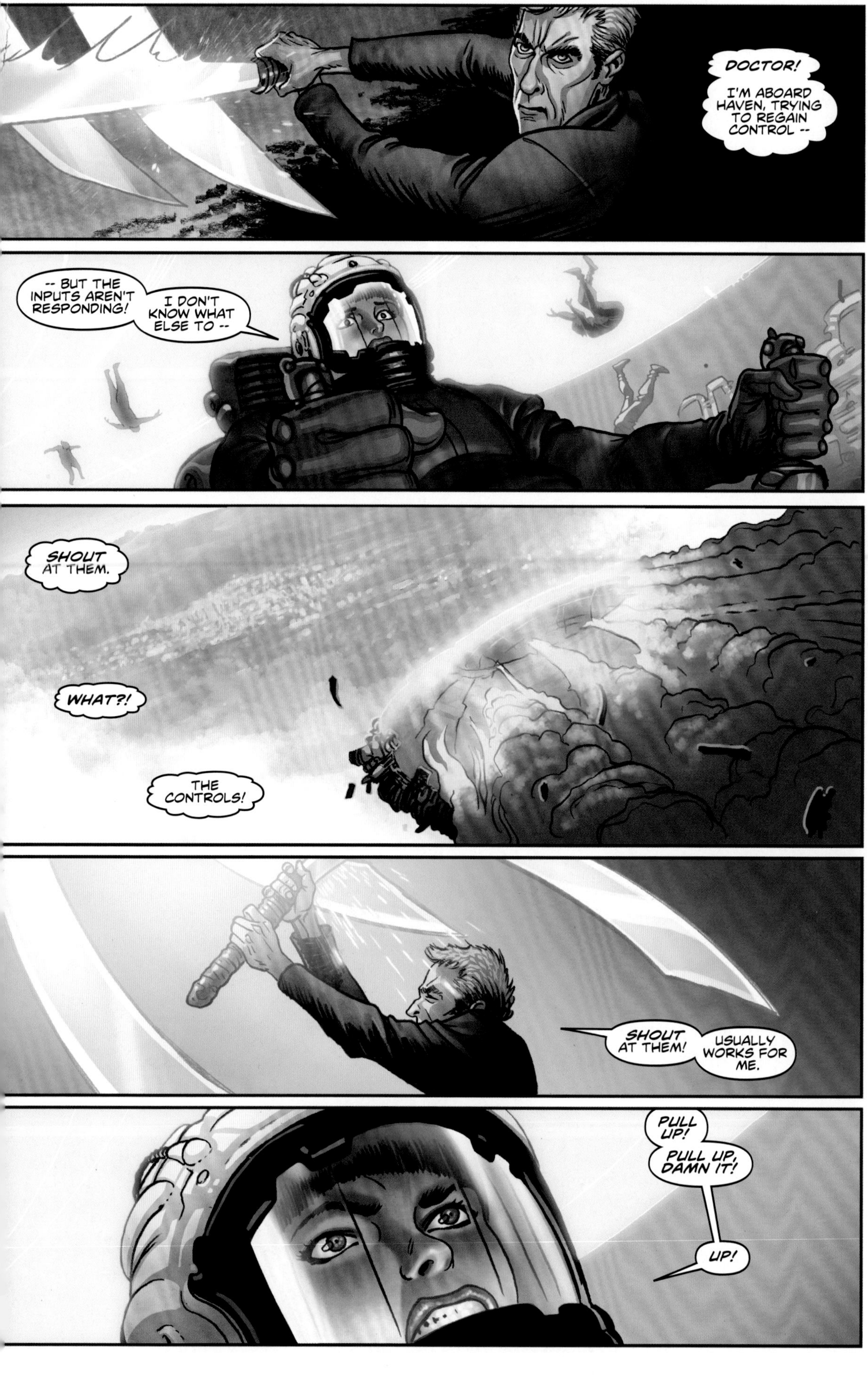
DOCTOR!
I'M ABOARD HAVEN, TRYING TO REGAIN CONTROL --
-- BUT THE INPUTS AREN'T RESPONDING!
I DON'T KNOW WHAT ELSE TO --
SHOUT AT THEM.
WHAT?!
THE CONTROLS!
SHOUT AT THEM!
USUALLY WORKS FOR ME.
PULL UP!
PULL UP, DAMN IT!
UP!

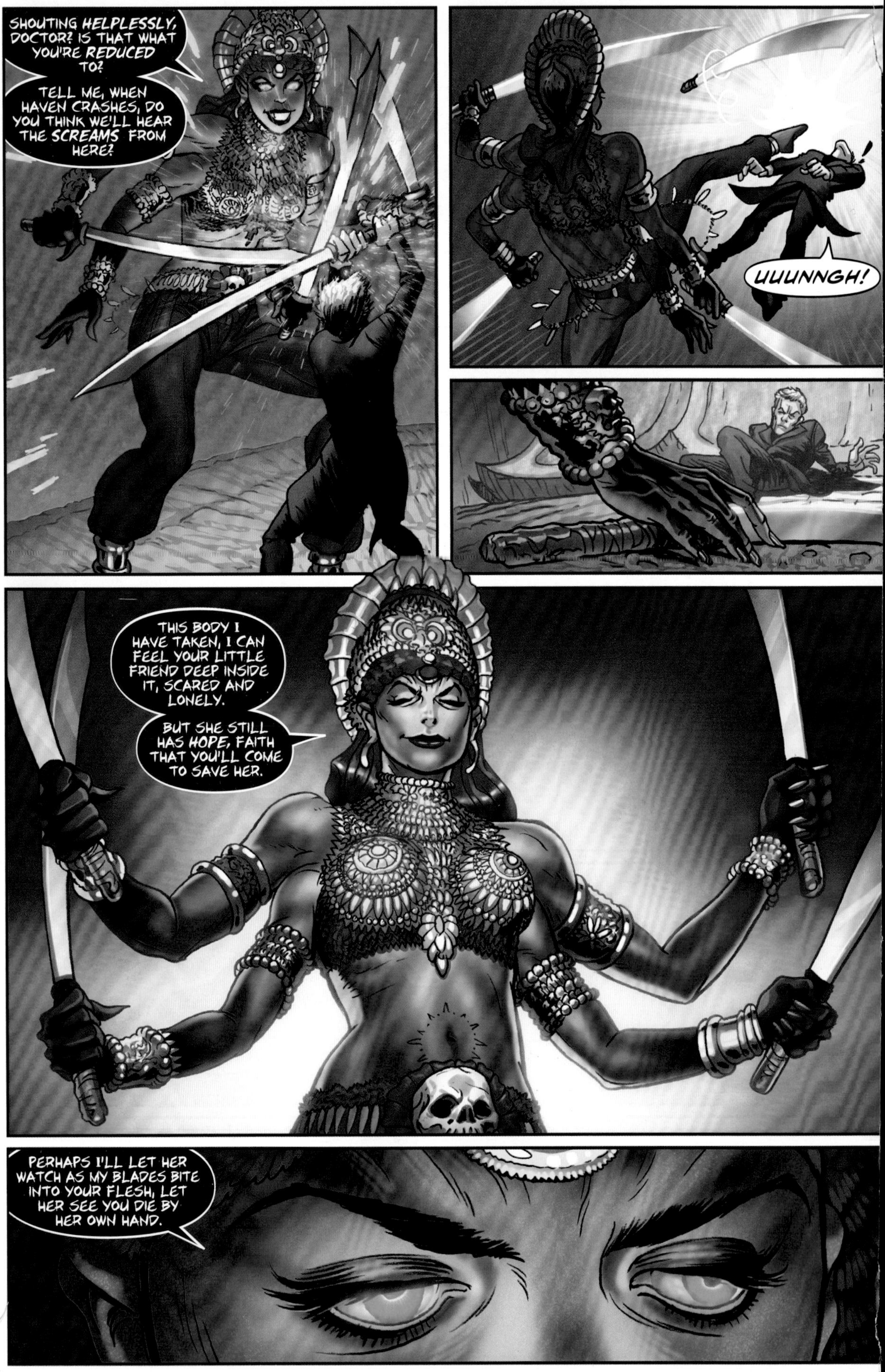
SHOUTING HELPLESSLY, DOCTOR? IS THAT WHAT YOU'RE REDUCED TO?
TELL ME, WHEN HAVEN CRASHES, DO YOU THINK WE'LL HEAR THE SCREAMS FROM HERE?
UUUNNGH!
THIS BODY I HAVE TAKEN, I CAN FEEL YOUR LITTLE FRIEND DEEP INSIDE IT, SCARED AND LONELY.
BUT SHE STILL HAS HOPE, FAITH THAT YOU'LL COME TO SAVE HER.
PERHAPS I'LL LET HER WATCH AS MY BLADES BITE INTO YOUR FLESH, LET HER SEE YOU DIE BY HER OWN HAND.

OH, SHE DOESN'T NEED *ME* TO SAVE HER.

A GODDESS OF DEATH AND DESTRUCTION AGAINST CLARA OSWALD? *NO CONTEST.*

ALL THE EVIL IN THE UNIVERSE COULDN'T OVERCOME THAT *IMPOSSIBLE GIRL.*

GGGRRRAAAAAHHH!

MS. CLARA OSWALD, I PRESUME?

D-DOCTOR... I CAN'T HOLD HER... SHE'S...

IT'S LIKE THERE ARE *KNIVES* IN MY MIND AND SHE'S *CUTTING...*

CUTTING...

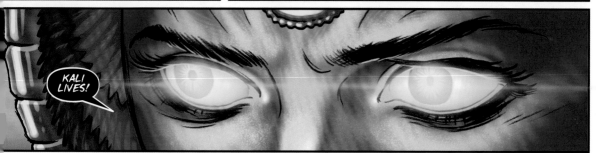

KALI LIVES!

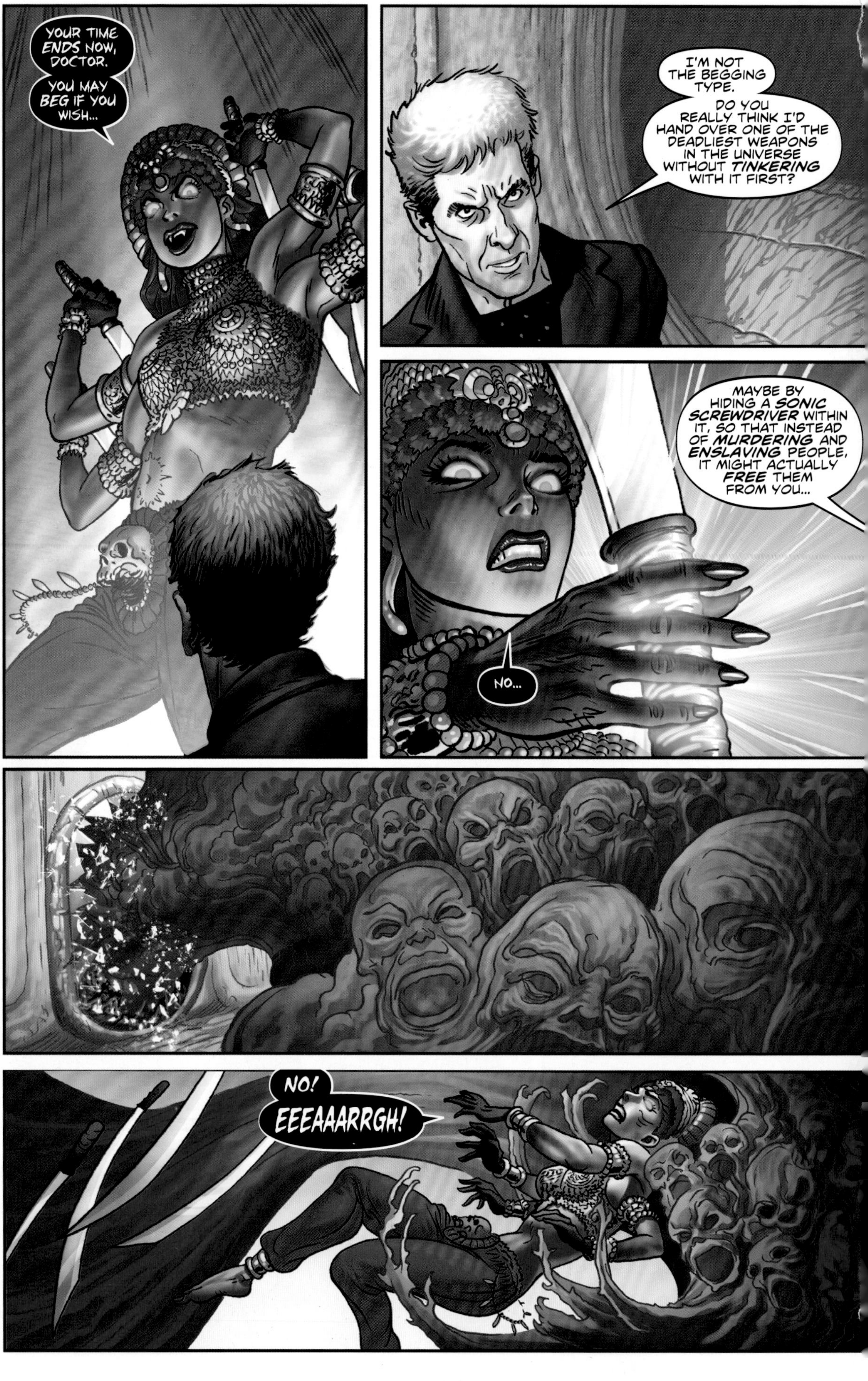
YOUR TIME ENDS NOW, DOCTOR.
YOU MAY BEG IF YOU WISH...
I'M NOT THE BEGGING TYPE.
DO YOU REALLY THINK I'D HAND OVER ONE OF THE DEADLIEST WEAPONS IN THE UNIVERSE WITHOUT TINKERING WITH IT FIRST?
MAYBE BY HIDING A SONIC SCREWDRIVER WITHIN IT, SO THAT INSTEAD OF MURDERING AND ENSLAVING PEOPLE, IT MIGHT ACTUALLY FREE THEM FROM YOU...
NO...
NO!
EEEAAARRGH!

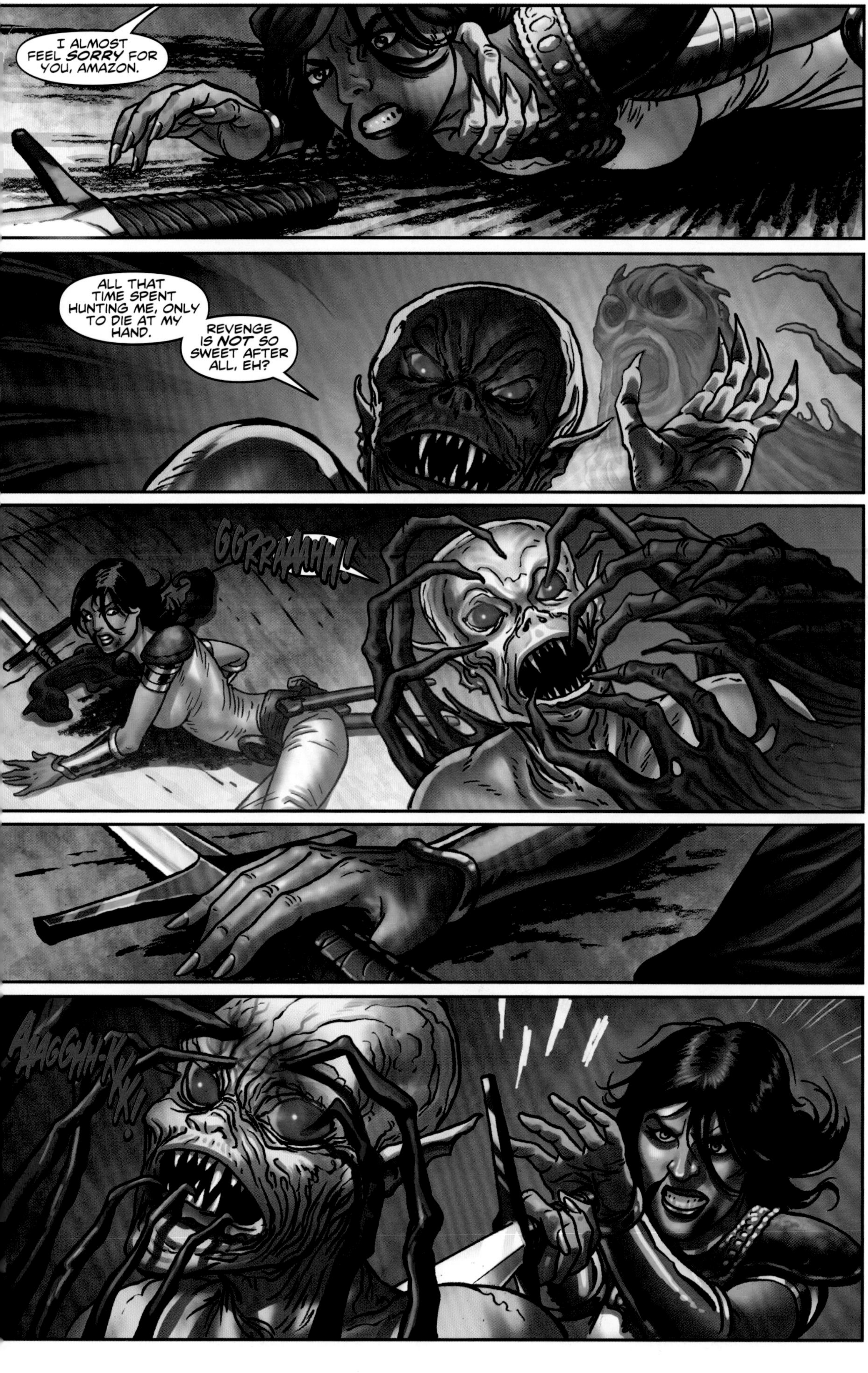
I ALMOST FEEL SORRY FOR YOU, AMAZON.
ALL THAT TIME SPENT HUNTING ME, ONLY TO DIE AT MY HAND.
REVENGE IS NOT SO SWEET AFTER ALL, EH?
GGRRAAAHH!
AAAGGHH-KKK!

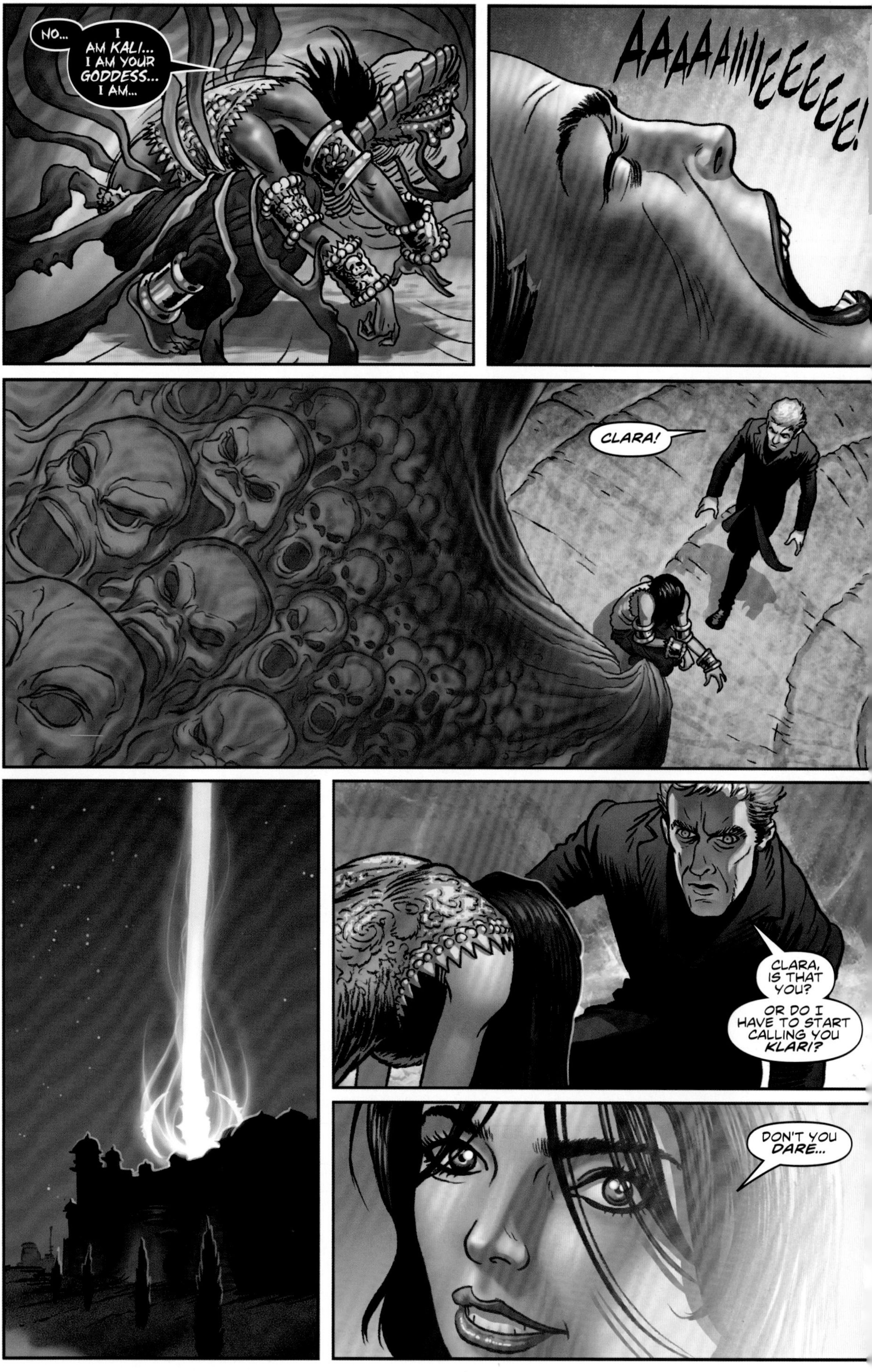
NO... I AM KALI... I AM YOUR GODDESS... I AM...
AAAAIIIIEEEEEE!
CLARA!
CLARA, IS THAT YOU?
OR DO I HAVE TO START CALLING YOU KLARI?
DON'T YOU DARE...

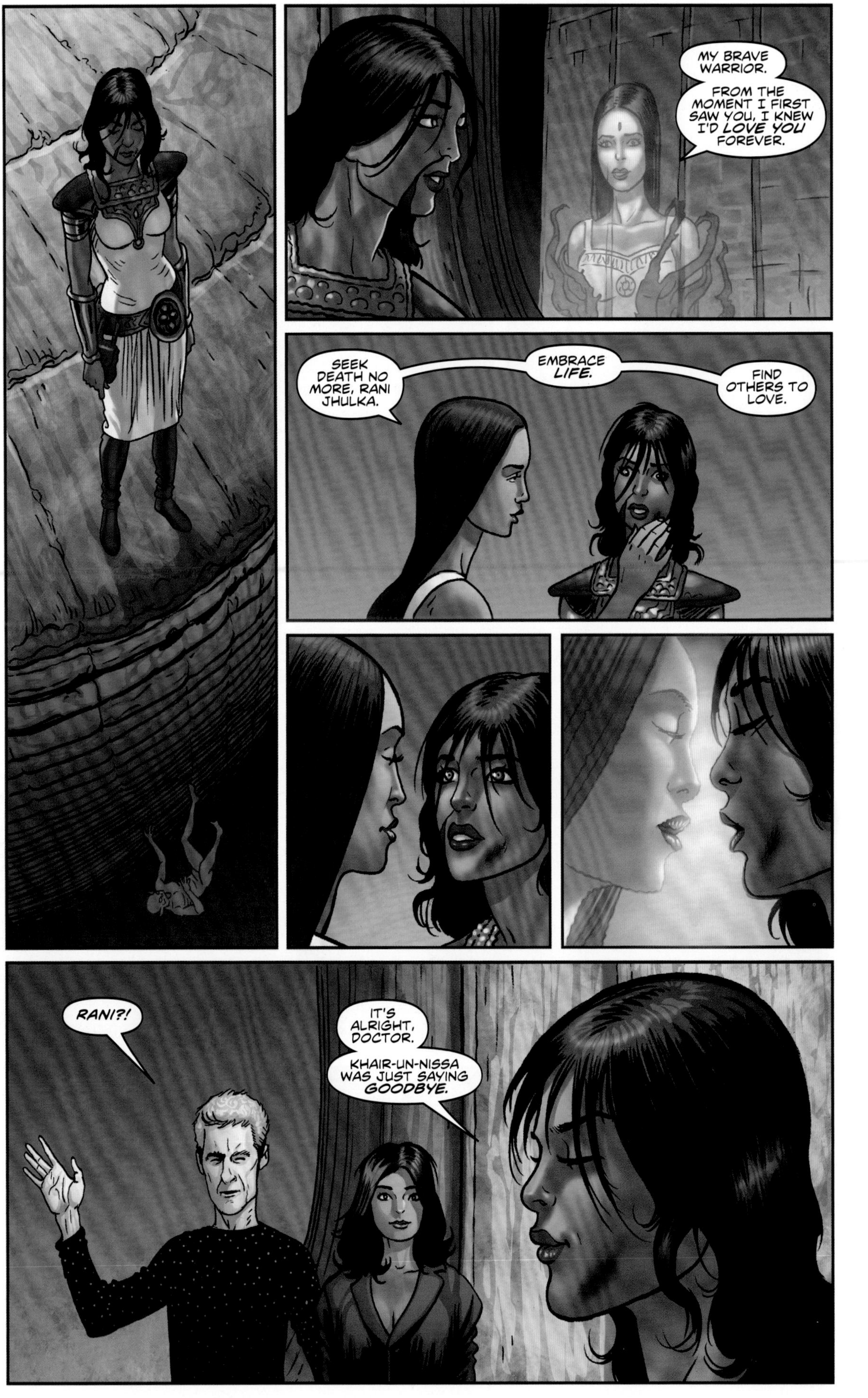
MY BRAVE WARRIOR.
FROM THE MOMENT I FIRST SAW YOU, I KNEW I'D LOVE YOU FOREVER.
SEEK DEATH NO MORE, RANI JHULKA.
EMBRACE LIFE.
FIND OTHERS TO LOVE.
RANI?!
IT'S ALRIGHT, DOCTOR.
KHAIR-UN-NISSA WAS JUST SAYING GOODBYE.

SO, DOCTOR...

PRIYANKA!

IT SEEMS THE CONTROLS OF THE MOST SOPHISTICATED SPACE STATION EVER BUILT RESPOND BEST WHEN YOU *SHOUT ANGRILY* AT THEM.

DIDN'T WORK AT FIRST, SO I TRIED A *SCOTTISH* ACCENT...

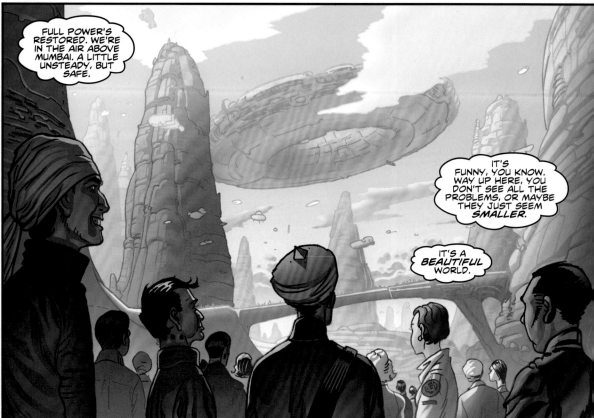

FULL POWER'S RESTORED. WE'RE IN THE AIR ABOVE MUMBAI. A LITTLE UNSTEADY, BUT SAFE.

IT'S FUNNY, YOU KNOW. WAY UP HERE, YOU DON'T SEE ALL THE PROBLEMS, OR MAYBE THEY JUST SEEM *SMALLER.*

IT'S A *BEAUTIFUL* WORLD.

WE REALLY SHOULD TAKE BETTER CARE OF IT.

WELL, SAID, PRIYANKA.

YOUR *FATHER* WOULD BE *PROUD.*

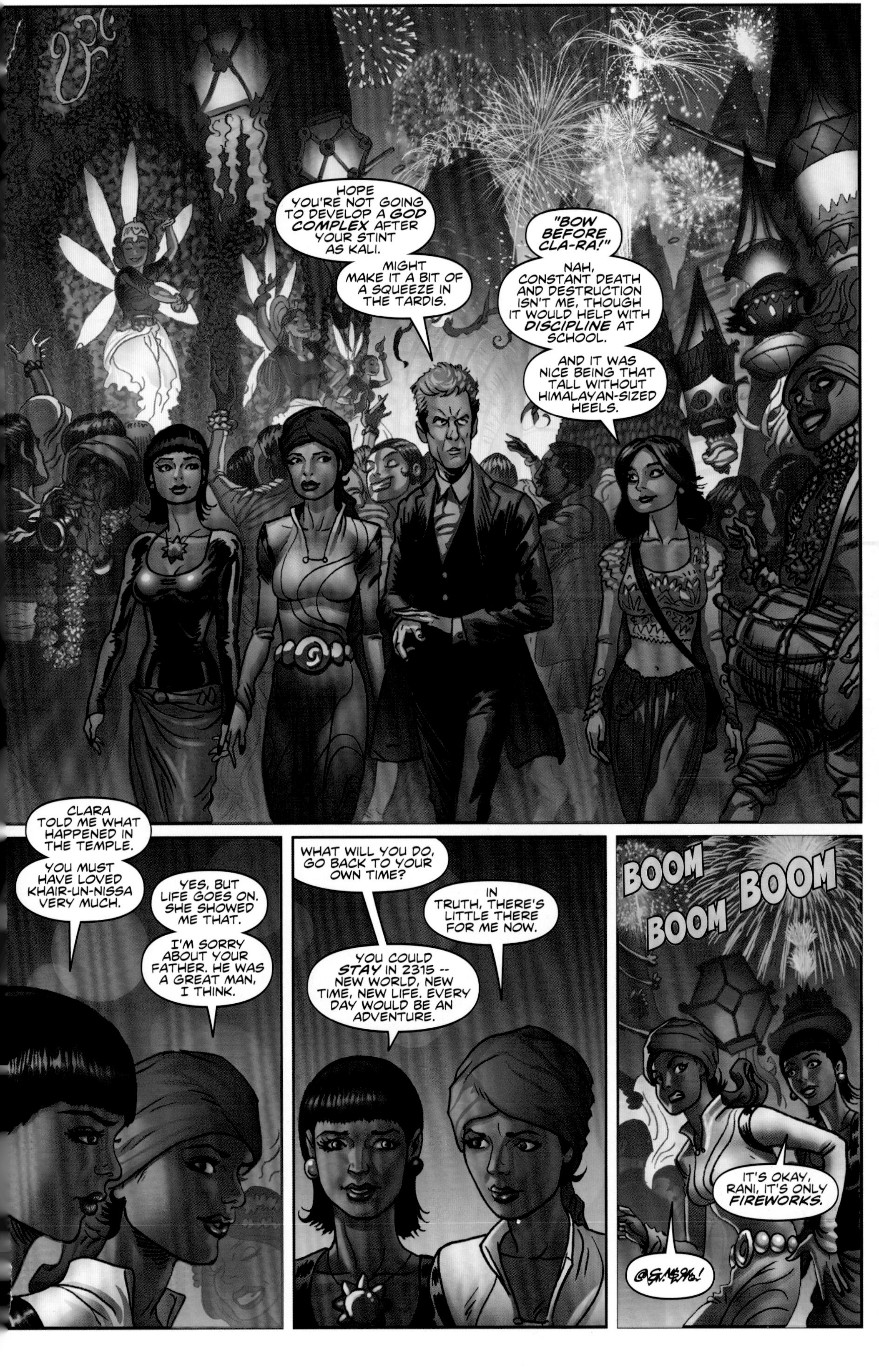
HOPE YOU'RE NOT GOING TO DEVELOP A GOD COMPLEX AFTER YOUR STINT AS KALI.
MIGHT MAKE IT A BIT OF A SQUEEZE IN THE TARDIS.
"BOW BEFORE CLA-RA!"
NAH, CONSTANT DEATH AND DESTRUCTION ISN'T ME, THOUGH IT WOULD HELP WITH DISCIPLINE AT SCHOOL.
AND IT WAS NICE BEING THAT TALL WITHOUT HIMALAYAN-SIZED HEELS.
CLARA TOLD ME WHAT HAPPENED IN THE TEMPLE.
YOU MUST HAVE LOVED KHAIR-UN-NISSA VERY MUCH.
YES, BUT LIFE GOES ON. SHE SHOWED ME THAT.
I'M SORRY ABOUT YOUR FATHER. HE WAS A GREAT MAN, I THINK.
WHAT WILL YOU DO, GO BACK TO YOUR OWN TIME?
IN TRUTH, THERE'S LITTLE THERE FOR ME NOW.
YOU COULD STAY IN 2315 -- NEW WORLD, NEW TIME, NEW LIFE. EVERY DAY WOULD BE AN ADVENTURE.
BOOM
BOOM
BOOM
IT'S OKAY, RANI, IT'S ONLY FIREWORKS.

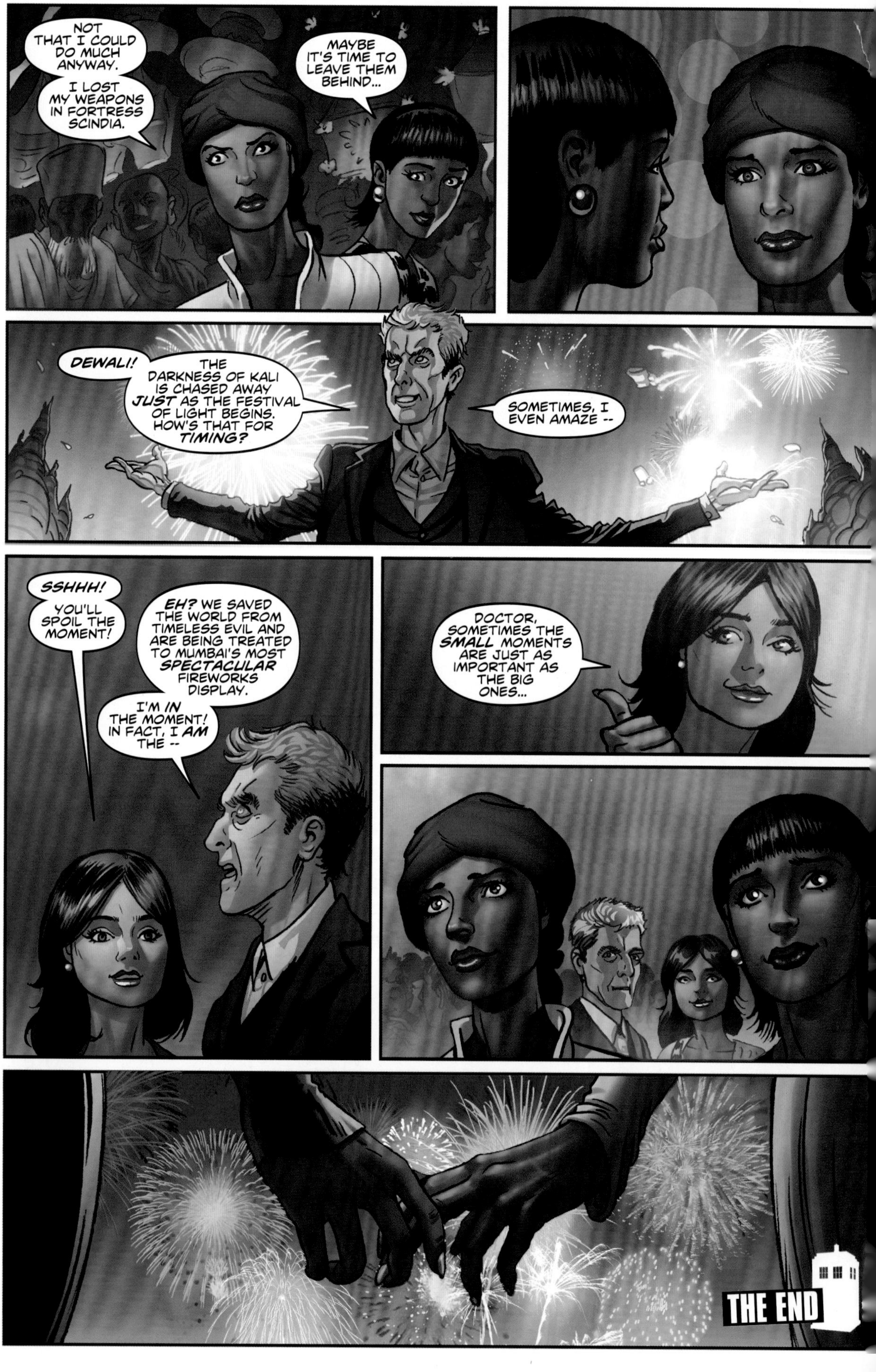
NOT THAT I COULD DO MUCH ANYWAY.
I LOST MY WEAPONS IN FORTRESS SCINDIA.
MAYBE IT'S TIME TO LEAVE THEM BEHIND...
DEWALI!
THE DARKNESS OF KALI IS CHASED AWAY JUST AS THE FESTIVAL OF LIGHT BEGINS. HOW'S THAT FOR TIMING?
SOMETIMES, I EVEN AMAZE --
SSHHH!
YOU'LL SPOIL THE MOMENT!
EH? WE SAVED THE WORLD FROM TIMELESS EVIL AND ARE BEING TREATED TO MUMBAI'S MOST SPECTACULAR FIREWORKS DISPLAY.
I'M IN THE MOMENT! IN FACT, I AM THE --
DOCTOR, SOMETIMES THE SMALL MOMENTS ARE JUST AS IMPORTANT AS THE BIG ONES...
THE END

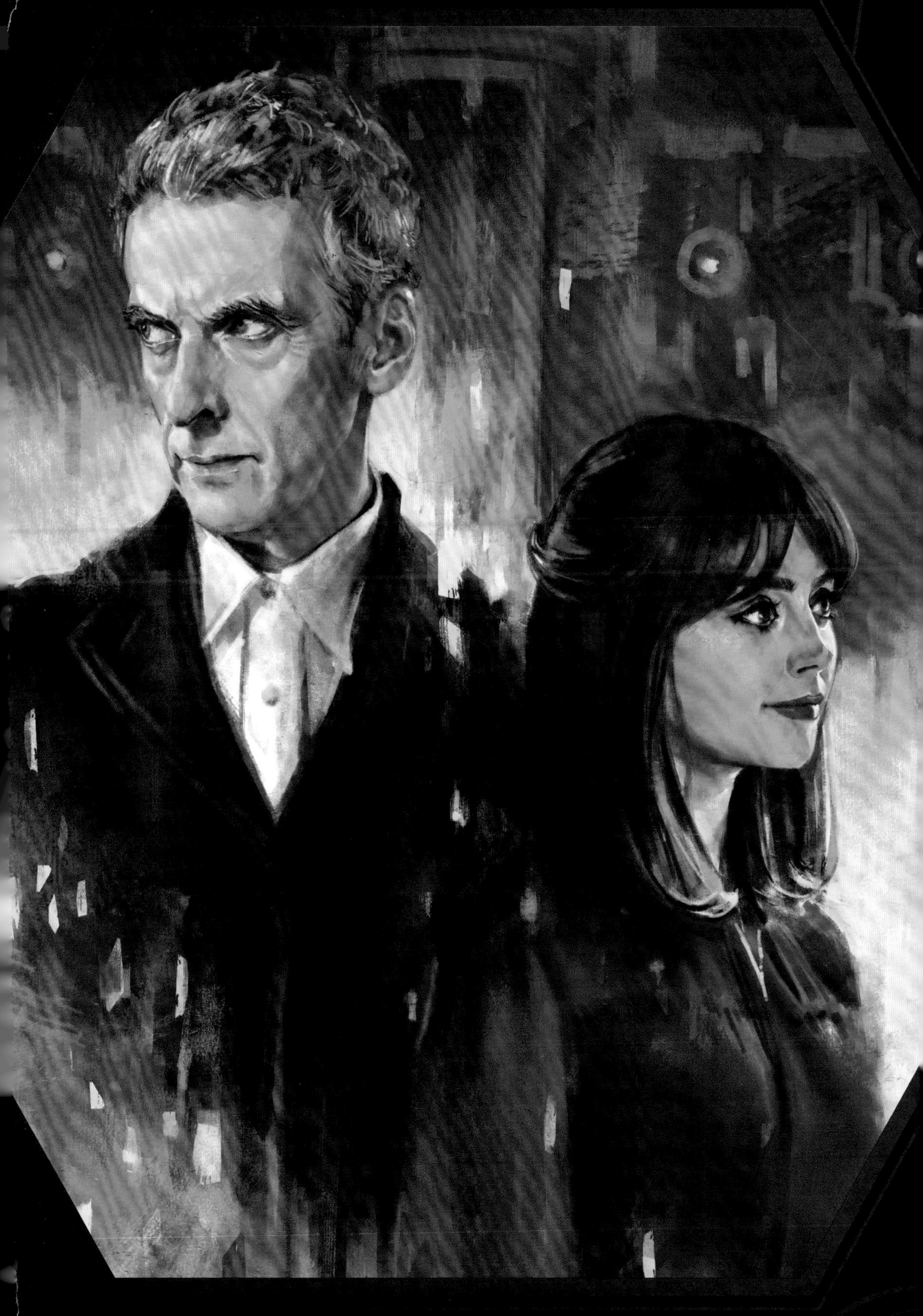

12D #5 Cover Art by Alice X. Zhang

COVER GALLERY

1A

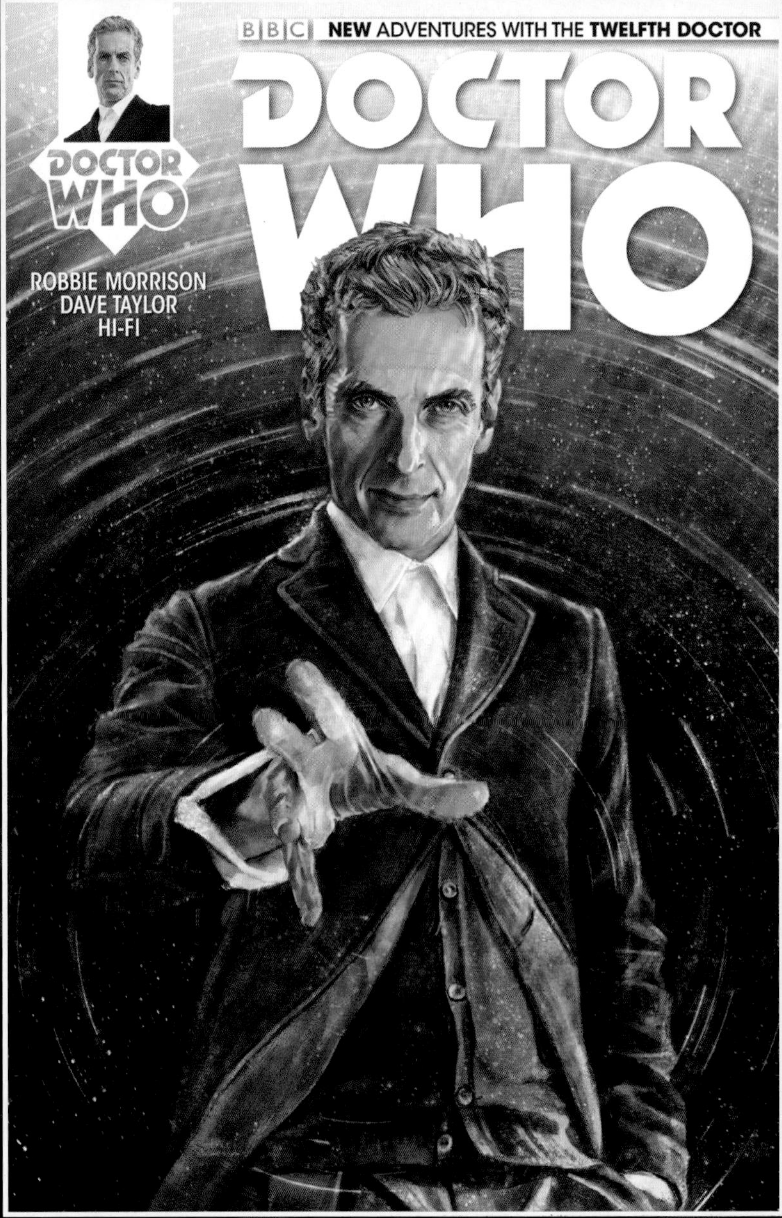
BBC NEW ADVENTURES WITH THE TWELFTH DOCTOR
DOCTOR WHO
DOCTOR WHO
ROBBIE MORRISON
DAVE TAYLOR
HI-FI

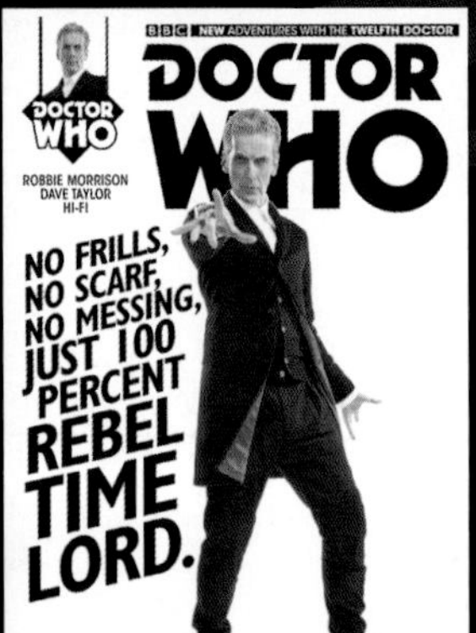
BBC NEW ADVENTURES WITH THE TWELFTH DOCTOR
DOCTOR WHO
DOCTOR WHO
ROBBIE MORRISON
DAVE TAYLOR
HI-FI
NO FRILLS, NO SCARF, NO MESSING, JUST 100 PERCENT REBEL TIME LORD.

1B

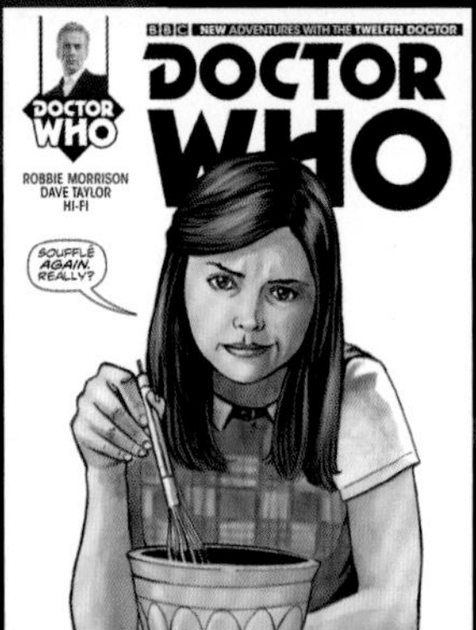
BBC NEW ADVENTURES WITH THE TWELFTH DOCTOR
DOCTOR WHO
DOCTOR WHO
ROBBIE MORRISON
DAVE TAYLOR
HI-FI
SOUFFLÉ AGAIN. REALLY?

1C

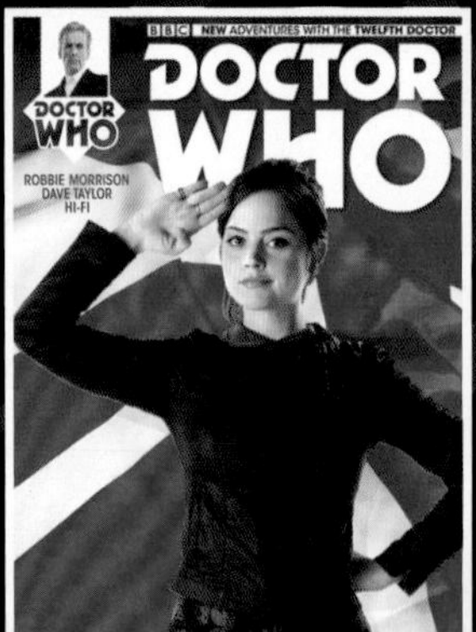
BBC NEW ADVENTURES WITH THE TWELFTH DOCTOR
DOCTOR WHO
DOCTOR WHO
ROBBIE MORRISON
DAVE TAYLOR
HI-FI

1D

#1 A: Alice X. Zhang

#1 B: AJ

#1 C: Mariano Laclaustra

#1 D: AJ / Rob Farmer

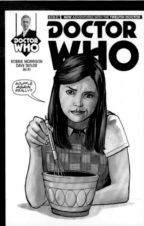

COVER GALLERY

#2 A: AJ   #2 B: Rob Farmer   #2 C: Rob Farmer

COVER GALLERY

3A

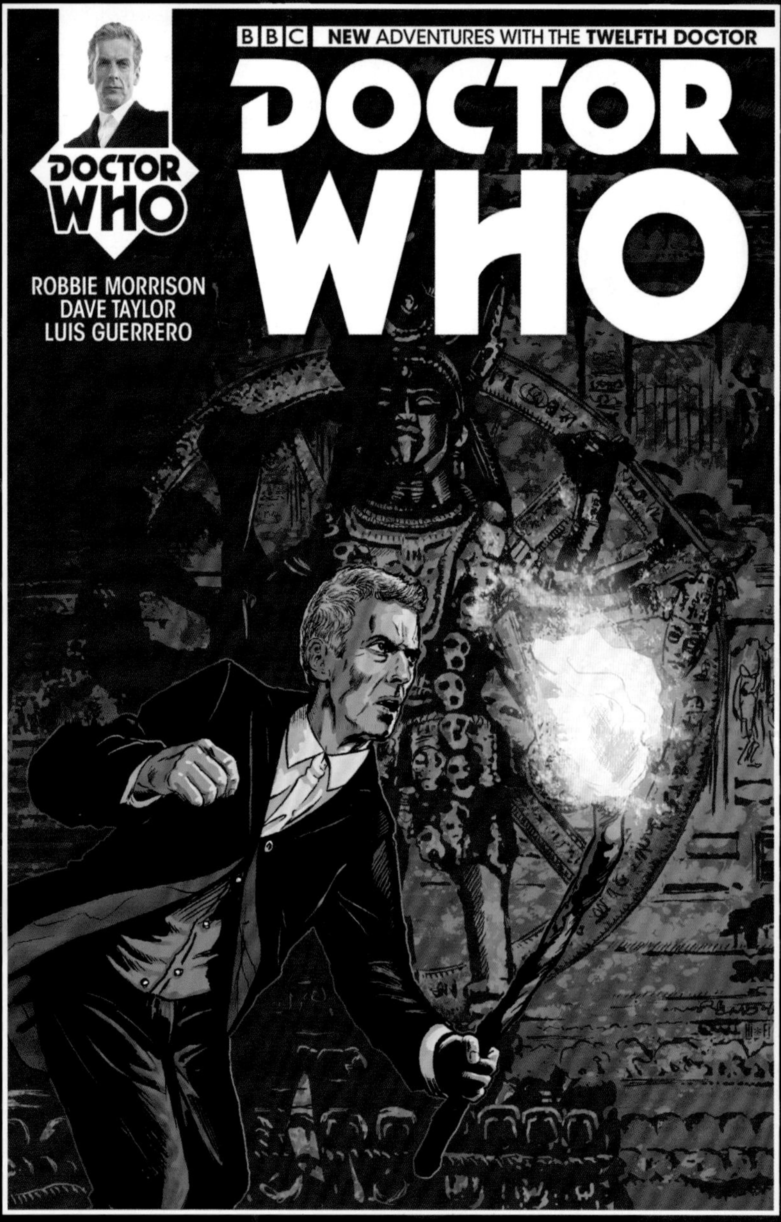
BBC
NEW ADVENTURES WITH THE TWELFTH DOCTOR
DOCTOR WHO
DOCTOR WHO
ROBBIE MORRISON
DAVE TAYLOR
LUIS GUERRERO

3B

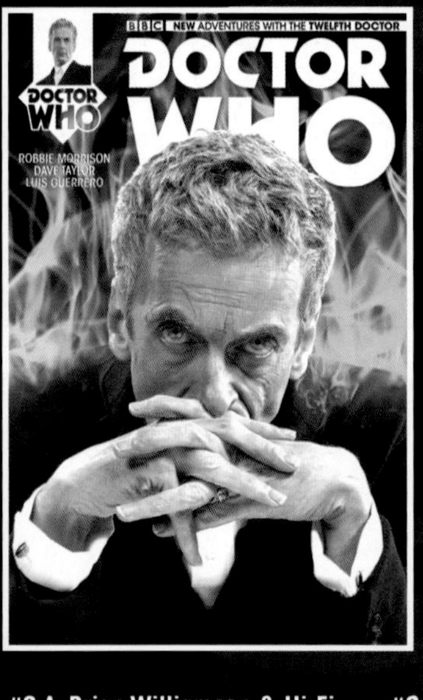
BBC
NEW ADVENTURES WITH THE TWELFTH DOCTOR
DOCTOR WHO
DOCTOR WHO
ROBBIE MORRISON
DAVE TAYLOR
LUIS GUERRERO

3C

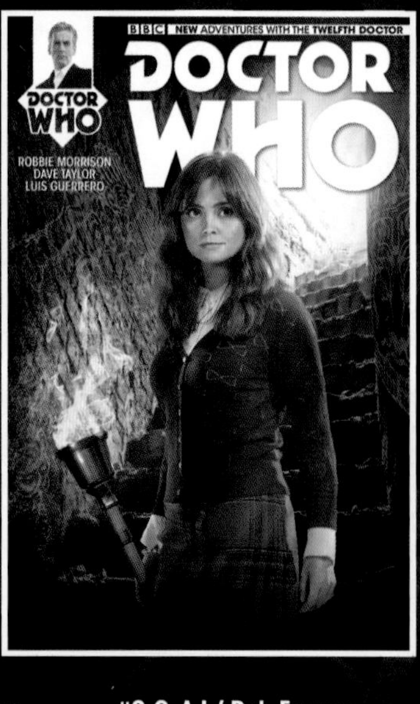
BBC
NEW ADVENTURES WITH THE TWELFTH DOCTOR
DOCTOR WHO
DOCTOR WHO
ROBBIE MORRISON
DAVE TAYLOR
LUIS GUERRERO

#3 A: Brian Williamson & Hi-Fi

#3 B: AJ / Rob Farmer

#3 C: AJ / Rob Farmer

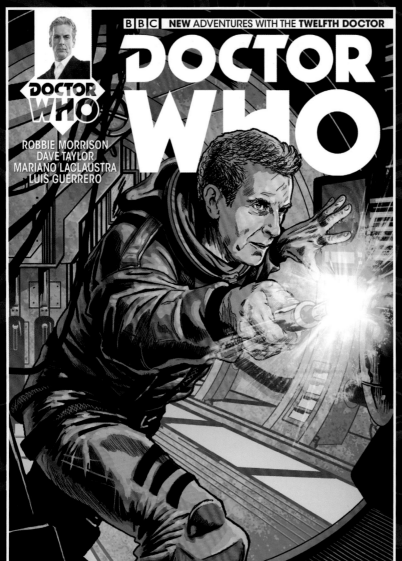

COVER GALLERY

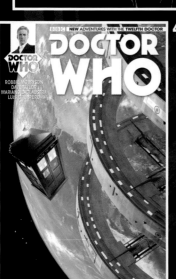

4B

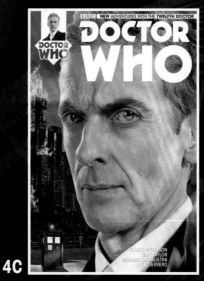

4C

#4 A: Brian Williamson & Hi-Fi   #4 B: AJ / Rob Farmer   #4 C: AJ / Rob Farmer

DOCTOR WHO: THE ELEVENTH DOCTOR VOL. 1: AFTER LIFE

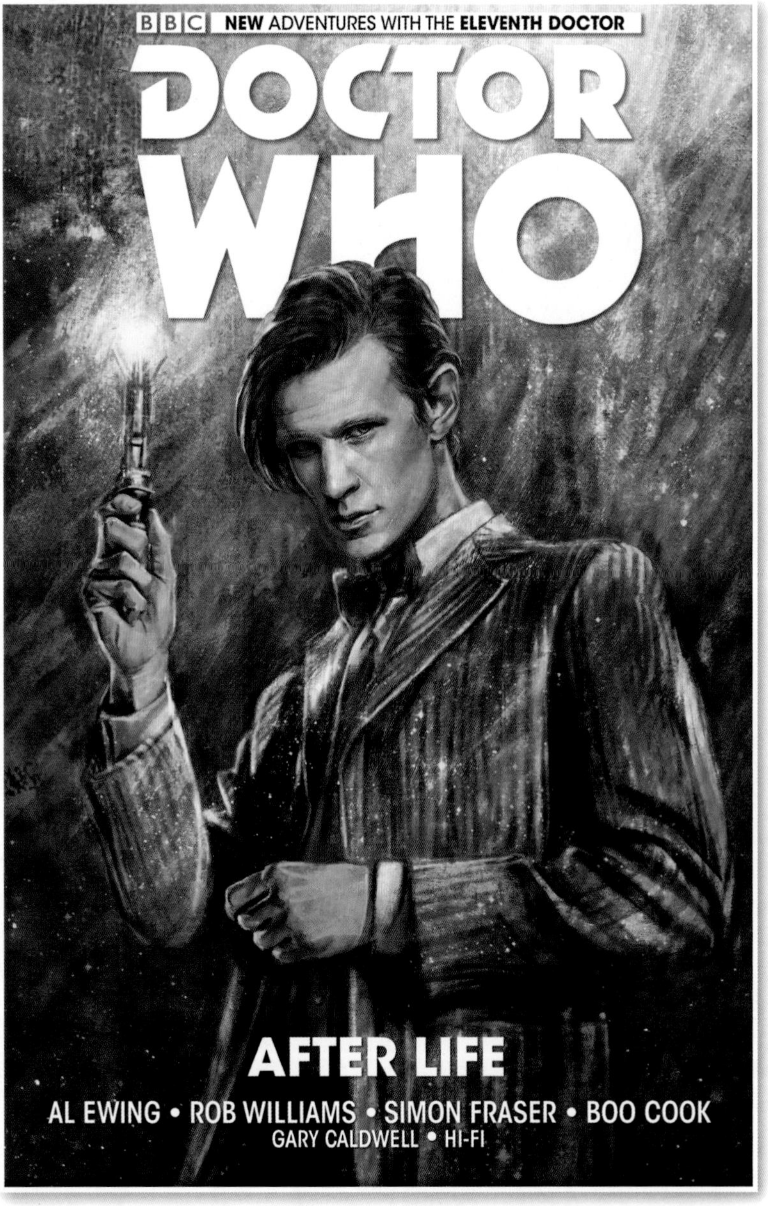
BBC
NEW ADVENTURES WITH THE ELEVENTH DOCTOR
DOCTOR WHO
AFTER LIFE
AL EWING • ROB WILLIAMS • SIMON FRASER • BOO COOK
GARY CALDWELL • HI-FI

ISBN: 9781782761730

AL EWING
(LOKI: AGENT OF ASGARD)

ROB WILLIAMS
(THE ROYALS, ORDINARY)

SIMON FRASER
(2000AD, NIKOLAI DANTE)

BOO COOK
(ELEPHANTMEN)

COLLECTS DOCTOR WHO: THE ELEVENTH DOCTOR ISSUES #1-5

ON SALE NOW - $19.99 / $22.95 CAN

TITAN COMICS

AVAILABLE IN ALL GOOD COMIC STORES, BOOK STORES, AND DIGITAL PROVIDERS!

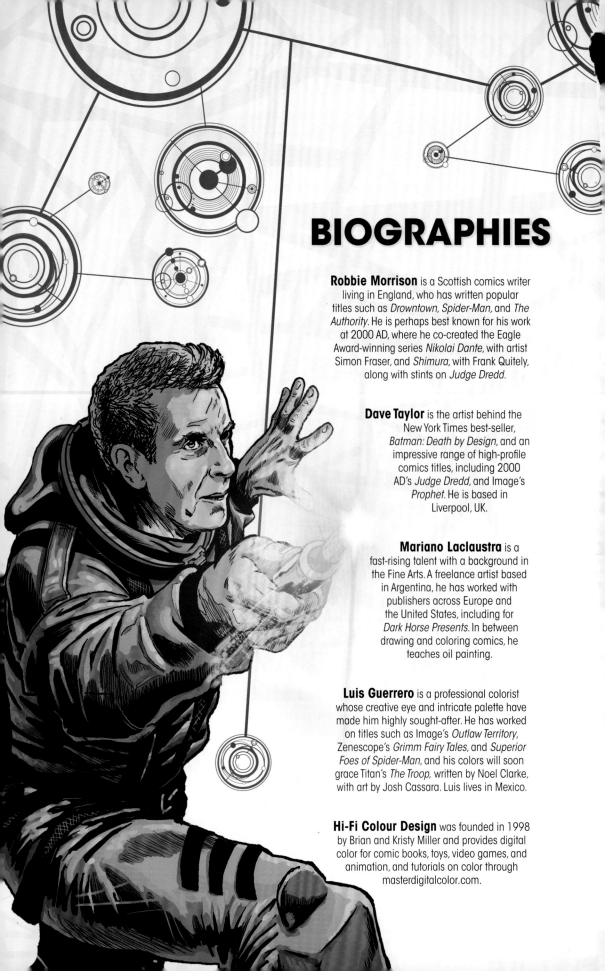

BIOGRAPHIES

Robbie Morrison is a Scottish comics writer living in England, who has written popular titles such as *Drowntown, Spider-Man,* and *The Authority.* He is perhaps best known for his work at 2000 AD, where he co-created the Eagle Award-winning series *Nikolai Dante*, with artist Simon Fraser, and *Shimura*, with Frank Quitely, along with stints on *Judge Dredd.*

Dave Taylor is the artist behind the New York Times best-seller, *Batman: Death by Design*, and an impressive range of high-profile comics titles, including 2000 AD's *Judge Dredd*, and Image's *Prophet.* He is based in Liverpool, UK.

Mariano Laclaustra is a fast-rising talent with a background in the Fine Arts. A freelance artist based in Argentina, he has worked with publishers across Europe and the United States, including for *Dark Horse Presents.* In between drawing and coloring comics, he teaches oil painting.

Luis Guerrero is a professional colorist whose creative eye and intricate palette have made him highly sought-after. He has worked on titles such as Image's *Outlaw Territory*, Zenescope's *Grimm Fairy Tales*, and *Superior Foes of Spider-Man*, and his colors will soon grace Titan's *The Troop,* written by Noel Clarke, with art by Josh Cassara. Luis lives in Mexico.

Hi-Fi Colour Design was founded in 1998 by Brian and Kristy Miller and provides digital color for comic books, toys, video games, and animation, and tutorials on color through masterdigitalcolor.com.